D1603974

ERAU-PRESCOTT LIBRARY

SHARKS AMONG MINNOWS

SHARKS AMONG MINNOWS

Germany's First Fighter Pilots and the
Fokker Eindecker period, July 1915 to September 1916

Norman Franks

GRUB STREET · LONDON

Published by
Grub Street
The Basement
10 Chivalry Road
London SW11 1HT

Copyright © 2001 Grub Street, London
Text copyright © 2001 Norman Franks

British Library Cataloguing in Publication Data
Franks, Norman L. R. (Norman Leslie Robert), 1940-
    Sharks among minnows: the Fokker Eindecker period,
    July 1915 to September 1916
    1. Fokker Eindecker (Fighter planes) 2. World War, 1914-1918 –
    Aerial operations, German
    I. Title
    940.4'4943

ISBN 1 902304 92 6

All rights reserved. No part of this publication may be reproduced,
stored in a retrieval system, or transmitted in any form or by any
means, electronic, mechanical, photocopying, recording, or otherwise,
without the prior permission of the copyright owner.

Typeset by Pearl Graphics, Hemel Hempstead

Printed and bound in Great Britain by
Biddles Ltd, Guildford and King's Lynn

CONTENTS

ACKNOWLEDGEMENTS

I have been piecing together the events of this early period of aviation history for some years, among other projects, but have never been really confident that I had covered all the known claims and casualties from the German side. While I was in contact with A E Ferko, an expert on the German Air Service, on several occasions, I never mentioned this area of interest because it seemed to me too vast a project.

However, on his sad passing, all his files and records went to the University of Texas, in Dallas, and once they had been catalogued I discovered Ed Ferko had indeed been listing the claims and losses of the German Air Service for all the war years, and these files were made available by the University staff. There is no way of knowing how current his work on these files was, but it seems from some notations that he must have added items to them every now and again. What appealed to me, of course, was that I could now dove-tail his notes with my own, and feel far happier with the result, and more confident that I wasn't missing much. Or at least, if he had missed something, I probably would not have found it in any event.

As this era of the so-called Fokker Scourge continued to interest me, I felt able now to proceed with detailing the events of this period in book form. I have, therefore, to thank and acknowledge the late Ed Ferko for his work on this fascinating period. Also to the University of Texas, for their kind co-operation.

My thanks also go to my good friend Frank (Bill) Bailey, for allowing me access to his researches into French claims and losses, which he also made available to Ed over the years, from which it was possible to make comparisons with German claims.

On the photographic side, I was, as always, able to call on the archive of Jack Bruce and Stuart Leslie, Stuart being his usual helpful self in finding a number of pictures of crashed allied aeroplanes. Neal O'Connor likewise made his Fokker photographs available, for which grateful thanks, while other pictures and help came from Trevor Henshaw, Tony Mellor Ellis, Greg VanWyngarden, Johan Visser, Phil Jarrett, and Reinhard Zankl.

Further help came from Jack Bruce, Simon Moody, formerly of the RAF Museum, Barry Gray, Jeff Taylor and Rick Duiven, a friend and fellow author, each having my sincere thanks.

INTRODUCTION

The start of the Great War in August 1914 was just like any previous war. The men of the British regular army marched to the war front, in this case Northern France, to support its ally, France, while a goodly number of the civilian male populace eagerly enlisted, keen to get into the fight before the conflict ended. Again, like many previous wars, there was rumour of it all being over quickly 'by Christmas', and if one wanted to have a crack at the dastardly Hun, one had better get a move on.

However, the war did not end by Christmas, at least not Christmas 1914, although the guns did finally fall silent a few weeks short of Christmas 1918 – four years hence. This war was also very different to any previous conflict. After those first few late summer weeks of 1914 while armies were able to move fairly freely across the flat landscape of France and Belgium, then with the Allies' inglorious retreat from Mons, the war began to grind to a halt. With winter on the way, there was no going home till at least the spring, and with the ever present danger of Germany continuing to press south and west, the German and Allied nations' fighting men did what no others had ever done before. They dug into the ground; the infamous trench warfare began.

By early 1915 the ugly scar of these trench systems and earthworks stretched from the North Sea coast to the Swiss border, leaving great chunks of both France and Belgium under the occupation of German troops. The trench systems were made all the more terrible due to barbed wire entanglements, each side unwinding mile upon mile of this cursed barbed fencing to hinder their opposing counterparts should they try to attack. The other, even more deadly accoutrement to this 'modern day' war was the introduction of the machine gun.

Both Germany and Britain had developed this deadly weapon in the 1880s, Maxim in Germany, Vickers in Britain. Initially they were unreliable, but certainly the Germans saw the potential of this rapid-fire gun, and both countries had continued to develop both heavy and light machine guns, so that by the commencement of the First World War, both sides had them ready for action. Once on the battle field, these guns altered forever the way combatants used their infantry, and cavalry. Even so, all belligerents in the Great War suffered horrendous casualties due to these weapons.

Once the war became bogged down, with trenches, barbed wire and the deadly sweeping fire of the machine guns, two things quickly emerged. Firstly, the cavalry could no longer make reconnaissance forays to see what the enemy was doing, so the generals were suddenly without any intelligence; they were blinded. Due to this the second thing happened. The aeroplane, another new innovation to the conduct of war, which up until now these same generals – or most of them – had tolerated, and sometimes even took notice of reports brought in by their pilots and observers, suddenly realised that these flying contraptions were the only means of obtaining knowledge of what was going on 'on the other side of the hill'.

Aeroplanes of both sides in the conflict had been flying over each other's territory since the war began, although in very small numbers. It was all a brand new concept and the flyers were learning each day, how to see, how to read signs, what to look for. Their aeroplanes were fragile, and engines not always reliable, but the early military aviators knew they were developing a useful new weapon. With the coming of the trenches, they found themselves suddenly in vogue.

It does not take a genius to realise then, that each side needed to stop the other from looking at their ground forces. However, these early aeroplanes were still fairly frail and few had been designed with any serious thought of putting guns in them, either for offence or defence. The more aggressive airmen began to take up pistols or rifles in order to take pot-shots at any hostile aircraft they might find snooping around, but it was very much a game in those early months. But it soon became apparent that the use of a stripped down machine gun would be advantageous, and with the help of the mechanics who were able to work with steel, local modifications were made so that these guns could be carried. Even so, the main problem was the weight of both gun and ammunition – mostly ammunition drums at this stage – which affected the performance of the craft. However, in due course the necessity to carry such weaponry overtook such considerations, and back in England and the German homeland, gun mountings became standard and produced as a matter of course.

A handful of French and British pilots started to fit guns to their aeroplanes in early 1915 and enough had been learnt and understood for them to know that the best way of hitting another aeroplane accurately with a machine-gun burst was to point the aeroplane directly at the opponent. The problem, however, was the whirling blades of the propeller. A few Frenchmen, one being Roland Garros, got around this by having metal deflector plates fitted to the wooden propellers, so that any bullets that came from the muzzle of the gun when the blade was directly in front of it, were deflected away – harmlessly! Garros had two or three successes before his aeroplane was brought down by ground fire and he taken prisoner. With the secret of his success suddenly laid bare to his German captors, the idea was shown to the young Dutch aircraft designer, Anthony Fokker, who was building aeroplanes for the German Air Service. (His earlier offers of help to the French and British had been turned down!)

Fokker and his team of engineers knew at once that deflector plates were not the way forward. Pre-war, LVG Aircraft Works had designed, on paper, an early interrupter gear and now Fokker's engineers re-developed the idea, providing a cam and push-rod mechanism so that the gun was stopped from firing each moment the propeller was in front of the gun muzzle. As it happened, Fokker had recently designed a monoplane machine, to be used as a fast, light reconnaissance craft, but it was ideally suited to be the test-bed for the interrupter gear. Thus his monoplane, designated M5L, was kitted out with gun and gear in the early summer of 1915. In the early days he used the Parabellum air-cooled light machine gun, but as supplies ran short due to demand, later machines had to have converted heavy water-cooled guns which had their water jacket stripped away along with other unnecessary parts, although it was still some 50% heavier than the lighter gun.

Fokker had another good reason for ignoring the deflector plates in favour of an effective interrupter gear, and that was the ammunition Germany used. The French used bullets with copper jackets which being fairly soft, easily deformed and did little or no damage as they ricocheted off the steel plates. The Germans on the other hand, had steel-jacketed bullets which resisted deformation to a larger extent, which in turn would damage similar plates and do little good to the wooden propellers.

The famous story of Fokker having to fly the monoplane to the battle front in order to demonstrate the gun gear is well known, and fortunately for Fokker – still a Dutch neutral in reality – he did not find a suitable target, and then managed to talk himself out of 'doing the deed'. However, the unit to which he had flown his Fokker machine had been Feld-flieger Abteilung Nr.62 – Field Flying Unit 62 – based near Douai. This two-seater reconnaissance unit had its full complement of pilots and observers, two of the former being men by the names of Oswald Boelcke and Max Immelmann. These two, and another pilot by the name of Otto Parschau based at Stenay, who had accompanied Anthony Fokker to the front in a two-seater, all saw the potential of the Fokker monoplane, none more so than Boelcke, who was about to show little short of genius in the developing air war.

From flying lumbering two-seaters on reconnaissance or light bombing missions to being able to fly solo in a light and nimble single-seat scouting aeroplane fitted with a machine gun firing through the propeller blades, was excitement enough. The air war was about to turn into something quite different and quite extraordinary over the next months. Air warfare had arrived already, but now one side had an aeroplane that could out-perform and out-shoot the opposition; air fighting had begun.

For almost a year the Fokker monoplane – now designated as E-types – and its fighter pilots dominated the sky over the French battle fronts and the first successful pilots became heroes and household names in Germany. They became the sharks flying amidst the allied minnows.

Air combat was still in its infancy as they arrived. Both sides grew up very fast.

Chapter One

THE FIRST GREAT AIR WAR BEGINS

As mentioned in the Introduction, German, British and French airmen had already begun to shoot at each other, firstly as a matter of course, for they were 'the enemy', and also because it was soon clear that each side needed to stop the other from looking freely at their own side of the trench lines. This was very hit-or-miss. Nobody had done this before in history and it took time to work out where to fire at a moving and often turning target, in order for the bullet(s) to strike home. There were many vital areas that were highly susceptible to a bullet hit – the pilot or crew, petrol and oil tanks, engine, control wires and so on, but there was also a vast amount of non-vital areas, such as fabric covered fuselage and wings. To bring down an aeroplane a single bullet from a pistol or carbine had to hit one of the vital parts, causing sufficient damage either to make the aeroplane fall to the ground, or at least force the pilot to head for home as rapidly as he could.

In the beginning there was no suggestion of 'victories' as became the norm as the war progressed, and it was not until better fighting machines and airborne machine guns began to be used, that anyone even imagined that a pilot or crew could possibly bring down more than the odd hostile aeroplane. So, in this same beginning, a victory could represent not just an aeroplane brought down, but also the driving off of an opponent, for this meant that the opposing crew had been forced to abandon their task of either reconnaissance – later photo-reconnaissance – or bombing.

It must also be borne in mind that in the early days of the war, aircraft were not so plentiful as in mid-to-late 1916, and certainly not in the numbers as would be found in 1917-18. Sometimes airmen from both sides could fly several missions without even seeing a hostile aeroplane, let alone being in a position to engage or attack one, or be attacked. And even if they did, some felt it safer to stay clear. Not that many had even the means to attack the opposition. The sky is a big place, full of haze, cloud, rain, glaring sunshine, and once aeroplanes began to paint their upper surfaces in colours that helped merge the craft into the ground landscape, they almost became invisible at a distance. In addition, their engines did not have the power to go chasing around like the future pilots of 1917-18. There are many reports of pilots of both sides making long chases and not gaining on an opponent in any way, certainly not before that opponent had made it back to his own side of the lines, making it necessary to abandon the pursuit.

A handful of British and French airmen did begin to take guns aloft, in an attempt to see off any hostile machines they found, not necessarily to bring them down. That was an ideal not yet thought truly realistic. The Frenchman, Roland Garros, a pre-war aviator now flying with Escadrille MS23, which used Morane-Saulnier monoplanes, soon decided to be more aggressive in the air, and believed the best way of attacking German aeroplanes was to fit a machine gun on top of the fuselage and engine cowling, right in front of his cockpit, aim the machine, and fire. The problem of hitting the propeller was not solved, but after talking with the Saulnier people, he and they came up with a sort of solution as mentioned earlier. That is, fitting metal deflector plates to the blades of the propeller so that any bullets which did leave the muzzle while the blades were opposite it, would be deflected away. The majority of the bullets would obviously pass through undisturbed. In this way he had two or three successful air combats, much to the surprise, we are told, of the opposing airmen.

Once the Fokker monoplanes arrived on the scene, things changed dramatically, although at first they were just unarmed aircraft used for reconnaissance. The first Fokkers (M5K) had a 100 hp Oberursel rotary engine which could give it a speed of over 80 mph (130 km per hour), and later versions improved on this. The Royal Flying Corps went to war with its squadrons equipped with a variety of aeroplane types, and it took some while for a squadron to have a full complement of the same types. Many of these, once equipment became established, were the ubiquitous Blériot Experimental (BE) two-seaters made by the Royal Aircraft Factory at Farnborough, in Hampshire. The type most commonly seen and used in the first years of the war were the BE2 series (BE2c, BE2d, BE2e, BE2f and BE2g). They were lovely aeroplanes to fly, with no particular vices, and being so stable were useful for airmen while studying the terrain below them. However, these traits were less advantageous if attacked in the air, and the best way to defend against engagement was to see the opposition first and dive down and away as fast as the pilot could do so.

As the early BE2 machine could only get around 70 mph from its 60 or 70 hp Renault engines, a diving Fokker monoplane pilot was easily able to overhaul a BE. The French reconnaissance aeroplanes were mainly the Farman, Caudron or Voisin types. The Caudron G.3 had a single 80 hp Gnôme engine, giving it perhaps a speed of 65 mph, while the G.4 machines had two engines, 80 hp Le Rhônes, but they only produced a speed a little over 70 mph. The Farman and Voisins were 'pusher' types. That is to say the engines were to the rear of the machine, and pushed the aeroplane through the air, rather than the tractor types with the engine(s) in front, that pulled the craft.

The 'pusher' type concept had, however, one good feature, which was that the forward view, and therefore the forward gun-firing area too, was free of whirling propeller blades. Thus a pilot and/or observer had a clear field of fire of virtually 180 degrees to the front. The downside of course, was that any attack from behind was obscured by the engine, and it was the engine that was generally hit first in any surprise attack. At least with the tractor machines with a two-man crew, they had a better all-round view, and mostly a better rear defensive field of fire. The Henri Farmans (HF), and the Maurice Farmans (MF) – two brothers who built their own aeroplanes while initially using the same factory premises – had similar engines to the Caudrons, as did the early Voisin machines. However, when war was declared, Gabriel Voisin had developed his machines with the 120 hp Canton-Unné engine – type LA.3 – and was about to send a batch to Russia. Once war came, Voisin offered them to the French Government, and, at his own expense, equipped them with 37 mm Hotchkiss machine guns. Their speed was no better than the other French machines, as probably any improvement with the higher horse-powered engine was countered by the weight of gun and ammunition.

Nevertheless, it was a Voisin LA.3 (No. V89), flown by Sergent Joseph Frantz and his observer, Sapper Louis Quénault, of Escadrille V24, who scored the first aerial victory of the war for France on 5 October 1914. They engaged and brought down a German Aviatik two-seater from Fleiger-Abteilung 18 (FA18), over Jonchéry-sur-Vesle, near the town of Reims, Quénault using the machine gun which Voisin had mounted on a pivoting fork. The German crew of Feldwebel Wilhelm Schlichting and his officer observer, Oberleutnant Fritz von Zangen, both died.

Both the British and the French had smaller, single-seat biplane and monoplane aeroplanes, one not dissimilar to the Fokker monoplanes. The RFC had a few Bristol Scout biplanes, used for scouting (general reconnaissance), most carrying some form of armament – a cut down rifle, or a machine gun, but fixed to fire obliquely forward in order to miss the propeller blades. In order to fire at an opponent, the pilot had to fly behind and to one side, rather than directly behind. At least one other had a light machine gun mounted on the top wing, fixed to fire over the propeller. The RFC and the French had Morane-Saulnier Type N monoplanes, as well as the type L which Garros had used, although the type L had a parasol wing arrangement, ie: the wing was above the fuselage. The type N had a wing configuration similar to the Fokker's, ie: shoulder-wings, each stretching out from the sides of the fuselage next to the cockpit. The type N only came to the Front in 1916, no doubt purchased from the French in order to emulate the success of the Fokkers.

The aeroplane which looked most like a Fokker monoplane was the Morane-Saulnier type H, which had been around since 1911. Looked at quickly one could be forgiven for saying it was indeed a Fokker. However, while one or two models saw service with the RFC in France in the summer of 1915, it did not carry any armament other than, perhaps, a pistol; any other similarity to the Fokker ended there.

The RFC also used the Martinsyde S.1, with an 80 hp Gnôme engine, which did give it a speed at sea level of almost 90 mph, and it could mount a Lewis machine gun on the upper wing. An early example went to France in January 1915, but it proved not too stable in the air, but because it could carry a gun, was tolerated. The few that were used did not last long and by the summer of that year had been withdrawn.

EARLY COMBATS

During those early, rather clumsy, air actions in the opening weeks of the war, and with, in addition the field guns which now pointed skyward to fire on aeroplanes (anti-aircraft fire), not to mention rifle fire from ground troops, the Germans claimed a few early successes right from the start. The day before the war started German infantry fire brought down a French aeroplane near Berillion. On the first day of the war Escadrille MF2 lost a Maurice Farman shot down close to the frontier between France and Germany. Before the month was out two or three more had come down. 27 August saw the first French airman captured, Lieutenant Faurit in a Blériot monoplane.

In September and October, ground fire and accidents caused others to come down. In October a brand new Morane Parasol was shot down by Leutnant Arthur Schreiber's gun battery south of Roye. Schreiber said it was the fourth hostile aeroplane the Germans had accounted for. On 22 October a two-seat Blériot was shot down 50 metres in front of the German lines at Bois Mortmare, from which the crew were shot dead by infantry fire.

The Germans had their air losses too. The RFC brought down its first hostile aeroplane on 25 August. Three aircraft from No.2 Squadron engaged a German Taube and so alarmed the pilot with feint attacks that he made a forced landing. One of the British aeroplanes landed nearby but the German had run off into some woods and escaped them.

Both sides also received ground fire attention from their own troops. All aircraft looked the same to soldiers and if they were overhead, were assumed hostile. These sorts of incidents continued well into the spring of 1915.

NUMBERS IN THE FIELD

Mention was made earlier of the lack of aeroplanes in the sky during the early months of the war. To quote my friend Jack Bruce (the oracle on WW1 aeroplanes) in his book *The Aeroplanes of the RFC Military Wing* (Putnam, 1982):

> 'In the summer of 1915 there were nine squadrons of the RFC in the Field with the BEF [British Expeditionary Force] in France. Between them on 30 June they mustered 105 aircraft of fourteen different types, of which only six Bristol Scouts, and two Martinsyde S.1s could be described as true single-seat scouts, and neither could be effectively armed. In such circumstances the new Morane-Saulnier [type N] with its forward-firing machine-gun must have seemed an aircraft of lethal potential. The RFC ordered three; deliveries were made on 18 and 19 September, 1915 . . . .'

Once the battle front had settled down in the spring of 1915, so had the areas of responsibility. The British and Belgian forces held the line north of Amiens, the French the line to the south of this city. Occasionally the

French had some troops within the British sectors but generally speaking, this was how the front was manned.

On the German side, the various Army Groups kept vigil along its various sectors, with little change. On the North Sea coast, to a line south of Ypres was the German 4th Army; from here to just south of Cambrai, the 6th Army; from Cambrai to the River Oise, the 2nd Army; south of the Oise, the 7th Army; opposite the French were the 3rd and 5th Armies, then army detachments 'A' and 'B' from Verdun southwards. Each army corps and HQs had units of the German *Fliegertruppe* (Aviation Service) attached to them, two-seater abteilungen for use in reconnaissance. Like their opponents, they carried no weapons other than perhaps the odd pistol. Once the war degenerated into trench warfare, aircraft of both sides were also used for artillery co-operation, crews recording the fall of shot and by use of morse code, the gunners could adjust ranges until they were on target. This too quickly became a reason to down, or at least chase off, aircraft from either side, which effectively stopped accurate artillery fire.

At the start of the war the Germans had few machine guns suitable for aeroplanes, but soon, captured British and French aeroplanes, downed by anti-aircraft fire, or from an engine malfunction, gave the Germans examples of Lewis and Hotchkiss guns. Pre-war – around 1911 – Germany had started to produce its own guns suitable for airships and aircraft, the Parabellum LMG14 (7.92 mm), and the 'Spandau', although production was slow. The Spandau was in reality a 7.92 mm Maxim, a gun modified for aircraft use, but being marked with the name 'Spandau', the name of the arsenal at Spandau, near Berlin, it was mistakenly thought to be the gun's name by the Allies.

The Parabellum belt-fed gun was light by comparison to others, weighing only 11 kilograms with its water jacket empty, 12.8 kg with it full. This compared favourably with the Maxim's full weight of 21.5 kg. Its rate of fire was 700 rounds per minute. It was this gun which was fitted to the early EI machines.

Later the standard MG 08 Maxim – 'Spandau' – was converted for aircraft by draining the water jacket, taking out the water pump, and making the jacket air-cooled by cutting slots in it, which also had the effect of reducing its weight down to 15 kg. As the later Fokker EI, EII and EIIIs started to arrive, it was this gun which was being fitted to them, and used with the Gestänge Steurung (push-rod control system) interrupter gear. Its rate of fire was around 400-500 rounds per minute. The Fokker usually carried a 500-round belt, so the pilot had around a minute's worth of fire. (As a comparison, the Browning machine gun as used in the WW2 Spitfire had a rate of fire of 1,100 rounds per minute and carried enough bullets in each of its eight guns for around 16-18 seconds of fire; ie: around 350 bullets per gun.)

By the early summer of 1915, with air actions increasing, the Fokker monoplane finally arrived, and the air war truly began in earnest.

FOKKER DISTRIBUTION
Building of the Fokker monoplane had been slow, but once its potential was

realised, it was put into serious production. There was no question of the aircraft being formed into one dedicated unit, overall numbers dictating that one be sent to each flieger abteilung as they became available, and used for escort work or for chasing off Allied aeroplanes who were making themselves a nuisance over the front. The first arrived in June, and by the end of July, just 15 Fokker monoplanes were flying over what was now being termed the Western Front.

Let us be clear. The Fokker M5K monoplane was nothing really outstanding as an aeroplane. Certainly it had a little more speed than many of its opponents, but what really made it a success was the fixed machine gun firing through the propeller arc. And so secret was this, that Fokker pilots were forbidden to cross the trench lines for fear of their aircraft falling into British or French hands, whereupon the secret would be out. This fact, plus the limited number of Fokkers around, was responsible for the German fighter arm to begin to fly a defensive war, almost all of which was fought on the German side of the lines. Very few forays were made across the lines except for attacking Allied balloon locations. It did give the German fighter pilots several advantages, however. They could choose when and if to engage, and were generally helped by the prevailing wind which tended to blow from west to east, making it necessary for Allied pilots to fly home against this wind, and if German pilots were forced down to land, it was generally over 'friendly' territory, whereas the Allied airmen, if forced down, almost always became prisoners.

As the Fokker monoplanes began to arrive, the question was who would fly them. There was no fighter training, and some two-seater pilots had no desire to fly the single-seater anyway. However, there was no reluctance on the part of some pilots, who could perhaps see the opportunities opening up before them for more warlike actions, not to say, even fame and glory. The Prussian outlook of the dashing hussar not only defending his homeland but reaping glorious victories in battle too, was ever in the forefront of men brought up on stories of famous past heroes. Those who may have imagined themselves in dashing cavalry charges had long since seen that picture fade with the coming of the trenches, and lancers and uhlans who had seen the odd action in the first weeks of the war, were either now languishing in back areas awaiting developments, or had seen the light, many exchanging a horse for an aeroplane.

Others had become interested in aviation pre-war, and had, like so many Englishmen, Frenchmen, and even Americans, already taken to the air, not for any futuristic warlike ambitions, but just to delight in the world's new adventure of pure flight. It was not difficult, therefore, for the commander of Flieger-Abteilung Nr.62 at Douai to find at least two of his young pilots not only willing, but eager for the chance of flying the Fokker monoplane. Oswald Boelcke and Max Immelman.

FA62, formed at Döberitz in May 1915, had moved to an airfield near Douai equipped with a couple of armed LVG C-type two-seaters for reconnaissance duties and, not long afterwards, a couple of Fokker EI machines. The unit was commanded by Hauptmann Kastner.

BOELCKE AND IMMELMANN

Oswald Boelcke was born in the town of Giebichenstein, near Halle on the Salle, in Saxony, on 19 May 1891. He was the fourth child of a professor in the local high school, and two more would follow. A sister and two brothers had been born in Buenos Aires, Argentina, where their father had been the rector of the German Lutheran School in the city. Oswald was the first child born in Germany.

The family moved to Dessau in 1895, his father becoming a professor in the Antoinette School, Oswald graduating from education at Easter 1911. Like so many Germans with an adventurous streak, there was no question of going into anything except the military. Thus in March 1911, two months short of his 20th birthday he entered the Prussian Military Cadet Corps, and after his initial training he was assigned to the 3rd Telegrapher's Battalion at Koblenz. His first contact with aviation came on the occasion his duties took him to Darmstadt, where there was a flying school. Determined to become a pilot himself his desire was thwarted for some while but eventually, in June 1914 he finally obtained a transfer to the flying school at Halberstadt. It took him just six weeks to complete his flight training, although his parents did not know anything about it, and as war began at the beginning of August, he was posted to Darmstadt and then Trier with a reserve unit.

As the war progressed, Leutnant Boelcke, now a member of FA13, in which his elder brother Wilhelm was an observer, began to fly missions on the French Front, often as pilot to Wilhelm, flying over the Argonne region. He remained with FA13 for seven months, and received the Iron Cross 1st Class and 2nd Class. He was also introduced to a Fokker monoplane, long before it became famous as a fighting machine. Fokker had designed and built his Fokker M5K before the war and a few had passed into military service. He flew one in December 1914, powered by a French rotary engine. With this and the Taube, Boelcke flew recce sorties and artillery observation duties until April 1915. On 15 April he was posted to Berlin and another unit – FA62. It was with this formation, newly created, that he met Immelmann and Otto Parschau. By June he was at Douai, the airfield located 15 miles north-east of Arras and 12 miles south-east of Lens. The airfield was to the south-west of the town itself, at a place called La Brayelle, on the Douai-Brebières road. He was back on two-seaters, but that would soon change.

He and his observer had a prolonged but successful air fight on 4 July in the vicinity of Valenciennes, which resulted in them downing a French Morane Parasol. Both Frenchmen were killed in the crash near Beaulicourt. Both men had been hit by bullets from Boelcke's observer's fire. As Boelcke recorded, his observer – Leutnant Heinz Helmut von Wühlisch – had fired 380 bullets, 27 of which hit the Morane. The machine came from Escadrille MS15, the crew having been Lieutenants Maurice Tétu and Le Comte Georges de la Rochefoucauld Beauvicourt. Boelcke had been flying an LVG C1, Nr. 162/15.

Max Immelmann was also a Saxon, born in Dresden on 21 September 1890, so was a few months older than Boelcke. His father had owned a factory, but he had died while Max was still a small child. In 1905 Max went into the Cadet School in Dresden, and was made an ensign in 1912, following his assignment to the 2nd Railway Regiment in 1911. He also took a course at the War Academy, returning to his regiment upon the outbreak of war. However, he too had discovered aviation and by November 1914, having applied for a transfer, found himself learning to fly at Johannistal, Berlin. Completing his training at Adlerdorf, he was assigned to FA10 in March 1915, but within a month he was sent to FA62 where he met his colleague Boelcke. The two men became firm friends and developed a friendly rivalry with the arrival of the armed Fokker machine.

Both men became intensely interested in Anthony Fokker's monoplane which he flew to Douai in May, armed with a gun fixed to fire through the propeller. In reality this was the same Fokker-type Boelcke had been flying during the winter of 1914-15, but without the gun. Also the monoplane now had a German engine. Immelmann inherited Boelcke's LVG, while Boelcke himself took over the Eindecker full time from 7 July. Immelmann, far from disgruntled, felt content in the knowledge that he would now be flying an armed two-seater as escort to the unit's un-armed machines so would be able to continue his offensive spirit. However, the better news was that he was promoted to Leutnant, and on the 15th he received the Saxon Friedrich August Medal in Silver.

As Anthony Fokker took his leave of Douai, he left behind two Fokker EIs and one of the unarmed monoplanes, probably a type M5K. One of the former was numbered E.3/15, and Boelcke was assigned to this machine. After a few familiarization flights in the M5K he took up E.3/15 for the first time on 31 July. Early the next morning he was up again and ran into British aeroplanes but his machine gun jammed and he had to break off the action. With the report of British aircraft in the area, Immelmann immediately took off in E.13/15, arriving at the scene just as Boelcke was breaking away. He chased the RFC machines, and cut off a BE2c just as the formation was turning for the lines after bombing targets near Douai. Of the five BE machines on the raid, two carried six bombs but no observer, one would carry three bombs and an observer, while the other two, acting as escort, had observers and machine guns.

Armed with just two automatic pistols, Lieutenant William Reid, of No. 2 Squadron RFC, was one of the bomb-carrying BEs with no observer aboard, but was no match for a machine-gun armed Fokker monoplane, and he had little or no help from his comrades. A burst of gunfire from Immelmann slammed into the BE and wounded Reid in the left arm, and a second burst smashed his gravity fuel tank. The engine immediately stopped and Reid had no alternative than to force land near Brebières, almost within sight of FA62's airfield. Immelmann landed his Fokker nearby and actually helped Reid out of his cockpit and saw to it that he was sent off to the nearest medical unit, which was the 1st Bavarian Reserve Corps Field Hospital.

From here Reid was later operated on in Douai town hospital, then sent to a military hospital in Münster where his shattered arm kept him for the next five months. Meantime, Immelmann took one of FA62's LVG two-seaters over the British lines the next day and dropped a message saying what had happened to Reid, and that although wounded, he was otherwise safe and well. He was later repatriated to Switzerland in May 1916, where he continued to receive medical treatment, and he finally came home to Britain in March 1918. Once home, he made the following report:

> 'On Satuday evening, 31 July, Major Becke called five pilots into the orderly room and gave instructions for a bombing raid the following morning – Captain Hearson, Captain Smith, Lieutenant Leather, Lieutenant Gallie [and me]. We were to meet over Arras at 6 am and proceed to a German airfield between Douai and Vitry. Hearson and Gallie carried machine guns and observers but no bombs. Smith carried a machine gun and three bombs, Leather and self six bombs, no gun, no observer.
>
> 'Over Arras at 6 am I counted only three machines so waited but saw other three aircraft head for the lines. I saw Leather drop his bombs on target, I was at 7,500 feet, he a little lower. I dropped my bombs over the sheds. I saw two escort machines above and ahead heading for the lines, then looking back, saw a German Fokker about fifty yards behind me. I immediately took my automatic pistol in my right hand and controls in my left and started to turn towards the German. He opened fire with machine gun and [the burst] broke my left arm in four places. I pointed my nose down and steered for the lines hoping escorting machines would see me. The German kept 50 yards behind and then my engine stopped – he had put a bullet through my gravity tank.
>
> 'I had to go down, the German following and firing all the time. I managed to land and the German landed half a minute later and helped me out of my machine. He turned out to be Leutnant Immelmann and he dropped a letter over our lines that afternoon saying I had been shot down and severely wounded in the left arm. I was taken to Douai hospital, operated on, and then transferred to a military hospital at Münster [where I stayed] for five months.'

After Reid had been driven away, Immelmann had a look over the BE. He found about 40 bullet hits – two in the propeller, three in the petrol tank, four or five in the fuselage and six in the wings. All the instruments had been shot to pieces and further hits had cut several bracing wires and control cables, and damaged the bomb rack and the left wheel.

Flying back to his airfield, Immelmann then drove back to the location by car as his CO had gone there. Later, as Reid had said, Immelmann flew a biplane over St Pol where he dropped a note informing the British what had happened to their pilot. Immelmann had been a Fokker pilot for just three days; the award of the Iron Cross 1st Class quickly followed.

This is believed to be the first 'official' victory scored by a Fokker monoplane pilot although it is possible that the achievement of first bringing down a hostile machine was made by another Fokker pilot, Leutnant Kurt Wintgens. Kurt Wintgens was born on 1 August 1894, in Neustadt, the son of an army officer. (Thus Immelmann's first victory was scored on Wintgens' 21st birthday!) He became an army cadet in 1913 with the Telegraphen-Battalion Nr.2, in Frankfurt and was actually attending a military academy in August 1914 but quickly rejoined his unit and once in action on the Eastern Front he received the Iron Cross 2nd Class.

In late 1914 he transferred to aviation, firstly as an observer on the Western Front, and later in Poland. In March 1915 he began to train as a pilot and then transferred to the Fokker Flying School at Schwerin, then, due to his obvious skill was sent to FA67 to fly a Fokker monoplane which had been assigned to the unit. He then moved to the Bavarian, FA6, to fly its Fokker. One of his instructors at Schwerin had been Mario Scherff, who had been with the Turkish army in 1912, as a pilot of Mustafa Kemal Pasha (later Kemal Atatürk). In May 1915 he went to Döberitz in order to specialise in Fokker monoplane flying.

Back with FA67, on 1 July Wintgens engaged a French aeroplane over the front, a Morane L from Escadrille MS48, flown by Captiaine Paul du Peuty and Sous-lieutenant Louis de Boutiny whilst flying Fokker EI 2/15. They were forced down in French lines east of Lunéville at 18.00 hours, both men wounded. Having come down on the French side, Wintgens' claim was not allowed. Had it been, he would have been the first pure fighter pilot to down an Allied aeroplane. He tried hard again on the 4th, against another Morane L Parasol, but this claim was not confirmed either.

Many years ago, that wonderful German air historian, the late Heinz J Nowarra, had access to letters written by Wintgens. On 2 July 1915 Wintgens had penned:

> 'Yesterday the great moment came. Time 6.00. Place: near east of Lunéville. Altitude between 2,000 and 2,500 metres. Suddenly I saw a monoplane in front, about 300 metres higher than I; and in the next moment he dived down on me, and his machine gun was buzzing intensively. But as I immediately rushed under him in the opposite direction, he had no chance. After four attacks I climbed, banking to his altitude, and now my machine gun also came into action. I came so close to him that I could look into his face. After my third attack he did the most stupid thing that he could do – he ran away. I banked on the point and had him now fine in the gunsight. Four seconds I fired, and he went down head foremost. I could follow him firing until 500 metres altitude. Then I got intensive fire from the ground because the fight had taken place behind the French lines.'

If the French reports are correct, the French crew were only armed with a carbine so Wintgens' saying the attacking aircraft came at him with a machine gun buzzing, seems a trifle exaggerated. They did, however, confirm they had been engaged by a Fokker over the Fôret de Parroy and that de Peuty was wounded in the right thigh. After the exchange, de Boutiny was also hit in the leg but they got back across the lines and managed a good landing with just a damaged engine.

Wintgens now moved, on the 4th, to FA48 at Mühlhausen, although he seems to have had something of a roving commission for then he was with FA67 where he was credited with his first official victory on 15 July, another Morane Parasol at Schlucht. He was flying Fokker EI 5/15. However, with Immelmann well known as having scored the first Fokker kill on 1 August, we must assume that Wintgens was piloting a two-seater and not a monoplane. There is no obvious French or British loss, so the date may be incorrect.

At some period between 15 July and early August Wintgens was credited with a second victory, date unknown, still with FA48. Either that, or somehow someone has included his unconfirmed 1 July claim in his total. However, on 9 August he engaged and shot down a French Voisin from Escadrille VB112, in flames near Gondrexange, for victory number three. The crew of Marechal-des-Logis (MdL) Louis Pasco and Sergent Phillipe Toureille were killed. In a letter home, Wintgens recorded:

> 'It was a very interesting and exciting fight which ended with a 'little' explosion of the French battle biplane. The fellow almost took me with him when he went down in flames from 2,700 metres, for the last 50 rounds I fired at him were from a distance of only two aeroplane-lengths. But I saved the situation via an involuntary looping. It was really wonderful, due to my superior speed and manoeuvrability I could continuously keep my position in the blind spot of his machine gun. Shortly I shall get a small monoplane with a 160 hp engine.'

He did not score again until the new year of 1916, following a bout of influenza, but Wintgens' star was soon to rise.

Meantime, the increase in German air activity had not been lost on RFC HQ. In late July, Colonel H R M Brooke-Popham (a future Air Chief Marshal), one of three RFC wing commanders had written:

> 'The German aeroplanes are becoming far more active, and are making a regular habit of attacking our machines when on reconnaissance, and we are having to fight for all our information.'

To use a phrase popular more than half a century later, 'He hadn't seen anything yet!'

Chapter Two

THE BEGINNING OF THE 'FOKKER SCOURGE'

BOELCKE'S FIRST FOKKER KILL – 19 AUGUST 1915

Oswald Boelcke took nineteen days to equal his rival Max Immelmann in scoring a victory in a monoplane – or as he called it in a letter home, his good luck. He wrote:

> 'I fly mostly in the evening to chase the Frenchmen who are out range-finding, and that evening there were a lot of them out. The first one I went for was an English Bristol biplane. He seemed to take me for a Frenchman; he came toward me quite leisurely, a thing our opponents generally don't do. But when he saw me firing at him, he quickly turned. I followed close on him, letting him have all I could give him. I must have hit him or his machine, for he suddenly shot off his engine and disappeared below me. As the fight took place over the enemy's positions, he was able to land behind his own lines. According to our artillery, he landed right near his own artillery. That is the second one I am positive I left my mark on; I know I forced him to land. He didn't do it because he was afraid, but because he was hit.
>
> 'The same evening I attacked two more, and both escaped by volplaning. But I cannot say whether or not I hit them, as both attacks took place over the French lines.'

One might ask what was so different between Wintgens' claim of 1 July, and this one of Boelcke's. While Boelcke seems certain that his fire caused the British pilot to land it is by no means certain. In these early days of air combat, with some form of chivalry still in place, airmen of both sides felt fairly safe in getting out of danger by going down to land. It might well be that the 'Bristol' was damaged, or even the engine or fuel line may have caused the propeller to stop, giving the pilot no option but to land. It was not usual for a pilot to turn off his engine just for the sake of it.

In these early days too, in fact for much of the war, airmen were not all that accurate in correctly identifying the type of aeroplanes they were up against. It was not all that essential, and when someone is trying their best to kill you, your mental capacity for detailed inspection of the other man's aeroplane is probably not uppermost in your thoughts. During much of the war German airmen in particular were more likely to record an aeroplane 'type' rather than a specific name. For some time during the first half of the war a 'Vickers' covered virtually any sort of RFC 'pusher' type, be it the Vickers FB5, the FE2, FE8 or DH2. Later, the name Sopwith meant virtually any sort of single-seater RFC fighter – Pup, Triplane, Camel, DH5 – or even the SE5.

Bristol biplanes – Scouts – were in use at this stage, but employed mostly for scouting rather than artillery observation. If indeed it was helping to range artillery as Boelcke believed, then it was quite likely to have been a BE2 machine. However, if its pilot did in fact edge towards Boelcke's Fokker, was it to engage, as a Bristol might have done, or did the RFC pilot think the other machine was a Morane? If he did, there was no real reason to fly towards it.

A machine of No.2 Squadron was in combat with a German aeroplane on the 19th, and the gunfire severed its fuel pipe, forcing the crew to land near Arras without further mishap. The crew comprised Captains J G Hearson and Barker. Were they Boelcke's opponents? Cutting their fuel pipe would certainly stop the engine, and force them to land. If they were, it is interesting to evaluate this 'victory'.

As mentioned earlier, in these early days few thought that the counting of victories – in terms of numbers brought down by any one pilot – was going to be of interest and that interest was still in the future, even if it was the immediate future. Encounters with opposing aeroplanes, while on the increase, were still not as yet a daily occurrence and surely it could not be comprehended that within a year or so, some fighter pilots would have individual 'scores' of 20 or more. Then again, when I started to study air fighting and aviation history, I believed, naively perhaps, that if I read that such-and-such a pilot had scored 20 victories, this meant 20 aircraft destroyed. This was simply because I had been brought up studying the WW2 system of things, where probables – or even damaged – were noted but not counted in a pilot's score. Equally naively I believed unquestioningly that someone somewhere, had evaluated these victories and there was no question as to their validity. After more than 40 years of study, I now know better.

However professional these various airmen were, and in what ever war, they were still comparative youngsters, filled with enthusiasm and fear, optimism and a full measure of adrenaline. However certain a pilot was that the aeroplane he had fired upon had gone down to crash or even be seen to burn in the air, within a moment's hesitation, checking the sky about him before looking again, all sorts of things can happen. Over-claiming air victories was fairly common due in the main to more than one person seeing the same thing differently. If, in an air battle, a number of pilots fired on an enemy aeroplane, and shortly afterwards, they saw an aircraft going down in flames, or perhaps in WW2 a parachute suddenly appearing, each could think it was his victim. Even in WW1, at this early stage, a pilot could see what he wanted to see, that is human nature. If in this case, Boelcke felt certain his fire had disabled either crew or aeroplane, he had no way of confirming it, all he could do was to report what he had seen; in this case, the aeroplane landing with a dead engine. Either or both of the crew might well have been mortally wounded and the aeroplane so badly damaged that it was of no further use and was struck off. But Boelcke had no way of knowing if any of this applied to his victim on this day. That someone in 'authority' had deemed to credit him with a 'victory' must be taken in the light of what had actually been achieved. As far as this 'authority' was concerned, an English aeroplane had been forced to abort its artillery spotting task, been seen to go down with its engine stopped and force land. Being behind the Allied front line, that was all that could be properly assessed. No doubt someone on the German side of the trenches had been asked if anyone had seen an aeroplane falling into Allied lines, and if they had done, that would be all the confirmation 'authority' needed, especially in this early stage of the air war. 'Authority' would later become more stringent, but whatever the outcome, on this day, Oswald Boelcke had scored and been credited with his second air victory, and his first in a Fokker monoplane. Future combats that are covered in this book will also need this open minded view of things, as we shall read.

Meantime, a few more Fokker machines arrived at the front. In the 6th Army area, north of FA62 at Douai, FA5, FA9 and then FA24 received Fokkers for escort work. And eager young pilots to fly them.

FIRST REPORTS OF FOKKERS BY THE RFC

Mention that it could have been Captain J G Hearson and his observer that were in action with Boelcke on 19 August is interesting because it was Hearson who was one of the first RFC pilots to report meeting an armed Fokker monoplane just over two weeks earlier. On 29 July he and his observer, Lieutenant Marshall, were escorting another BE2c engaged on a photographic reconnaissance over Seclin. Both BEs fired at the Fokker and Hearson's observer later reported driving off two more Fokkers. While undoubtedly these were the two FA62 machines, the report put in indicated three Fokkers in all. Hearson's claim that both were driven down is jargon for the period. It merely meant that the opposition lost height and flew off, which could mean anything. In this case it certainly meant in reality, that at least one of the Fokkers regained height and came back with a companion before breaking off again, perhaps this time due to nothing more sinister than a low fuel state. What was significant was that Hearson reported the Fokker was armed with a machine gun!

This same day a 4 Squadron BE crew also reported encountering a Fokker. Captains Reese and Kennedy in a Vickers saw a Fokker following a BE2 and attacked it. They saw the Fokker make a steep spiral downwards, and fire a quick burst at the Vickers, one bullet hitting the lower wing, going through two spars, cutting two bracing wires and shattering one wing rib. When last seen the Fokker was descending towards an aerodrome at Cambrai. The 'Vickers' was presumably a Vickers FB5 'Gunbus' pusher.

Captain L G Hawker and Lieutenant Noel Clifton of 6 Squadron had a series of air fights on 11 August, the last being against a monoplane scout whose pilot tried to get behind their FE2 machine. However, Lanoe Hawker, who had recently won the Victoria Cross for his prowess in air fights, suddenly turned sharply and the monoplane flew across in front of the FE at about 50 feet. After being fired on the monoplane made a vertical nose-dive. This must have been seen by others in the air or by troops on the ground for reports received indicated that the monoplane had been hit. Again bearing in mind the vagaries of air combat it is of interest that Hawker and Clifton were credited not only with the monoplane destroyed (between Lille and Roubaix), but also a two-seater Aviatik over Houthem earlier that morning – also destroyed – although the Aviatik too was last seen only in a nose-dive. Later these actions were said to have ended with the Aviatik landing near St Yves while the monoplane had crashed on the outskirts of Lille. There do not appear to be any German casualties this date – that is airmen killed or wounded.

Another encounter with a Fokker monoplane (although they thought it a Fokker Parasol) came on 22 August, a 2 Squadron crew having their BE2c badly shot about over Seclin. The British crew got back safely but they reported the German pilot had been using steel core bullets. The German pilot, Vizefeldwebel Gustav Nestler, was flying with FA5. Although he was sure he had hit the BE it had finally escaped him.

IMMELMANN'S SECOND VICTORY

Both Boelcke and Immelmann were out hunting on the evening of 26 August. It was their favourite time, but whether this had anything to do with being free from other dutes by the evenings, or simply because they felt the conditions were more favourable is not known for sure. Both had already chased hostile aircraft back and down over the French lines, then Boelcke's gun jammed as they went for another. Immelmann fired 300 rounds and saw the enemy pilot throw up his arms as if he had been hit, and also discard his flying helmet as his machine began to spiral earthwards. Watching it go down the two men suddenly saw it fall and plunge into the ground close to Souchez.

Taking off a flying helmet and discarding it was to become a fairly common occurence for airmen wounded, having the urgent desire to feel cold air upon the face. Throwing up arms could represent being hit, although it could just as easily be an equally urgent signal that he had had enough and was giving up – leave me alone! Coming down inside French lines it was obviously difficult for the Germans to identify the victim, and there is no record of any French airman (or RFC) being killed this day, or for that matter, wounded. So it has never been possible to discover who Immelmann had been shooting at, but, again, German front-line observers had confirmed the fall, and Boelcke too had seen the airman throw up his arms and go down, so victory number two was confirmed. Soon after this fight, Immelmann received the Saxon Albert Order, Knight's Cross 2nd Class with Swords, to add to the Saxon Friedrich August Medal in Silver received on 20 July.

Oswald Boelcke became a local hero on 28 August. After lunch he watched a youth by a river bank, which ran in front of FA62's mess building, suddenly fall in and disappear. Diving into the water and seeing bubbles rising, he dived under the surface and pulled the 14-year-old boy up and then to a boat a comrade – von Teubern – had pushed out. Boelcke later received the Prussian Life Saving Medal.

On the last day of August one of the early French aces, Sous-lieutentant Adolphe Celestin Pégoud, was brought down. This pre-war airman had been flying a Morane with Escadrille MF25 and MS49 and the French credited him with six victories in air combat. However, on this day he engaged a two-seat Aviatik of FA48 piloted by Unteroffizier Kandulski. His observer, Leutnant Bilitz, got in a telling burst on the Morane which forced the Frenchman to crash to his death near Belfort. Strangely enough Kandulski had been a former flying pupil of Pégoud's before the war.

Two RFC flyers, Second Lieutenant E R C Scholefield and Captain F J C Wilson, No. 8 Squadron, had a fight in the air on the morning of 30 August (in BE2c 1704) which was indecisive. Two days later it was a very different matter.

LEUTNANT PRESTLE'S FIRST VICTORY

Again flying BE 1704, Scholefield and Wilson set off on a recce sortie soon after dawn and failed to return. Somehow, indications were that they had been brought down by an Albatros (two-seater?) near Bapaume, and were last seen in a nose dive way over the lines. However, Captain Wilson (6th Battn Scottish Rifles, and who hailed from Lanarkshire), upon being repatriated in late 1917, recorded the true story:

> 'I was a qualified observer in No. 8 Squadron, then stationed in the village of Marieux behind the Somme front. I had been detailed with my pilot, Lieutenant Scholefield, for a reconnaissance of gun emplacements north-east of Bapaume. Our machine was a BE2c. We had almost completed our reconnaissance when attacked by a Fokker that had hovered round for some time.
>
> 'The fight took place at a height of 8,000 feet, and lasted for ten minutes, during which the mounting of the Lewis gun became damaged and had to be fixed by handkerchief. I had almost finished my ammunition, without vital effect, when the enemy cut our rudder wires and we began to quickly descend out of control. We crashed badly. I was thrown out and sustained a severe concussion of the brain, my pilot escaped without much hurt. Throughout the engagement, Lieutenant Scholefield handled his machine with the greatest skill, and during the descent did all in his power to lessen the crash. Lieutenant Scholefield is still a prisoner of war.'

Edward Rodolph Clement Scholefield had learnt to fly in France, and held French Pilot Certificate No.819, dated 5 April 1912. The BE was credited to Leutnant Prestle of FA1, its fall noted as by Courcelles le Comte, north-west of Bapaume. While some German records of this period do not always mention the type of aeroplanes pilots flew, Wilson clearly noted it as a Fokker, and as there is no other German airman named, Prestle was presumably flying alone in a single-seater. Therefore we can deduce he was in an early Fokker Eindecker, one – or even the one – attached to FA1. The only suspicion is that if Prestle was an officer observer, and his NCO pilot did not receive a mention, then the Albatros connection may be true, although that doesn't explain why Wilson named the machine a Fokker unless it was a two-seat M8.

When finally Scholefield was released from prison camp he merely noted that they had been on a gun pit recce, had been attacked by an enemy aircraft and brought down due to aileron and rudder controls being cut.

It is understood that Karl Prestle was an observer early in the war and was with FA1 from September 1914 until he was severely wounded on 18 September 1915. This put him in hospital until November at which time he spent a year with FEA1b. Promoted to Hauptmann in 1918, he served with FA(A) 289b in the spring of 1918 then commanded FA(A) 292b from 31 May till the Armistice. Interestingly, an RE5 crew of 7 Squadron had a fight with a Fokker on 18 September 1915.

FOKKERS GROUNDED

For a while in September 1915 the Fokker monoplanes had to be grounded due to three fatal crashes at training units in Germany, but the pressure for their re-instatement was so great that the order was soon rescinded. Meantime, on 6 September, the 6th Army Fokker pilots met at FA5's airfield to discuss tactics and to see if formation flying was possible. They arranged that if warning of approaching enemy aircraft was received in time, they should meet over Lille and make a combined attack. Meanwhile, Boelcke was happily inspecting his new 100 hp engined Fokker – 37/15 – his previous one only being of 80 hp.

The very next day Allied aeroplanes were reported heading for Douai-Lille and Messrs Nestler (FA5), Constantin Krefft (FA5b) and Richard Dietrich (FA24) met over Lille and spotted four hostile machines. As the Fokker pilots had spread out somewhat it was not possible to make a formation attack. Dietrich saw what he identified as a Hanriot machine turning eastwards, caught up with it between Orchies and Marchiènnes and in a frustrating engagement with it and a Vickers machine that joined in, Dietrich, with a troublesome gun, finally had to break off.

In the German system, most pilots who were later fighter pilots had first to fly a period of duty with two-seater units. While not rare, it was not usual for fighter pilots not to have done a stint in a C-type aeroplane. This gave them good experience of war flying and was probably a better system than the RFC and RNAS used, to merely select pilots to fly single-seaters straight from training. By the time German pilots volunteered to fly single-seaters they generally knew their way about in the air, had gained their 'air eyes', and knew the way opposing two-seater crews worked.

Many successful German air fighters 'cut their teeth' in two-seat combat, and one during September 1915 was Emil Thuy, then a Gefreiter, later a 35-victory Leutnant and *Pour le Mérite* winner. On 7 September, flying with Oberleutnant Cranz in FA53, this twosome shot down a French Maurice Farman of MF8 in flames. The crew of Capitaine Jean Saillier, the Escadrille CO, and Sous-lieutenant Le Galle, were both killed.

Boelcke's Third Victory

Oswald Boelcke made a claim for his third kill on 9 September, again during an evening hunt to the front lines. He and Immelmann became embroiled with French machines, and when one attacked his comrade, Boelcke went to his rescue and following his burst of fire, saw the French pilot throw up both arms and then the aeroplane went straight down, hitting the ground about 400 metres in front of the German lines. He recorded it as a Morane two-seater, stating too in a letter to his family that both airmen had been killed and the aircraft wrecked. The victory was confirmed by Immelmann, near Souchez.

However, the date for this action is in doubt – it may have been on the 10th or the 12th. The problem is not helped by there being no obvious candidates, either French or British, on any of these dates. Escadrille MF25 did lose an aircraft on the 12th, with the pilot killed, reported down at Mont Faucon Wood, near Verdun, which if correct seems too far south. Obviously from the various locations noted by both Boelcke and Immelmann, they operated their two Fokkers not only from Douai but on occasions from further south. FA62, of course, had the luxury of having two Fokkers available, whereas other flieger-abteilungen had only one.

Some confusion remains too because of Immelmann's recollections in a letter home in which he comments on fights on the 9th and the 10th, involving Boelcke, which tends to confirm hostile aircraft forced down, but in Allied lines. On the 9th Immelmann appears to have fired at a twin-engined aircraft for an unconfirmed claim and then an aircraft forced to land the next evening, again unconfirmed as a victory.

That the Allies still did not know of the Fokker's interrupter gear is evidenced by a combat on 13 September between a Fokker and the crew of a 10 Squadron BE2c, Second Lieutenant J C Quinnell and Lieutenant W H Sugden-Wilson. During a recce sortie over Lamain a Fokker dived on them, its fire hitting the two-seater repeatedly and piercing its lower fuel tank as well as hitting an engine bearer. Sugden-Wilson returned fire and saw the Fokker turn away and start to glide in the direction of Tournai. They reported the Fokker had '. . . a machine-gun and deflector propeller', thinking it must have been a similar set-up used by some of the Morane pilots.

Sugden-Wilson would not be so lucky eight days later, falling to Immelmann to become a prisoner of war. On that occasion he was not flying with John Quinnell, who would survive the war as a Major with the DFC, and make the RAF his career, retiring as an Air Commodore CB in 1945.

Buddecke's First Victory

Hans-Joachim Buddecke, from Berlin, born 22 August 1890, had joined the German army in 1904 and six years later was commissioned. Leaving the army in 1913 he went to the United States of America where he worked at his uncle's car factory, and also learnt to fly, even purchasing his own French Nieuport aeroplane. He even had plans to start an aeroplane factory but the war stopped all that.

Returning to Germany he volunteered for the air service and was assigned to FA23, commanded by Hauptmann Seber. One of the pilots in this unit was Leutnant Rudolf Berthold (who we shall meet later) and when a Fokker arrived at their base at Roupy Lager, near Bertincourt, Berthold suggested that Buddecke should fly it, as he had flown a similar monoplane pre-war. Once they had the Fokker, they kept it in a hangar at Châteax Vaux, although there was little real interest in the machine, but the unit, operating from Vaux became a small detachment from the main abteilung, with the Fokker and Berthold's AEG twin-engined G-type machine, which carried a crew of three. Buddecke began flying the monoplane, although it was three weeks before he had a successful air action with it. Buddecke was to gain fame in another theatre of war, but his first victories were scored in the Fokker during the autumn of 1915, victory number one coming on 19 September. It also won for him the Saxon Knight's Cross of the Military St. Henry Order on 16 October. While not a Saxon himself, FA23 had close association with Saxony, hence the award.

His first victory was over a BE2c (No.2008) of No. 8 Squadron RFC. The crew of Lieutenant W H Nixon and Captain J N S Stott came down near St Quentin, Nixon being killed, Stott wounded and captured. Buddecke's citation for his award noted:

'On 19 September, 1915, Lt. Buddecke set out on a Fokker fighter monoplane (single-seater) against an English plane which had forced another plane of his section down after a short fight and was bombing the city of Cambrai. Lt Buddecke got within ten metres of the English plane. During the combat he fired almost 700 rounds. The enemy plane received 109 hits and was forced to land behind our lines (pilot dead, observer captured). Only his extraordinary handling of his aircraft and personal courage allowed such a result against a comparably equipped enemy.'

Returning from captivity, Captain John Stott (a reserve cavalry officer) confirmed that Nixon had been killed while they were on a long reconnaissance from Marieux to Avesnes, hit as they had been attacked by a single-seater.

Three days prior to Buddecke's award, on the 13th October, Max Immelmann had also received the same decoration, the first such award to a fighter pilot, although by that date, Immelmann had four victories. It has to be noted that these awards given to aviators and in particular to fighter pilots, resulted in much prestige and fame. Little wonder that many fighter pilots hunted opponents with such determination.

Another pilot to join Buddecke in FA23 was Leutnant Ernst Freiheir von Althaus, a northern Bavarian, and he took over a second Fokker machine, joining the detachment at Vaux.

Shortly before this, Leutnant Berthold, who was to become a most successful fighter pilot despite a number of injuries, got into a fight flying his AEG GII and both his observers were killed. Although Berthold had liked the type, this action finally changed his mind, and he began to fly the monoplane when available.

IMMELMANN'S THIRD VICTORY

Two days after Buddecke scored his first, Max Immelmann got his third – on his 25th birthday! He was flying an escort mission to German artillery observation machines, and upon approaching the front lines he saw a British aircraft and immediately attacked. The location of the fight was just east of Neuville at around 8 am German time (British time was one hour ahead.)

The combat lasted several minutes, Immelmann suffering with a gun jam for some seconds, but finally his fire wounded both British airmen in the 10 Squadron BE2c (No.2004) which forced a landing between Acheville and Willerval. Immelmann was for the second time able to land close to his recent opponents, whose aircraft had been badly smashed and set on fire. The observer, Lieutenant William Hodgson Sugden-Wilson had been thrown clear, but Second Lieutenant Stanley Winther Caws was dead. The dead pilot was no youngster, being 36 years of age and had seen duty in the South African War as a trooper in Paget's Horse. The BE crashed and burnt, near Vimy Ridge. Later the observer, whose only injury was a broken bone at the bottom of his spine, wrote to his parents:

> 'We were attacked by hostile machines and had a great fight lasting 15 minutes during which we expended all our ammunition. My pilot, Lieutenant Caws, was shot dead when we were 11,000 foot up, a bullet passing through his neck down to his heart, through the instrument panel, and hitting my leg!'

In the BE2 machines the observer sat in the front cockpit.

Two days later, Immelmann himself was on the receiving end. Engaged by a Vickers FB5 'Gunbus' on the afternoon of the 23rd, Second Lieutenant R E A W Hughes-Chamberlain and Captain C W Lane put a telling burst of gunfire into Immelmann's Fokker, around the cockpit area, the German pilot having to break away and dive rapidly, later admitting to being 'shot about'.

It was on the 23rd too that the French made the first mention in a communiqué of a Fokker monoplane, as one forced down a machine from Escadrille C56 into French lines where it landed. Of the crew, Lieutenants Albert Coué and Louis Escolle, the former was wounded.

The RFC were also becoming very aware that this new Fokker monoplane was firing a gun through the propeller but were still not certain it was anything other than the Germans using deflectors. Also on the 23rd, a 4 Squadron crew noted as much in a combat report. In BE2c 2035 at 2.15 pm between Douai and Arras, Second Lieutenants A T Whitelock and K F Balmain were the men involved.

Returning from a bomb raid they wrote that a German monoplane had been sent up from Douai aerodrome and was waiting to intercept them over

Cantin. The Fokker circled round in order to attack them from behind and then it opened fire. Balmain fired 2½ drums of Lewis at it in short bursts. Reaching Guémappe, two more hostile aircraft were seen in front and as their Lewis ammunition was running low, Balmain opened fire on the opposition with a rifle. AA fire then began to explode around them and the monoplane retreated towards Douai while the other two Germans broke off and headed for the deck.

Immelmann wrote of a fight this date, with a big English fighter east of Arras, but he described the British machine as having two engines and two guns. This was undoubtedly the 11 Squadron VFB5 'Gunbus', flown by Second Lieutenant R E A W Hughes-Chamberlain and Captain C W Lane (5456) mentioned above. They reported a fight near Ham with a Fokker which was probably hit as it nose-dived earthwards over Roupy from 5,000 feet at 1.15 pm. (This was followed by two more brushes with hostile machines before the British duo got back over the lines.)

Immelmann noted that the RFC machine had shot-up his undercarriage, cutting bracing wires, hitting the oil tank, petrol tank, engine and cowling, with further holes in the fuselage. Had Lane's fire been just that little bit more accurate, the name of Immelmann would not be so well known today as it is.

In reading through some of these early RFC combat reports, it is evident that Fokker pilots seldom pressed home attacks if surprise had been lost, and the British crew appeared able to defend themselves. In itself this seems quite sensible. Why endanger oneself? There will always be 'another one along in a minute', to quote a bus conductor's cry.

It should be remembered, that while during this period a Fokker monoplane was quite a fast 'bird', it was not as fast as fighters would become in the months to come, so the Fokker pilot knew quite well that his machine's approach speed was nothing a good man with a gun in an aeroplane could cope with and hit, provided he kept his nerve. Nor did the Fokker pilots possess the knowledge or have the ability in themselves or their aeroplane to fly aerobatically around, behind and over a would-be victim. That would come later to the next generation of fighter pilots on both sides.

For the most part, they played a stalking game, hoping to catch the opposition unawares, get in quickly, fire and break off. The Boelckes and the Immelmanns usually only pursued hard if they could see their opponents fleeing rapidly and perhaps not paying as much attention to returning fire as they might.

VON CRAILSHEIM'S FIRST VICTORY

Feld-fleiger Abteilung 53's Fokker was being flown by Leutnant Freiherr von Crailsheim on 22 September 1915. Kurt von Crailsheim came from a military family, whose men suffered severely during WW1. Kurt served with Infanterie-Regiment Kaiser Wilhelm, König von Preussen (2 Würrtembergisches) Nr.120 initially but was wounded in one leg in August 1914, being deemed unfit for front line service afterwards. He therefore transferred to aviation in December 1914 and following pilot training, was sent to FA53 at Monthois, France. Due to his work on two-seaters he was chosen for single-seater work and following a conversion course at Mannheim, returned to FA53 as a fighter pilot.

He had just received the Gold Military Merit Medal on 20 September and for the feat two days later, he won the Iron Cross 1st Class. According to his letters home, he and five other Fokker-trained pilots stayed at Vrizy, and each day von Crailsheim drove by car to Monthois, which was nearer the front, to fly the Fokker. On the 22nd he fought and downed a Voisin of VB114 south-east of Vouziers, flown by MdL Michel Doré and Soldat Eugene Valot; the latter later died as a prisoner. According to von Crailsheim this was his unit's fourth victory, but the first with a monoplane.

Early the following month the motor of his Fokker failed and in trying to land he hit some telephone wires then a tree, so it was back to two-seaters until another Fokker was assigned. This arrived on 10 October. He had no further successful combats and then on 30 December suffered a bad crash. With both thighs broken plus facial injuries, he died on 4 January 1916.

BOELCKE'S FOURTH AND BÖHME'S DOUBLE

We know more about Oswald Boelcke's fourth victory than his third. On 23 September he was suddenly transferred south to Metz. The 25th of September (the day the Battle of Loos began in the north) was full of activity for the German Fokker pilots, and Boelcke shot down a Farman near Pont-à-Mousson, in French lines. His own Fokker had yet to arrive from Douai but his CO loaned him another, which he took up early on the 25th to test fly. Once in the air he saw AA fire in the distance, and then hostile aeroplanes. Climbing to gain height on at least three French aircraft, which later increased to seven, he closed to 100 metres on one and began firing. Seemingly hit, the Frenchman began to glide down to his side of the lines, and Boelcke, in following, suddenly realised he was over enemy territory. Not only that but this was an area he was unfamiliar with and he had not brought a map with him. However, he found his way home and then came a report that front line observers had confirmed seeing an aircraft 'flutter' down to Hill 368, and its pilot had been seen dragged from the wreckage and into a trench. This crew, which is thought to be from a machine of MF16, was Sous-lieutenant Paul Mouilères and MdL Paul Samacelli.

Meantime, this same day saw a Fokker pilot with FA9b, which was commanded by Oberleutnant Franz Hailer, down not one, but two French machines – his name, Eduard Böhme. FA9b had been operating with the German Alpine Corps in the Dolomites area of northern Italy, but it returned to the Vosges region in August 1915, based at Ensisheim, ten miles north of Mülhausen, Alsace. One of Böhme's companions with FA9b was Otto Kissenberth.

FA9b, re-equipped with Fokker monoplanes, was given the task of defending German cities and targets in south-western Germany. On the 25th the French mounted a raid upon the town of Rottweil's gunpowder factory, situated to the north-east of Freiburg. Vizefeldwebel Böhme began by attacking a Farman 11 (No.750) of MF29, flown by Sous-lieutenant

Gustave Charles Devin, with Soldat (mechanic) Marcel Clémont Vérité as observer, who had taken off at 05.40. His first burst missed and Devin yelled at his observer to fire back. Vérité had not seen the Fokker, thinking the gunfire came from the ground. Böhme's next burst of fire killed Devin with a bullet to the chest and the observer had then to grab the stick by bending over his collapsed pilot, and headed the machine to the ground where it crashed.

Böhme then turned his attention onto another Farman 11 (No.742) which was also shot down – near Triberg – and with it its crew of Capitaine Henri Pigot (prisoner, but possibly died of wounds later) and Soldat (mechanic) Marcel Vermet, killed. They had put up a fight together with another Farman piloted by Capitaine Maurice Happe, MF29's commander. Vermet's gun jammed after 23 rounds and as he began to fire back with a carbine, a burst from Böhme hit the machine and put a bullet through the observer's head. With fuel tanks holed, the wounded Pigot had to go down and made a good forced landing near Elzach.

Happe later had a stiff fight with an AEG G1 of FA48 and both machines were damaged. Happe and the German crew each managed to get back to their bases, Happe's machine having some 60 bullet holes in his Farman. Böhme's official report of the action reads:

'On 25 September at 0727 hrs., I took off with Fokker E 14/15, 80 hp Gnôme (700 cartridges) to pursue three enemy biplanes which had been reported approaching from the south at 0655 hrs; they were seen from the airfield shortly afterwards. Not to lose sight of them I climbed directly towards the French aircraft flying north of Colmar towards the east. Above Elzach in the Black Forest I reached an altitude of 3,000 m, and caught up with them, flying about 500 m below. It must have been 8 am as the combat began. I had only one thought, to attack and not let one get away.

'I attacked one of them with vigour but realised that the others were turning on me and starting to fire. Several times I heard bullets whistle by, so I attacked one, then the other, and fired 50-150 shots from such close range that my machine was shaken by the slipstream of their propellers.

'The next time I attacked from the front, and we raced against each other, both firing. After two biplanes had crashed I was attacked by the third, flying very low above the top of the Black Forest. I realised that my gunbelt was empty, the last bullets had been spent. I decided to land close to one of the crashed machines, and as my Fokker touched down in a field very close to Maurice Farman Nr.742, my undercarriage collapsed (0830 hrs). The observer was dead but the pilot was alive and shook my hand.'

At this stage of the war, combat victories were still an event in themselves, but to bring down two aircraft was nothing short of sensational. As far as is known, this was certainly the first time a German pilot had downed two hostile aircraft in one fight. His immediate reward for his actions was to receive the Grand Duchy of Baden's Silver Karl Friedrich Military Merit Medal on 6 October. This was followed by the Silver Military St Henry Medal on the 22nd, from his home state of Saxony. He was also the first aviator recipient of this decoration.

Böhme came from Herold, Saxony, born 9 September 1893 and had worked in the family limestone and marble quarries. Taught to fly before the war although unfit for military service, he nevertheless flew as a test pilot with the Pfalz Aviation Company in 1915. Once with the air service he joined FA9b, and was one of the pilots, along with Otto Kissenberth and Ferdinand März, to take part in a bomb raid to Cortina d'Ampezzo on 31 July. He then trained as a single-seat pilot with Kampfeinsitzer-Abteilung Mannheim and by late September was back with FA9b at Colmar-North.

Sadly his moment of fame was relatively short-lived. Like von Crailsheim, Böhme was seriously injured in a Fokker crash as he took off from his home airfield on 24 January 1916 and died later that day in hospital.

One of the two-seater pilots with FA9b was Martin Zander, and it is understood that he and his observer brought down an 8 Squadron BE2c (4301) during the opening round of the Loos Battle, while on a bomb raid against the Douai-Valenciennes railway system. Second Lieutenants J N Washington and M W Greenhow were its crew, both being taken prisoner, although Washington later died of his injuries. They came down at Moeuvres, near Cambrai. Maurice Wyvil Greenhow, upon his return to England in late 1918, reported:

> 'Air fight with two German Fokker two-seaters which attacked alternately from different directions. Left rudder control severed. Both pilot's legs broken by gunfire and also hit in the stomach. Throttle shot away.'

This was Zander's first victory and he would later command Jasta 1 and become an ace. In the German system, there were no shared victories with other pilots or crews. If in this instant, two two-seater crews accounted for the BE, the decision of who should get the credit would either be made by one or other crew acknowledging the other crew should get it, or it would be solved with the toss of a coin.

On 6 October a German machine was brought down in French lines which carried a machine gun from this BE, the German saying it had been taken from the machine. A crew from FA62 had also been captured on 3 October.

OCTOBER 1915
The month of October began quietly enough although flak fire and two-seater combats resulted in some losses. Then on the 10th the air war flared up. It was a date on which another future German ace gained his first victory while still an observer – Robert Greim, flying with FA3b. As his

unit suggests, Greim was a Bavarian, born in June 1892, the son of a police captain. Following army cadetship he served with the 8th Bavarian Field Artillery Regiment from 1912 and saw active duty in France in the early months of the war. Artillery men were always welcomed by the air service as observers, especially those engaged on artillery spotting duties.

On 10 October, flying with Oberleutnant Fritz Hempel they claimed a French Farman of MF63 shot down near Deuxnouds aux Bois, its crew being killed. He spent several more months flying two-seaters before becoming a pilot. He ended the war with 35 victories and the *Pour le Mérite* plus the Max-Joseph Order and a knighthood, therefore his title became Ritter von Greim.

IMMELMANN'S FOURTH AND VON BÜLOW'S FIRST TWO

Max Immelmann made it four on 10 October by downing another BE2c (2033) flown by Lieutenants John Gay and David Leeson of 16 Squadron. They were sent out to photograph defences around Lille, while Immelmann had taken off to patrol between La Bassée and Lens. He spotted the two-seater amidst bursting AA shells, attacked and let fly 400 rounds of ammunition. Jock Gay was killed and Leeson's gun shot off its mounting. The aeroplane came to a shattering crash in a wood outside the village of Verlinghem, near Lille, the Canadian observer injured but alive – and very lucky to be so.

A report from the 50th Division that afternoon confirmed seeing a British aeroplane brought down after a fight with two enemy aircraft and a message dropped two days later and picked up by soldiers in the 3rd Corps area, informed them that Gay had died of wounds and that Leeson was slightly wounded and a prisoner.

Leutnant Walter von Bülow-Bothkamp was born on 24 April 1894, at Borby, near Eckernforde, Holstein, and had studied law at Heidelberg University and despite his young years was well-travelled. When war came he joined the Saxon Hussar Regiment Nr.17 – the famous 'Death's Head' Hussars – and saw action in Alsace where he was commissioned. Joining the air service he was assigned to FA22 following his pilot training, and flying AEG G11 two-seaters, operated on the French Champagne front from September 1915.

He went straight on to fly one of the Fokker monoplanes and on 10 October shot down a Farman which appears to have fallen or landed inside French lines. MF50 did have an observer wounded this date. The next day he was up again shortly after mid-day and this time engaged a Caudron from Escadrille C61. It and its crew of Sergent Thamin and observer/gunner Soldat Lasserre, crashed on the Somme-Py to Souain road.

PARSCHAU'S FIRST VICTORY

Otto Parschau had been flying with FA42 and FA261 since the start of the war. Born on 11 November 1890, in Klutznitz, East Prussia, he had originally served with the 151st Infantry Regiment in 1910, and commissioned the following year. He had taken an early interest in aviation and learnt to fly in 1913, obtaining licence No.455 on 4 July of that year.

With FA261 he had flown a Fokker, but then moved to Kampfgeschwader Nr.1 (KG1), a bomber unit, and flew Fokkers with them on escort and scouting missions. He later took command of KG1.

Flying over the Champagne area on 11 October he came across a Farman, noted as being from Escadrille MF2, which he shot down with the loss of its two crewmen, although the lack of French recorded losses makes this difficult to reconcile. (MF2 lost a crew on the 12th, noted as being downed by a Fokker, so perhaps a date somewhere has been recorded incorrectly.) The only loss was the Caudron of C61 which is mentioned above in connection with von Bülow's action.

Flieger-Abteilung 9b was back in the news on this 11 October too, with Hauptmann Martin Zander and his observer, Oberleutnant Lerche, shooting down a RFC BE2c (2047) near Villeret, north-west of St Quentin (Zander's second victory). The crew of Second Lieutenants A I Burnie and B O Wilkin were taken prisoner. Upon his return from PoW camp, Arthur Inglis Burnie stated:

> 'Shot down in fight with two-seater during a long reconnaissance. Gun jammed and then engine was hit so forced to land. Two-seater landed in same field so could not burn aircraft. Supposed to have escort by 11 Squadron FEs but no sign [of them] after flying through AA fire.'

Bertram Osborne Wilkin's recollections were:

> 'Slight damage by AA fire from over Bapaume. Engine started missing in one cylinder and later, over St Quentin, attacked by two-seater biplane. Drove it off with gun. Continued recce. and again attacked by same machine quarter of an hour later. Enemy had advantage of height and used it to gain speed. I opened fire and gun jammed after three rounds. Enemy aircraft smashed our engine and badly damaged propeller then dived clear, passed and climbed to our rear. We were both taken to the civil jail in St Quentin and two weeks later to Mainz, then Crefeld Camps.'

Wilkin later went to Ingolstadt and later still, in April 1918, was interned in Holland.

BOELCKE'S FIFTH

Although still on the strength of FA62, Oswald Boelcke is shown as being part of BAM in mid-October 1915 (Brieftauben Abteilung Metz – Carrier Pigeon unit, Metz). Similar in title to Brieftauben Abteilung Ostende (BAO), in reality these names were a cover for mobile combat units. It was while he was still at Metz that Boelcke got his fifth victory on 16 October, a French Voisin (No.V839) over St Souplet. This machine, from VB110, was crewed by Caporal Gaston Vibert and Sergent Robert Cadet.

On the British Front Fokkers were encountered on the 21st by a Morane crew from No.3 Squadron – dropping hand grenades on La Bassée! – and although they were shot up, were rescued by the arrival of a BE2c. Both men were wounded but they landed safely. Interestingly they reported that the Fokker had deflector plates on its propeller, so obviously the Fokker's interrupter gear was still unknown. An 11 Squadron FB5 also had a combat with a Fokker and an LVG two-seater this same day.

The next day an 8 Squadron crew fought two Fokkers near Le Cateau, one of which was seen to go down in a nose dive towards Cambrai and crash into trees in a cloud of dust, while its companion flew off.

By October the number of RFC squadrons in France had risen to around 25, and with the number of British and French aircraft on the increase, this was helping to keep the Fokker Eindecker menace in check. Because it was still in small numbers and also due to engine problems, the full impact of the German fighter was not being felt yet, but it certainly concentrated the mind of pilots and observers if they saw a Fokker approaching them, always assuming they saw it in the first place. Boelcke and Immelmann, as well as the other Fokker pilots, were starting to write the combat doctrines. Everything was new, and everything had to be tested. By now, knowing they had the slight edge on speed, the Fokker pilots were able to stalk the allied machines a little more, rather then just attack immediately. In this way they found they could secure a good attacking position, and also be able to surprise an opposing crew. After all, the allied two-seater airmen's main task was to look at the ground trying to locate targets for the artillery, information for the generals, and positions to be photographed. Sometimes only a cursory glance around them was all they managed, and in between times a Fokker pilot might pounce.

BUDDECKE'S SECOND

Hans-Joachim Buddecke of FA23 attacked and shot down a 13 Squadron BE2c (2017) on the 23rd, flown by Captain Cecil H Marks and Second Lieutenant W G Lawrence, south of St Quentin. They had been escorting a recce. machine that afternoon, and they were the first crew lost by the Squadron. William George Lawrence was the brother of (Colonel) T E Lawrence, who was to gain fame as 'Lawrence of Arabia'.

Buddecke had been assisted by von Althaus and he may have inflicted some of the 212 bullet holes later found in the wreck. Buddecke had seen that the British crew were badly hit and had flown off to one side hoping its pilot would make a good landing. However von Althaus, unsure of the situation, made an attack and the machine crashed.

On the 26th a 10 Squadron crew were hit by a Fokker near Lille, the pilot being wounded in one arm and shoulder. He soon fainted and the observer succeeded in flying the BE to the French lines after correcting a spinning nose dive. The observer was injured in the forced landing but at least they survived. They do not appear to have been claimed by a German pilot.

IMMELMANN'S FIFTH

This same day Immelmann got his fifth, a Vickers FB5 (5462) from No.11 Squadron. It was flown by Captain C C Darley, with observer Second

Lieutenant R J Slade. Charles Curtis Darley was a flight commander and as his unit was in the process of moving base, he had to take a new observer from another flight. Patrolling between Cambrai and Péronne he was beginning to have trouble with his engine as he climbed towards Arras. Crossing the lines just south of the town he began to follow the long straight road towards Cambrai, while being fired on by German AA gunners.

Gradually leaving the 'archie' fire behind he saw the German airfield at Cambrai and moved closer but moments later a Fokker was behind them, and firing. Taken by surprise, the engine was hit and promptly stopped as the fuel line was cut, and Darley received wounds, a bullet passing through his right upper arm, while another virtually severed his right thumb. He tried to glide west but had no hope of making the lines before he was forced to put down near Ecoust St Mein.

His injuries hampered efforts to set the Gunbus alight before German cavalry rode up to take both men prisoner. Immelmann landed nearby too, strolling over to introduce himself and saw to it that Darley's wounds received attention before arranging for the two men to be driven by car to hospital. Because of his serious injuries, Darley did not spend a full term as a prisoner, being exchanged into neutral Switzerland in May 1916, and was finally repatriated in June 1917. He later rose to Air Commodore CBE AM in the RAF. His Albert Medal was awarded in 1922 following a plane crash in which his brother Cecil was trapped in a smashed cockpit. Despite valiant efforts by Darley, he was unable to free his brother from the flames, during which he suffered burns which were to keep him in hospital for 18 months.

After being repatriated from prisoner of war camp, Darley made the following report of his flight of 26 October 1915:

> 'At midnight 14/15 October, I received orders that there were four patrols and recces for the 25th by C Flight. Only two observers were available so I sent round to the other Flights to borrow two more. As most had moved to a new landing ground, I could only get two partially trained observers, one, Second Lieutenant Slade, I took myself on a two-hour patrol between Cambrai and Péronne.
>
> 'Took off around 07.30 but engine was not running well so went north, nearly to Arras, before getting to 6,000 feet. Crossed the lines three miles south of Arras following the road to Cambrai and climbing a little. AA did considerable amount of shooting and machine hit frequently. Shooting dropped when a few miles over and no more until near Cambrai. No hostile aircraft about and I was steering for the German aerodrome to challenge them.
>
> 'AA fire lasted a few minutes then suddenly stopped and almost immediately a machine gun in the rear opened fire and my engine stopped. Pressure gauge showed no pressure in petrol tank which must have been hit. I banked machine and turned to bring fire to bear on enemy aircraft but it was now

above me and turned once more behind. Observer had two machine guns but nothing for the pilot.

'One bullet had gone through my right upper arm and another nearly cut off my right thumb. Two cylinders and three valves had been hit too.

'Engine couldn't be restarted so I headed for the lines 20 miles away and I was only at 6,500 feet. Fokker followed firing all the time; a north-east wind helped a little but ten miles short of the lines, had to land in a field. Aircraft badly shot-up and I fired six rounds [from a pistol] into fuel tank but it was empty. Tore wing fabric and tried to light it with matches but failed. It was difficult with one hand. Then a German cavalry soldier came up.

'Later the Fokker landed nearby and Immelmann came over and did what he could. I was then taken to a field hospital by car. My observer was unwounded.'

Reginald James Slade came back after the war and confirmed being shot down by a fast enemy scout which smashed their engine, and pierced the petrol tank. He said he was slightly wounded and Darley seriously so.

BOELCKE'S SIXTH

No sooner had Immelmann levelled Boelcke's score, than Oswald inched ahead with his sixth victory. Still at Metz, he claimed a Voisin south of Tahure on the morning of the 30th. He and others were flying in support of a ground attack and Boelcke attacked several French machines as he dived through some clouds. Closing to within a few metres of the Voisin he almost collided with it and had to break away quickly. Although he lost sight of the Frenchman, a crashed aircraft was later seen about 200 metres inside French lines, one wing pointing skywards. The crew appears to have escaped serious injury, although a crew of MF8 were killed this date, Lieutenants Alfred Dullin and Leclerc. Whether this had anything to do with Boelcke is unclear.

Chapter Three

WINTER 1915

CONFUSION TO THE HISTORIAN

Aircraft of No. 6 Squadron RFC were out on the late morning of 4 November. One crew were in a BE2c (2031), another in an FE2a pusher (5644). In the pusher were Lieutenants C H Kelway-Bamber and H J Payn (RE) on a patrol and photo sortie. East of Zillebeke at 12.45 they saw the BE being closely pursued by a Fokker monoplane.

They dived steeply to attack the German machine, but its pilot flew directly underneath the FE, no more than 30 yards away. Payn fired half a drum of Lewis at it, then the Fokker began to circle the big fighter, both aircraft gradually losing height. Finally the Fokker climbed away into his own territory, followed by the other half of the Lewis gun's drum, as the FE swung in behind, about 80 yards away.

The Fokker then made a right-hand turn, went into a steep bank, turned onto its back and plunged earthwards out of control while still over the Allied side, south of Zillebeke.

Landing back at base, the FE crew found the Fokker had wounded their comrade observer in the BE, Captain C E Ryan, but the pilot, Second Lieutenant H Bright was unhurt. In the RFC Communiqués the fall of the German machine is recorded as having crashed and a battered machine gun recovered.

One would have thought that this was all pretty conclusive. But no! Firstly, while the 6 Squadron combat report clearly states the machine as being a Fokker monoplane, the communiqué says it was a two-seater – and that both pilot and observer were killed. As a gun had been recovered, one would assume there was no doubt that someone had found and buried two German airmen. Yet there are no German fatalities this day amongst the German air service, nor any known prisoners! And the only German airman noted as killed was a man hit by rifle fire – over Serbia.

The BE crew had initially been engaged by a large pusher machine, then by three tractor machines, so were they all two-seaters, or a mixture of two-seaters and monoplane single-seaters? I delayed writing this book for several years simply because I knew that these sorts of problems would arise, about a period notoriously short of real facts, real records or even clear record keeping. Everything was in its infancy in 1915, even the keeping of historical information it seems. The bureaucrats might like to think things will be recorded and kept, but the fighting man at the sharp end isn't overly sensitive to such things. He may be dead the next day!

IMMELMANN'S SIXTH VICTORY

Max Immelmann drew level again on 7 November 1915. While on patrol from Douai he looked down and saw a BE2c (1715) below and then spotted that it was being escorted by a single-seat Bristol Scout. Both machines were from No.10 Squadron, the two-seater crew being Lieutenant Owen V LeBas and his observer, Captain Theodore D Adams. In the Bristol was a veteran flyer, Captain C Gordon Bell, who had become a pilot in 1911, and was destined to be one of the RFC's first aces. Later, as an instructor, one of his pupils would be James T B McCudden who would win the Victoria Cross in 1917.

Choosing his moment to attack, Immelmann went for the two-seater and his fire hit home. He watched as the BE spiralled down to crash near Quiéry-la-Motta, just west of Douai, at 15.45 (German time). Neither airman had a chance to survive the impact.

Meantime, Gordon Bell had seen an Aviatik and distracted by this he had failed to engage the Fokker until after its pilot had shot down his charge. But almost at once his engine began to give him trouble and he was forced to head for the lines. Looking back he saw the Fokker circling the crash site. Moments later, Immelmann once again landed nearby to his latest victims, but they were beyond help. LeBas was 21, Adams 26 and they are buried side-by-side at Brown's Copse Cemetery, Roeux.

Further honour was soon bestowed on Immelmann, he being awarded the Knight's Cross, with Swords, of the Royal Hohenzollern House Order, a few days later, the second Saxon to be so honoured in the war. However, Boelcke had beaten him to it, having been awarded the same decoration on 1 November – the first airman to receive it.

German authority, and especially Prussian authority, held a strict regime of awards, and these had to be awarded in order of precedence. After the Hohenzollern House Order, there was only one higher award, the coveted *Orden Pour le Mérite*. Neither men knew if they would ever achieve enough to receive this award, certainly no aviators had yet achieved anything that merited such a high honour. By this date only three had been awarded to fighting men, one to a soldier, two to naval officers. Only time would tell if more would be awarded.

Meantime, in the war diary of Flieger-abteilung 32 for 10 November, it had been noted that during the morning, Oberleutnant von Althaus arrived at the airfield upon being assigned to the unit from FA23 and the Fokker had been placed at the disposal of the 14th Reserve Corps. He flew a few patrols and then returned to FA23 on the 21st.

BUDDECKE'S THIRD

Hans Buddecke of FA23 brought down his next victory on 11 November, yet another poor BE2c, and another from No.8 Squadron RFC. It was another BE (1725) being flown by just a pilot, without the defensive fire of an observer. In fact 8 Squadron lost two observer-less BEs, out on this bomb raid. Buddecke's victim, Lieutenant W A Harvey – armed with just a rifle, which was not the most convenient weapon to handle in the confines of a cockpit – was wounded and taken prisoner, but later in the war was sent to Switzerland to be interned. However, he was taken ill in late 1917 and died from tuberculosis on 7 November. The other BE was shot down by ground fire, Second Lieutenant V M Grantham being taken prisoner of war at Warlencourt, south-west of Bapaume. Both airmen had been part of a raid upon the German airfield at Bellenglise, a combined attack by aircraft of three RFC squadrons, but very poor weather proved their undoing, the escorts becoming separated from the bomb-carrying aircraft.

William Anthony Harvey came from Thetford, Norfolk, and was 26. Previously with the 4th Norfolk Regiment, he is buried at Vevey, Switzerland: at least not a hostile land.

This same day a FE2a was shot down in combat with two German C-types. This is a good example of how victories were not shared. Leutnants Bethke and Eckstein in an Albatros CI of FA24 were the crew who received credit for bringing down 5644 of 6 Squadron, after a dispute with an LVG pilot – Leutnant Ilse – of FA6.

Five days later, on the 16th, another airman whose star had yet to rise, gained his first victory in a two-seater. Hermann Göring was going to have a long war, survive it and become well known as part of Adolf Hitler's Germany as head of the Luftwaffe (airforce) before and during WW2. In 1915 he was just a lowly Leutnant in the air service having risen from observer to pilot after army service in the Vosges. In the autumn of 1915 his flying unit was operating in the Champagne sector with Albatros C-type two-seaters.

On the afternoon of the 16th he had with him an observer named Leutnant Bernert. While there was to be a successful fighter pilot by the name of Fritz Otto Bernert, it is not thought that he was one and the same, despite the fact that he too was an observer in the Luftstreikräfte at around this time. The two men engaged a French Farman over Tahure, which they claimed as shot down into French lines, although there is no apparent casualty listed.

On the last day of November a Farman crew from MF16, Sous-lieutenant Marcel Alphonse Gindner and Sous-lieutenant Villiers, were in a scrap with two LVGs and a Fokker monoplane of FA13, north-east of Arras. Three to one are never good odds and the two Frenchmen were brought down near Drocourt and taken prisoner. It is not known who was in the Fokker, or if he was credited with the victory or if it went to either of the two-seater crews. What is known is that Caporal Marcel Gindner escaped captivity in December 1915 and returned to duty, while his observer, Sous-lieutenant Villiers was listed as missing.

THE PFALZ MONOPLANE

As well as the Fokker monoplanes (the types EII and EIII were arriving at the front now) there was another similar-looking monoplane, the Pfalz EI and then the Pfalz EIV at the front. The EI was a development of the Pfalz AI of 1914, and some of the latter had been used for recce work since the start of the war. Once fitted with the same interrupter gear as the Fokker machines, it went into production as the Pfalz EI. Although EII and EIII variants followed, it was only the EIV which saw more action. German pilots much preferred the Fokker to the Pfalz.

Although the Fokker and the Pfalz differed considerably structurally – the Pfalz was a wooden airframe, whereas the Fokker was of welded tubular steel – the machines looked very similar in the air, and one expects that most Pfalz machines, when seen in combat by allied pilots and crews, were identified as the more famous Fokker type. Like the Fokker, the Pfalz machines were allocated in small numbers to flieger-abteilungen for protection and scouting duties, some units obviously having a small mix of both types of monoplane.

GUSTAV LEFFERS AND VON ALTHAUS' FIRST VICTORIES

On 5 December, Leutnant Gustav Leffers, flying with FA32, scored his first victory in a Fokker. Leffers came from the northern German port of Wilhelmshaven, born 2 January 1892, and prior to the war had been studying naval engineering. Volunteering for aviation duty, after pilot training he was assigned to FA32 in February 1915, to fly LVG two-seaters. He rose through the ranks, being commissioned on 25 July 1915 and in September he requested fighter pilot training. Leffers undertook this training at Mannheim, and on 5 November was told to fly a Fokker machine (an EIII 86/15) back to his unit. Coming in to land the gun cable got snagged, and caused the monoplane to bank so far to the left that the left wing hit the ground. The crash destroyed the aeroplane, although Leffers scrambled out unharmed. A couple of days later he flew another Fokker to the airfield (84/15), a machine in which he was to have much success. One month after his crash he made his first kill.

Coburg-born Ernst Fr von Althaus was the son of the adjutant to the Duke of Saxe-Coburg-Gotha. Born on 19 March 1890, he enlisted in the 1st Saxon Hussar Regiment, Nr.18 as an ensign when he reached military age, and in 1911 was commissioned. In action during the opening rounds of the war, he won the Saxon Knight's Cross of the Order of St Heinrich on 27 January 1915, but soon afterwards requested a transfer to flying. Promotion to Oberleutnant came on 6 August. Assigned to FA23 on 20 September, he soon began to fly Fokker monoplanes, and by this time he had, as we read in the previous chapter, already been in action.

Mid-afternoon of 5 December Leffers encountered a BE2c (2049) over Achiet-le-Grand and sent it down to crash. He had taken off from Vélu airfield, just a couple of kilometres north of Bertincourt, and flying west, by 3 pm found himself over Bapaume. Alerted by bursting AA shells he then saw British aircraft over Martinpuich, which were flying a photo sortie to Bellenglise, and started a chase. Flying over Grévillers, heading for Achiet-le-Grand, Leffers opened fire on one of the BEs, the gunner too firing back at him. More firing and Leffers saw that the pilot had been hit, the machine looking as if it was in difficulties. Caught in the prop-wash from the BE Leffers took a few moments to get his monoplane under control, and once he did, saw the BE plunge to the ground. The pilot, Second Lieutenant Arthur R H Browne, from Australia, did not survive, dying from wounds, nor did his observer, 1AM William H Cox, aged 19, from Derby. They were from No.13 Squadron, and this unit lost a second

BE (4092) in this action during their photo-op to Bellenglise, engaged and brought down by von Althaus. By one of those strange coincidences, both British aircraft had the same four numbers in their serials, 2049 and 4092.

Observers from the British 11th Infantry Brigade saw the fight and saw both aircraft fall behind the German lines. 18th Division artillerymen also saw the action, the BE flying very high and a small German machine coming up behind it. Both aircraft were seen to come down very steeply. Obviously Leffers must have been very low before he got his Fokker under control, and was out of sight of British troops when he did so.

This BE2c was shot down by von Althaus of FA23 west of Roye, 24 kilometres south of Bapaume. Lieutenant Gavin A Porter, another Australian, and 1AM Henry J Kirkbride also died. All four are buried in Achiet-le-Grand (Extn) Cemetery.

A message was dropped by a German airman concerning the loss of these airmen, which read: "With regard to the BE No.4092 and other aircraft brought down after a violent fight in the air. The pilots and observers, 4, met with an honourable flying man's death and were buried yesterday with all military honours."

ZANDER'S THIRD?

No.11 Squadron lost a Vickers FB5 on 14 December (5074), piloted by Second Lieutenant G S M Insall VC, with observer Corporal T H Donald DCM. Both men were wounded and taken into captivity, but who shot them down?

Gilbert Insall had won his Victoria Cross, and Donald his Distinguished Conduct Medal, for an action just a month earlier, 7 November, forcing a German two-seater to land four miles south-east of Arras. No sooner had the German crew climbed from their machine than Insall, circling, saw them about to fire at the Gunbus. Insall dived, giving Donald the chance to fire at the two enemy airmen, who then fled. Nearby German infantry then began to fire up at the aeroplane but ignoring them, Insall flew back over the two-seater and dropped a small incendiary bomb on the machine which was soon wreathed in smoke. Flying back, Donald took the opportunity of raking front line trenches with gunfire but then the Vickers was hit in the fuel tank and they were forced to land. They had made it to the British side, but then had to contend with German artillery fire but the aircraft was not hit. The two men erected a rough screen one side of the FB5 as darkness fell, allowing Donald to effect repairs by torchlight, and the next morning they took off for their aerodrome.

According to RFC records, Insall and Donald were attacked by a Fokker, or by AA fire, which damaged the FB5's engine – the same 5074 in which the VC action was fought – and they had to land. However, Insall later reported being hit during a fight with a German two-seater, and was forced to land. Their apparent victors were Martin Zander and his observer, Leutnant Lerche, of FA9, although they do not appear to have been awarded credit for it. It would have been Zander's third victory, but officially his third victory was not credited to him until August 1916. Did they have a dispute with some anti-aircraft battery, and did Insall have his machine hit by AA fire during the action with the two-seater and believe the damage was caused by the two-seater's fire? Did the two-seater crew hit the FB5 only to lose the dispute with the AA battery?

Whatever the facts of the matter, Insall and Donald were sent of to hospital, both men having been wounded, then to prison camp, where Insall, after several attempts, finally escaped and got into Holland in September 1917. For these efforts he received the Military Cross.

IMMELMANN'S SEVENTH

The day after Insall was captured, Max Immelmann brought his score to seven by shooting down a 3 Squadron Morane (5087) over Valenciennes. Both crew members, Second Lieutenants A V Hobbs and C E T Tudor-Jones, were killed. They had been on what was termed a 'long reconnaissance' to Valenciennes, and when the next day a radio report was heard by the Squadron that Immelmann had downed a Morane, everyone knew the fate of their recent companions.

Further confirmation came from a civilian refugee who reported seeing an aircraft with tricolour markings and bearing the number 8057 (*sic*) brought down by the Germans near Raismes; both occupants had been killed.

Alan Victor Hobbs, Royal Sussex Regiment, came from Tunbridge Wells, the eldest son of a local chemist. When war came he was at St John's College, Cambridge, and immediately volunteered for the Queen's Own Royal West Kent Regiment, then commissioned into the 10th Royal Sussex Regiment. Transferring to the RFC he joined 8 Squadron in July 1915, but then moved to 3 Squadron. He was 21.

Charles Edward Tudor Tudor-Jones was a year younger. The second son of a solicitor from Swindon, Wiltshire, he too was training in the legal profession when war came. Volunteering into the 7th Battalion, the Devonshire Regiment of the territorials, he had the temporary rank of captain but resigned to join the regular army, going to Sandhurst, where he was gazetted Second Lieutenant in the East Lancashire Regiment. Attached to the RFC he had joined 3 Squadron in September 1915.

With Immelmann now having a score of seven victories, and Boelcke six, it can be assumed that some attention to scoring victories was being seriously given not only by the newspaper journalists, but by 'higher command'. Up until fairly recently, it was something of a feat to bring down an aeroplane in an air fight, but these two were starting a trend and making it look a lot easier than was supposed. Confusion no doubt also began to creep into the way of things, for until now – remembering always that all this was still absolutely new and unprecedented – victories did not necessarily mean an aircraft destroyed. Merely putting an opponent out of action, or stopping him do his work, was a kind of 'victory'. Victories associated with an aircraft totally destroyed was not yet one and the same, although for the Germans it was practically so. It was not until post-WW2, after which victories in air combat had become more established, a victory actually representing an aircraft destroyed, that early aviation historians in the late 1950s merged these facts with victory scores from WW1, and totally confused the issue.

While it is true that interest in WW1 fighter aces had flared up in the 1930s, few enthusiasts really had any depth of knowledge of detail. RAF records had become secret and were not open to the general public, and wouldn't be until the late 1960s. And, it has to be said, these records became so closely guarded by the Air Ministry, that very few people had access to them. These early enthusiasts, come air historians, could only work with what they had, and while the more serious of these did pretty good jobs on the whole, the pulp-fiction writers of the day only helped to muddy the waters with their garish stories of daring-do. Even such established writers as W E Johns, himself a WW1 pilot (although not a fighter pilot), in creating his air hero *Biggles* (Captain James Bigglesworth DSO MC) in the 1930s, did little to lay ground rules, or make it clear how things had worked in the recent war. Not wishing to upset the sensibilities of readers, his hero came through as a sort of devil-may-care good guy overcoming the dastardly Hun on a regular basis. By and large the temperament of people was different in the 1930s, and of course, most of the surviving pilots of the Great War were still young men, few of whom wanted to, or felt the need to embellish their own part in the recent war. It had been a hellish experience in the first place without living it constantly in peacetime. Most were struggling to hold down a job and raise a family during the depression years.

It seems too that many of the fanciful names given to pilots dated from the 1930s. In WW1 Baron von Richthofen was often referred to as the Red Devil, the Red Baron sobriquet coming later. Immelmann too, referred to as *Der Adler von Lille* – The Eagle of Lille – is a little hard to fathom. Of his victories, virtually all were whilst flying from Douai, some 30 kilometres due south of Lille. And only one of his victims fell anywhere near Lille itself, the vast majority in the vicinity of Lens and Arras, with others even further south, to the east and west of Bapaume. His 'nickname' became established following the publication of his biography written by his brother Franz, translated into English in 1935.

PARSCHAU'S SECOND VICTORY
Otto Parschau, a month past his 26th birthday, and still operating with BAO up around the Channel coast, brought down his second British aeroplane on 19 December. His victims were the crew of a BE2c (2074) from No.12 Squadron, Lieutenants Norman Gordon-Smith and Duncan Flower Cunningham-Reid, who were both killed.

This day saw the opening of a German ground assault on a sector of the British 2nd Army which opened with a gas attack, a particularly nasty aspect of the Great War. Air operations from both sides were intense and Parschau had easily found a victim engaged on reconnaissance near the Belgium city of Bruges. They fell at Oostcamp (Oostkampe) and were buried in the local churchyard, the rear fuselage, elevators and tail initially erected to form a cross over them.

The airmen who signed themselves 'Flieger-Abteilung, Ghistelles' later dropped a letter into the British lines, which read: 'Today, 19 December 1915, at 11.00 am, the English aeroplane AVRO 2074 was shot down by us near Oostcamp, south of Bruges. The English occupants, Pilot Norman Gordon-Smith RFC, Observer Lt. Cunningham-Reid, 20th Lancers, were brought down after a gallant fight both being killed by shots through the head. The valuables which were found on the deceased will be handed to the relatives through the medium of the German War Office. Both killed pilots will be buried with military honours near Oostcamp, and in about a week's time a photograph of their grave will be dropped at the same place.' War had not yet destroyed chivalry among the airmen of both sides.

Many Great War aviators had well-to-do backgrounds and Cunningham-Reid was no exception. An obituary noted: 'Lieutenant Duncan Flower Cunningham-Reid, 29th Lancers, Indian Army, attached RFC, was the eldest son of Mrs Ernest Kingscote and the late Arthur Reid, grandson of the late Edgar Flower, of Mildenhall Park, Worcestershire, and R L Rede, Governor of Bombay and nephew of Lord Erskine, and the late Sir William Flower. He was educated for the Diplomatic Service, and was a good linguist, a fine horseman, and all-round sportsman. He was given a commission, being appointed to the Indian Division, and on September 18th, 1914, left to join his regiment at Marseilles. He transferred to the RFC in October 1915, and in December, 1915, his commanding officer wrote saying that Lieutenant Cunningham-Reid left in an aeroplane, which was to escort another machine some 40 miles into the enemy's country. The aeroplane which was being escorted returned safely, showing that it had been well protected, but the other machine was heavily engaged with a German aeroplane, and both [men] fell to the ground. The enemy paid high tribute to the bravery of the British airmen, and buried him with military honours.' Cunningham-Reid's brother Alec, later became a successful pilot with 85 Squadron in 1918, winning the DFC and post-war became an MP.

There were quite a number of reported combats this day, Fokkers and other types being met. One fight by a 3 Squadron Morane involved a pilot and observer, the latter being future ace and VC winner, Sergeant J T B McCudden, during an escort to Douai-Valenciennes. Three Moranes were flying the sortie, one machine having the distinguished crew of Captain H D Harvey-Kelly, famous for being the first RFC pilot to land in France in August 1914, with Lieutenant C F A Portal as his observer, later Viscount Portal KG GCB OM DSO MC, a future Marshal of the RAF.

Heading out, McCudden later recorded in his book *Flying Fury*:

'. . . my pilot pointed to his left front and above, and looking in the direction he pointed, I saw a long dark brown form fairly streaking across the sky. We could see it was a German machine, and when it got above and behind our middle machine it dived on to it for all the world like a huge hawk on a hapless sparrow.

'I now saw the black crosses on the underneath surface of the Fokker's wings, for a Fokker it was, and as it got to close range, Mr Mealing (Lt R H S Mealing] the pilot of this middle machine, turned, and thus saved himself, although the Fokker had already hit the machine.

'The Fokker had by now turned and was coming towards our machine, nose on, slightly above. Not having a gun mounting to fire in that direction, I stood up, with my Lewis gun to the shoulder, and fired as he passed over our right wing. He carried on flying in the opposite direction until he was lost to view.

'We were by now over Douai aerodrome, and looking down, I could see several enemy machines leaving the ground. I watched them for a while, and then noticed the Fokker climbing up under our tail. I told my pilot to turn, and then fired half a drum of Lewis at the Fokker at 300 yards range. The Fokker seemed rather surprised that we had seen him, and immediately turned off to my left rear as I was facing the tail.

'After this he climbed about 300 feet above us, and then put his nose down to fire. Having been waiting for him, I opened fire at once, and he promptly pulled out of his dive and retired to a distance of 500 yards, at which distance he remained, for every time he came closer I fired a short burst, which had the desired effect of keeping him at a distance.'

Completing their mission the three Moranes headed home, although the Fokker remained in the vicinity. It made no further move to attack, and finally its pilot dived down and headed back towards Douai airfield. McCudden wrote that the Fokker pilot had most likely been Immelmann, and that as the Squadron had lost a Morane a few days earlier, the German pilot was no doubt waiting for a repeat performance, but running into three rather than one Morane, was unsuccessful.

The same afternoon McCudden was up again, this time with Major E R Ludlow-Hewitt, his CO. This man too was to have a famous future with the RAF. With a GCB GBE CMG DSO and MC, Sir Edgar achieved the rank of Air Chief Marshal. Whilst they were over La Bassée, McCudden busily sketching a new trench system, something made him look up. There was a monoplane above:

'I was unprepared, for the weather was so dull that we did not expect to see a German machine, but I snatched up my gun from inside the fuselage, put it to my shoulder and fired just as the Fokker started to dive. My pilot, whom I had not time to warn, must have felt me jumping about, for as soon as I fired he did a turn which also put the Fokker off.

'By now the Fokker was trying to get behind us again, but my pilot was turning as quickly as the Fokker, whose pilot at last saw it was no good, and then went off to the east from just above us. As he drew away I distinctly noticed that the pilot sat very high in his machine, and was wearing the black flying kit.'

Returning to their airfield, McCudden wrote that they were almost certain the pilot had again been Immelmann, and believed that as far as he was concerned, the German would not fight even when the odds were even, or perhaps he meant, if he had lost the element of surprise.

While these actions may have been with Immelmann, there is no guarantee although it seems likely. If the German did not press home attacks on what he deemed an alert crew, especially an alert observer, there is no reason to decry his actions. There was always another day, and other opponents. Tomorrow he might surprise a less alert crew and bag a victory with no danger to himself. It made good sense.

Other RFC machines this day that had combats with Fokkers were from 2 Squadron, 5 Squadron, two by 7 Squadron, one being against 'three' Fokkers and a pusher machine. All survived. Air combat was now definitely on the increase.

VON ALTHAUS' SECOND VICTORY?
Flieger-abteilung 23's Ernst von Althaus made it two on 28 December, although there is some indication that it was not made official. Officially his second victory came on 2 February 1916, but he does seem to have been in combat with the 8 Squadron BE2c (2670) flown by Second Lieutenants George L Pitt and Mark Head, who were both killed. They came down at Sancourt, the RFC reporting a combat with an Aviatik (two-seater), so perhaps we have another dispute between two German pilots.

A German wireless message the next day confirmed that: "The English yesterday lost two aeroplanes. One was shot down north of Lens by our AA guns and forced to land. The other, a big fighter, was shot down in an air fight north of Ham." In addition a message was dropped over British lines, reading: "The two flying officers Pitt and Head were killed by a fall in an aerial combat. They were buried with all military honours in Douilly."

LEFFERS' SECOND VICTORY
Gustav Leffers found two British BEs on the 29th, having received a telephone call that hostile aircraft were over Vélu airfield. Taking off he saw two BE machines surrounded by exploding AA shells over Bertincourt as they headed towards Cambrai. Closing in he caught up with them near Marquion, over the long, straight, Cambrai-Arras road.

Despite the two BEs flying close together, combining their return fire, Leffers continued in and began firing himself. As he got behind one (2039), so the other attacked his Fokker, and a gun jam did not help matters. However, his final rounds had hit home and his target began to go down in a steep spiral, then crashed headlong from 300 metres.

The other BE crew quickly turned and raced for the lines, but without a gun Leffers was unable to follow. Later it was discovered that the downed pilot, Second Lieutenant David A Glen had been killed by a bullet to the heart, thus the sudden headlong plunge, but Sergeant E Jones survived to become a prisoner despite some injuries.

According to a report by FA32, it was understood that the second BE, after flying off, had been forced to land, but took off again and escaped over the lines. In his report Leffers makes no mention to any other Fokker pilot

with him, although 8 Squadron record two Fokkers attacking. The second
BE, which Glen had been escorting, was flown by Lieutenant W S Sholto
Douglas, with observer Lieutenant J Child. They reported a total of six
Fokkers being engaged during the flight, three chasing them down to 20
feet!

Sholto Douglas, of course, was another airman to gain high rank within
the future Royal Air Force, ending up as a Marshal of the RAF, Lord
Douglas of Kirtleside GCB MC DFC. In his book *Years of Combat*, he
relates this action, although he attributes the downing of Glen to
Immelmann and Boelcke. Douglas's own actions he noted thus:

> 'Archie very good near Cambrai. Then met six Huns. Glen, my
> escort, was shot down, followed by two of the Huns. I was
> then set upon by the remainder. Child, my observer, downed
> one Hun. We fought the remaining three for half an hour.
> Petrol began to get low and engine sump was hit. So, relying
> on the stability near the ground of the BE2c as against the
> Fokker, came down in steep spiral to ten feet above the
> ground. Came back from Cambrai to Arras just over the trees.
> Huns shot like mad. Child turned Lewis gun on to one lot of
> Huns by a farmhouse. Saw several small convoys and a staff
> officer on horseback. Fokkers left us a mile from the lines.
> Engine failed and landed among French heavy batteries just
> south of Arras. About 100 holes in machine. Engine sump
> pierced $1\frac{1}{2}$ inches from bottom.'

While there is no specific mention of them landing and taking off again, the
German report obviously meant it was seen to land on the allied side, not
the German. Equally obvious from his letters home, it was indeed Boelcke
who had chased the BE: Boelcke wrote on the 31st:

> 'The day before yesterday I had a fight with a very keen
> opponent, who defended himself bravely. He tried to escape
> by curving and manoeuvring, and even tried to throw me on
> the defensive. He did not succeed, but I could not harm him
> either. All I did accomplish was to force him gradually closer
> to earth. Finally he could not defend himself any more because
> I had mortally wounded his observer [then] I ran out of
> ammunition. Finally another Fokker (Immelmann) came to
> my rescue and the fight started all over again. I attacked along
> with Immelmann to confuse the Englishman. We succeeded in
> forcing him to within 100 metres of the ground and were
> expecting him to land any moment. Still he kept flying back
> and forth like a lunatic. Immelmann, by flying straight at him,
> wanted to put a stop to this, but just then my engine stopped
> and I had to land. I saw him disappear over a row of trees, and
> armed with a flashlight rode over on a horse. I expected that
> he had landed, but imagine my surprise! He had flown on. In

the evening the report came that he had passed over our trenches at a height of 100 metres on his way home. Daring of the chap! Not every one would care to imitate him. Immelmann had jammed his gun and had to quit.'

Boelcke had thought he had killed Child but as Sholto Douglas noted in his book, all the manoeuvring had so upset his observer that he fell over and was violently sick – all over his pilot. Sholto Douglas now had to discard his goggles in order to see ahead. Boelcke had interpreted this as the observer being killed. One assumes too that finally seeing Boelcke go down with his engine stopped, they thought that they had accounted for the German pilot too. Immelmann and Sholto Douglas may have met briefly on 12 December, Sholto recording in his log-book a brief skirmish with a Fokker that, after a couple of bursts, dived for the ground. Immelmann recorded that this day he had to abandon pursuit of a British biplane because his engine began to give out.

THE END OF 1915

By the end of 1915 the Fokker monoplanes had certainly made their mark over the Western Front, and upon air fighting in general. As far as is known, as the year ended there were 107 German single-seat fighters assigned to various two-seater abteilungen on the Western Front. Of these 86 were Fokkers and 21 were Pfalz machines. Not all pilots had had successes in combat with either British or French aeroplanes, but a list of those who achieved victories was published by the Germans as:

Obltn Max Immelmann	FA62	7
Obltn Oswald Boelcke	FA62	6
Ltn Hans-Joachim Buddecke	FA23	3
Ltn Kurt Wintgens	FA67/48	3
Vfw Eduard Böhme	FA9b	2
Ltn Walter von Bülow-Bothkamp	FA22	2
Ltn Gustav Leffers	FA32	2
Ltn Otto Parschau	KG1	2
Obltn Ernst Fr von Althaus	FA32	1

(Not listed was:

Ltn Kurt Fr von Crailsheim	FA53	1)

This made 28 'official' victories for Fokker monoplane pilots – shared between just nine of them. Martin Zander, with FA9b, had scored his two victories whilst flying two-seaters.

HONOUR CUPS

Another 'award' to successful German airmen upon bringing down a hostile aeroplane was the presentation of an *Ehrenbecher*, an honour cup. Reference to them began to appear at around the end of 1915, and amongst the first to receive them were Boelcke and Immelmann.

They were silver cups (drinking goblets) sponsored by rich industrialists from the German homeland and awarded to every pilot or observer in the Fliegertruppe upon being officially credited with a victory in air combat. Until well into 1917 all those eligible received one although later the qualification was raised to eight or nine victories. At that stage the cups were no longer made out of silver, but iron. They came with a certificate which noted: *Ehrenbechers für den Sieger im Luftkampfe* – honour for victory in air combat.

Chapter Four

1916

The winter weather in January 1916 curtailed war flights by both sides somewhat, with gales and rain. Flying started on the 5th, then stopped again until the 10th. On the 5th the RFC flew, and the recent poor weather did not stop the Eindecker pilots from getting at the two-seater recce machines of the Royal Flying Corps, or the French Air Service.

BOELCKE'S SEVENTH VICTORY

No. 2 Squadron sent off two BE2c machines at 08.15 am, one to fly a tactical recce, the other as its escort. The two aircraft were spotted by Oswald Boelcke, and the escort machine took his attention. Chasing the two machines he overhauled them near Henin-Liétard, firing at the machine, which was hit and began to go down. Staying behind the BE (1734), the other BE (2766) continued to fly off, and very soon the disabled machine was put down near Harnes, and collapsed, breaking its back.

Boelcke landed nearby. Some local villagers had already surrounded the machine, Boelcke finding both crewmen had been wounded, the observer seriously. He discovered the pilot, Second Lieutenant W E Somervill, could speak German and conversed with him. He said the gunfire had severed his control cables, making it impossible for him to escape. The following day Boelcke visited the wounded observer in hospital, taking him some English books and a photograph of the wrecked BE.

Upon his return from PoW camp, William Edmund Somervill reported that only two Fokkers had attacked him, and it was only after this that a third one attacked. He confirmed that his controls had been shot away and he'd been forced to land. He had also been slightly hit in the head. He also said that his wounded observer, Lieutenant G C Formilli, had been in hospital for three months.

Geoffrey Cecil Formilli, when he came home from Germany, reported:

'On a short reconnaissance to Lille, acting as escort to recce machine. Just after we commenced our return journey from Lille, we met a Fokker at whom I fired a drum of ammunition. The Fokker made off. Shortly afterwards, as we were making our way back to the lines, a Fokker appeared behind us and opened fire. I changed my Lewis gun to the rear mounting and started firing. When I had finished my first drum I found the strap of the drum was broken and was having difficulty in removing the drum, when I was hit with a bullet which went through my right shoulder. After this I found that I was absolutely unable to remove the drum with my left hand. [Lt Somervill was also grazed with a bullet along the right side of his head.]

'Lieutenant Somervill then attempted to use the machine gun, but it jammed. By this time our machine appeared to be out of control and we were coming down. I understand that our rudder control and one of the aileron control wires had been shot away. We landed in a field near Harnes and the machine crashed on landing, smashing the undercarriage, right wing tips and back of fuselage. Lieutenant Somervill tried to help me out of the machine so that we could burn it. However, the Germans arrived before we could manage this. The pilot of the Fokker was Lt Boelcke.'

According to the recce BE – crewed by Lieutenants C S Wynne Eyton (RFA) and W Davey, they had been attacked by three Fokker monoplanes – one or more being two-seaters. If this is correct, they may well have been Fokker M8 machines, a small number of which were used by the Germans as artillery co-operation machines. They looked very similar to the single-seat E-types and Boelcke is known to have liked the M8 as an aeroplane.

Davey reported that the first to attack was a Fokker two-seater, which passed behind their BE, firing sideways over his right wing as it went by. One drum of Lewis gun ammunition was fired back from about 100 yards and the Fokker dived away steeply and was lost sight of.

Another Fokker was seen to attack the escort machine and the third Fokker probably did the same. The fight was not followed further as Davey and his pilot were then attacked again but when the scrap ended, only two Fokkers remained airborne, and the other BE was nowhere to be seen. Charles Sandford Wynne Eyton later flew single-seat Bristol Scouts with 2 Squadron.

ERNST HESS' FIRST VICTORY

Only a couple of hours later, another 2 Squadron BE was brought down, this time by a Fokker pilot serving with FA62. Ernst Hess came from Wiesbaden, where he had been born on 8 January 1893. Leaving school early to become an apprentice engineer, he became interested in aviation, and moved to work at the Goedecker aeroplane factory near Mainz so that he could learn to fly. Acquiring flying certificate No.535 on 26 September 1913, he had earlier surprised everyone by making his first flight after only two taxi-runs across the airfield.

He joined Luftschiffer Battalion Nr.3 in Cologne on 1 October, and then went to FA3 on 1 April 1914 to train as a military pilot. He qualified for his Military Pilot's Badge in November and was sent to FA9b as an Unteroffizier, which was operating on the Lille-Arras front. He was commissioned in June 1915 and then managed to get himself posted to FA62 at Douai and be attached to the unit's Fokker Einsitzer Kommando along with Boelcke and Immelmann. At this time he made the fourth Fokker pilot alongside his two heroes and Unteroffizier Albert Österreicher, who was soon to be commissioned.

Shortly after lunch on 5 January 1916 he took off in Fokker EI 32/15, and encountered BE2c No.2019 on a special bomb raid on Douai, so Second Lieutenant A L Russell had no observer. Hit by Hess' fire, Russell went down out of control but managed to right his machine and landed it without damage near Vitry, luckily surviving as a prisoner of war. As he was carrying a large bomb under his machine, he was also lucky in that direction! Hess landed close by his victim which was not far from where Boelcke had landed also.

There is no doubt that Hess thought he was now on his way, but things did not turn out quite as he had hoped. Within four weeks he was sent to Fokkerstaffel 'C' in the 3rd Army area down on the Champagne front, where air fighting was comparatively rare, and it was to be a further four months before he was able to gain his second victory.

On the 9th Wintgens is supposed to have wounded Adjutant Maurice Faure and Lieutenant Daniel Dumêmes, a French Nieuport crew from Escadrille N26 near Bapaume, but this was not confirmed. Another difficulty was that they were supposed to have been wounded near Ostende! Next day, the 10th, Leutnant Rudolf Berthold had an unconfirmed claim against a French Voisin, near Zeebrugge.

* * *

Amidst the Fokker successes, there was a German two-seater crew which began to have some success in aerial combat in 1916, Leutnant Albert Dossenbach and his observer, Oberleutnant Hans Schilling. Dossenbach came from St Blasien, in the southern Black Forest region (Baden), a former medical student. Joining the army when war came he won the Iron Cross 2nd Class as an NCO and then the Military Merit Cross and Iron Cross 1st Class. Commissioned in January 1915 he transferred to aviation, and on becoming a pilot, served with FA5 and later FA22.

Schilling came from Zäckerick, born 24 September 1892. With FA22 in December 1914 he had received the Knight 2nd Class with Swords of the Ducal Saxe-Ernestine House Order. He also wore glasses, in common with a number of German aviators, including Kurt Wintgens, and which did not preclude them being allowed to fly. Schilling had previously served with 2. Thüringisches Infanterie Regiment Nr.32. An aviator from the start of the war he had received both Classes of the Iron Cross by or during 1915.

Details of their early combat successes are scant, but it seems probable that a Morane from No.1 Squadron RFC (5091) was their first victory on 10 January 1916. The crew of Second Lieutenants John C McEwen and F Adams were taken prisoner, being brought down near Tournai, Belgium, after an air fight.

WILHELM FRANKL'S FIRST FOKKER VICTORY
On 10 January Wilhelm Frankl scored his second air victory, but his first in

a Fokker monoplane. Born 20 December 1893, in Hamburg, he was the son of a Jewish salesman. After living in Frankfurt am Main, he moved with his family to Berlin to complete his schooling. His interest in aviation began pre-war and led to him learning to fly, at one stage being a student of Melli Beese at her flying school at Johannistal, and to acquire his pilot's licence on 20 July 1913. Upon the outbreak of war he joined the flying services and despite being a certified pilot, flew as an observer as well as a pilot in FA40 in Flanders, where he rose to the rank of vizefeldwebel by the end of 1915. He received both classes of the Iron Cross for his two-seater work and gained his first aerial victory on 10 May 1915.

Unusually, he had gained this victory with a five-shot carbine, downing a French machine recorded as a Voisin. Although Frankl was to record that the French admitted the loss of an aeroplane, it is not certain who or what it was, nor if it was a 'loss' or merely an aeroplane forced down inside French lines.

Volunteering to fly single-seaters when one arrived at his unit, his first success was over a cannon-armed Voisin 4 Ca2 (No.991) from RFD (36 CA – Section d'Avions Canon du 36 Corps Armée), crewed by Sergent Parent and Fusilier Bonnier, which came down near Woumen, south of Dixmude, Belgium, the crew taken prisoner. This same French unit claimed two Fokkers destroyed between Dixmude and Houthulst Forest. As one of the Fokkers was supposed to have been that which downed the Voisin, their claim appears over-optimistic! The Voisin, with a large number '5' on the gondola, was later on display in Germany in the German captured booty exhibition (Deutsche Luftkriegsbeure Ausstellung – DELKA).

Two days later the two stars of FA62, Boelcke and Immelmann both scored again, and, as a matter of interest, Hans-Joachim Buddecke, now flying on the Turkish Front, downed his fifth victory, a Farman of the British Royal Naval Service 3 Wing.

BOELCKE'S EIGHTH
Boelcke had had a late night and did not feel too much like rising, but his batman told him the weather was good so after breakfast he took off around 9 am and headed for Lille to see if any British aircraft would turn up. After some fruitless searching, he finally saw bombs exploding near Ypres and although he headed for the town, seeing the Channel further north, he did not see the aeroplane which dropped them. Heading back towards Douai he spotted two British machines and dived at the nearest one. The RFC pilot turned and rushed for the lines and with Boelcke following he reached the lines before the German was close enough to fire. The British machine headed down and landed while Boelcke turned his attention to the other aircraft.

Boelcke overhauled him north of Lille but this one also quickly headed west, and the observer didn't open fire until he saw the Fokker do so. Boelcke guessed he was up against an old hand so sat squarely on his tail before firing again. Old hand or not, Boelcke later recorded that the British pilot held his course and did not take evasive action, which allowed him to get on target. The British machine headed down and landed in Mouscron, north-east of Tourcoing. The time was 09.20.

His victims were the crew of a RE7 of 12 Squadron, piloted by Second Lieutenant Leonard Kingdon who was killed, and observer Lieutenant K W Gray, wounded and a prisoner. What is also interesting is that shortly earlier, a 1 Squadron Morane crew – Second Lieutenant Robert Barton and Lieutenant Eyre S Wilkinson – had come down on the British 2nd Army Front following a combat near Roubaix, and both had been pulled dead from the wreckage of their machine. Was this the aeroplane Boelcke first attacked and which he saw going down apparently to land in British lines? The difficulty here is that in July a gold cigarette case belonging to Barton was returned to his father via the War Office and American Ambassador, which seems to indicate it had fallen into German hands. If this is so, why wasn't this machine credited to a German airman, even Boelcke. Furthermore, if it had been the Morane crew which Boelcke had shot down, the same question arises; who downed the RE7 from which there is a prisoner?

Boelcke put down at an airfield near Lille to refuel, but landing back at Douai later, he learnt that Immelmann had also downed an opponent which once more levelled the score of both men.

IMMELMANN'S EIGHTH

Immelmann and Albert Österreicher had flown off in their monoplanes shortly after 08.30 following a report that hostile aircraft had crossed the lines in various places. By the time he had climbed to around 500 metres, Immelmann looked back at the airfield to see Boelcke climbing into his Fokker, but whereas he flew north, Immelmann and Österreicher headed south, towards Arras and then further south, towards Bapaume.

Halfway between these two towns, Immelmann saw bursting AA fire in the direction of Cambrai so he headed in that direction followed by his companion. From the AA fire, it seemed as if the hostile aircraft was heading roughly north-west towards Douai. Flying directly into the morning sun he could see no sign of the hostile machine, but then he was almost upon it. The British machine made a sharp turn west, Immelmann recognising it as a Vickers FB5, and then it was coming straight towards him. As the observer began to fire, Immelmann turned, banked round and came down behind the Gunbus and began firing too. The two machines began to circle each other, but it was Immelmann who pulled tightest and another burst of 100 rounds set the Vickers machine on fire. It fell well alight but Immelmann saw it make a landing and someone jump out.

Immelmann once again landed nearby and the FB5 was still burning when he arrived on foot to the scene. The observer, Second Lieutenant Sidney Hathaway, had been killed, the pilot, Second Lieutenant Herbert Thomas Kemp had managed to get clear and was clutching a slight head wound. It was just after 10 am, and the Vickers had come down near Roubaix. The machine was from No.11 Squadron, Herbert Kemp later stating he thought he'd come down near Beaumetz-les-Cambrai, and confirming he'd been attacked by two Fokkers.

According to Immelmann, he spoke to Kemp, telling him that he and his observer was his eighth victory. Kemp then asked if he was Immelmann. When the German said yes, Kemp confirmed that he was well known to the RFC and congratulated him on '. . . a fine sporting success.'

Kurt Wintgens wrote home that he had shot down a Caudron in the second week of January, its crew taken by surprise because, he said, they were making a bad job of paying attention whilst directing artillery. He was following it down over the French lines but was then hit by ground fire and so broke away. This was another claim that was not allowed by 'higher authority'.

THE FIRST *POUR LE MÉRITES*

With Boelcke and Immelmann now both having eight victories each, it seemed high time that some high award should be given to these two formidable fighter pilots. Scoring such a number of victories was something of a real milestone, and although somewhat small in comparison to the 80 victories Manfred von Richthofen was to achieve by the spring of 1918, in January 1916 a score of eight was impressive.

Both men had already received several decorations, including the Hohenzollern House Order, and the next highest – in fact Germany's top award – was going to have to be the *Pour le Mérite*, the famed Blue Max. Immediately these two flyers were awarded this prestigious award. Not only that, they were the first two airmen ever to receive the decoration.

Shortly afterwards both were invited to dine with the King of Bavaria, then the Crown Prince of Bavaria, and telegrams of congratulations came from such people as the King of Saxony, the Crown Princes of Prussia and Saxony, Prince Sigismund, the Chief of War Aviation, and so on.

The curious thing about German awards and decorations is that for these two men, like a number of other successful fighter pilots later in the war, once they had received the Blue Max there was no higher award they could be given. They could continue to receive lower awards from various German states, but that was it. There were no 'Bars' to these German decorations either. The British could award Bars to the Victoria Cross, and the French had varying (upwards) degrees of their Légion d'Honneur, but with the Blue Max, that was the top.

BOELCKE'S NINTH VICTORY

Two days later, 14 January, Boelcke was again successful – on the same day as he dined with the Bavarian Crown Prince. Lieutenant J H Herring and Captain R Erskine of 8 Squadron were in their BE2c (No.4087) on a recce mission and were attacked by a Fokker near Achiet-le-Grand just an hour after they had departed their base. Engine and cockpit area was shot up and the engine failed, forcing Herring to make a crash landing in the burning BE, in front line trenches. Both men were either wounded or injured but managed to scramble clear and get into British trenches, but German artillery then hammered the machine to destroy it completely.

Boelcke had earlier seen exploding bombs and headed towards the spot but the BE crew saw the Fokker and were heading for the lines. As he closed behind the BE, it suddenly turned and headed for Boelcke and then, as the German pilot was later to admit, began the hardest fight he had yet been in. A turning battle ensued, although Boelcke knew that he held the advantage, as sooner or later the BE had to make a dash for the lines. Finally the BE's engine was hit and the machine headed towards the front lines, but only reached the barbed wire in front of the British positions.

Ralph Herring later became a pilot and flew with No.66 Squadron in Italy. On 1 January 1918, this married 25-year-old from Glasgow, and later Wimbledon, south London, was shot down in his Sopwith Camel during a combat with pilots of Jasta 1 and died of his wounds. He was the son of Captain James Erskine, Gordon Highlanders.

Boelcke recorded that he had conserved his ammunition, not wanting to run out as he had done on 28 December. However, his Fokker now carried two guns, rather than the earlier one, both firing through the propeller. Boelcke also thought one of the crew had been burned up in the smashed and blazing machine as only one of the occupants had actually been seen to get to safety, but both men had survived.

Boelcke had been forced to land near Flers as his fuel ran out and because of his 17.30 date with the King and Prince of Bavaria, had to take a car back to Douai, then drive on to Lille for his appointment. The combat had taken place around 10.30 but it took him most of the day to get to Lille, and he had to change into his best uniform on the way. No doubt the day's events made useful conversation over dinner.

VIZEFELDWEBEL HUCK'S FIRST VICTORY

There was a lot of air fighting this day, and a lot of confused records too. A No. 1 Squadron Morane (5113) crewed by Second Lieutenants W Watts and Charles Oswald Hayward, on a special recce sortie were supposed to have been downed by AA fire over Wytschaete, falling near Dadizeele, having left their base at just after 7 am. However, there are indications that Vizefeldwebel Huck of FA5, or Kek 1, was credited with this victory, which came down inside German lines.

Wilfred Watts, from Blandford, Dorset, was 23, and had been awarded the French Croix de Guerre with Palm for distinguished conduct in September 1915. Hayward came from Lincoln and had been educated at Repton and Pembroke College, Cambridge. Aged 21 he had been in France since July 1915 with the 7th Lincolnshire Regiment. He had only transferred to the RFC two or three weeks before his death. Another 1 Squadron crew were also engaged by a German 'scout' monoplane at 09.40 near Hollebeke but they returned safely although shot up.

At around 11 am a 5 Squadron BE2c crew, having had a scrap with three Aviatiks, was then engaged by a Fokker as they headed for home, but they too evaded successfully. A Martynside pilot with 6 Squadron had a fight with a Fokker this same morning and he thought he had scored hits on the monoplane as he saw a spurt of flame and then the German went down. A crew from 9 Squadron also claimed hits on a Fokker, believing they had hit the enemy pilot. The ever aggressive Captain C Gordon Bell fought a Fokker in his 10 Squadron Bristol Scout, suspecting the German machine to have two guns – because of the noise! No. 15 Squadron also had several combats, with two-seaters as well as Fokkers.

WHOSE VICTORY?

Captain Vivian H N Wadham and his observer Sergeant N V Piper (BE2c 2105) were flying an escort sortie to a recce machine, taking off at 07.35. They failed to return and one suggestion is that they were shot down by Gustav Leffers of FA32 near Bapaume. However, his victory remained unconfirmed, a little strange considering Wadham was killed and Piper taken prisoner, ie: there was a wreck, a body and a captive.

Captain Wadham came from Shepperton, Middlesex and had previously been with the Hampshire Regiment. Aged 24, he had been promoted to flight commander in May 1915.

Another source indicates that Otto Parschau shot them down, but Parshau was not named as having a victory this day. A two-seater crew from KG1, Unteroffizier Krauss and Leutnant von Lersner did have a combat and were credited with a victory, their first, near Paschendaele/Westroosebeke. As only two British aeroplanes were lost, and two credited, it certainly seems that the laurels went to Huck and the two-seater crew, while the others are only speculative.

HÖHNDORF'S FIRST TWO VICTORIES

Another pre-war pilot who became a successful Fokker Eindecker pilot was Walter Höhndorf, who was born in Prutzke, on 10 November 1892. As a teenager he was a keen student of motor and engineering mechanics, and getting the aviation bug, learnt to fly in Paris, France, in September 1913, licence No.582, dated 3 November. After this he became a noted aerial performer in Germany and was among the first aviators to perform complicated aerobatic manoeuvres rather than just flying straight and level. Not only this, but he also helped to design and produce aeroplanes with the Union Flugzeugwerke, at Teltow.

With the start of the war he volunteered for flying duties, and in early 1915 was commissioned, but flew as a test pilot for the Siemens-Schuckert company. It was not until the end of the year that he got to the front and was flying with FA12, and then later with FA67, as a single-seater pilot.

Operating on the French front, his first claim – on the 17th – came over the Alsace region, bringing down a Voisin of VB105 (No.V1096), crewed by Caporal Follot and MdL Hennequet, who were taken prisoner. The Voisin landed intact and on the side of the gondola his groundcrew painted: *Erbeutet in Luftkamp von Feldflieger 12 durch Ltn Höhndorf* (captured in air battle with Feldflieger 12 through Ltn Höhndorf).

While there is some question about victory number two, Höhndorf is supposed to have gained his second kill two days later, on the 19th. Another Voisin, this time from VB101, fell over Medovich (or near Thiaucourt), the crew being Sergent Paul Henry Bernard Chevalier, and observer Sergent Agénor Corroenne. To add to the confusion, theirs was supposed to have been a night mission which began on the 18th, but without any times of these actions, it is difficult to know if they were going out, or coming back, in semi-darkness, thereby allowing the German pilot to engage.

OBERLEUTNANT KRUG'S FIRST VICTORY

No.15 Squadron was in the wars again on the 19th, several crews reporting combats with both two-seaters and Fokkers. One crew did not report a combat due to the fact that they failed to return. Flying on an escort mission, Lieutenant C W Wilson and Second Lieutenant W A Brooking were shot down near Tourcoing in BE2c 2694. Wilson was wounded in the pelvis, 18-year-old Walter Brooking RFA/RFC, the son of Brigadier-General H T Brooking CB, living and working in India, was killed.

Only upon his return from captivity was Charles Benjamin Wilson able to shed light on what had befallen him and his observer. He recorded that while on recce duty he was attacked and shot down by a Fokker monoplane and that Brooking was killed in the exchange. Wilson was wounded twice and became unconscious at 9,000 feet. When he regained consciousness, he discovered that he was a prisoner, the BE having landed itself without any help from its crew. Wilson also noted that this had been their third air fight.

Oberleutnant Michael Krug was, like Vfw Huck, a pilot with Fleiger-abteilung Nr.5b/Kek 1. He claimed his victory at 11.20 near Neuville, which is just to the north of Tourcoing. He had begun his war flying in August 1914 with FA2b, moving to FA5b on 8 December. He was attached to the Fokker staffel (AOK6) on 9 February as CO until 17 March on which date he moved to FEA 1b. On 1 April 1916 he became commander of KG6, Kasta 35, a post he held until the beginning of September. Later that month he became CO of Nr.IV Flying School until May 1917. From May to 28 January 1918 he was with Idflieg in Berlin (*Inspektion der Fliegertruppen* – Inspectorate of military aviation), then went onto the staff of Kofl 6 (HQ of all flying units of the 6th Army). From March to September 1918 he was with BG8, ending the war as CO of FA45b.

* * *

FRANKL'S THIRD VICTORY

On 19 January, Wilhelm Frankl was credited with his third kill, a Voisin, again over Woumen, where his second claim had been made on the 10th. Unhappily there is no record of a French loss this date and it may have been yet another of those claims where a machine appeared to go down over French lines, and being unable to pursue it over the trenches, the German could not determine its actual fate. (Either that or a confusion about the date, the 10th being wrongly re-read at some stage, as the 19th.)

Despite the ever increasing number of combats, the weather had played its part during January 1916. Kurt Wintgens reported that on his sector of the front, flying had only been possible on three days. Nevertheless, on 25 January he wrote a letter in which he related the story of another 'victory' the day before:

'. . . yesterday, once again I had a big success. I met my old opponent, the twin-engined large machine [Caudron G4] with which I had quite a run of combats, which had all ended without a decision due to a lot of various reasons. This time, however, engine and machine gun worked perfectly.

'Two of us were about 3,600 metres up and I attacked him from the left in such a manner that he could use only one machine gun. At a distance of about 80 metres I started to fire continuously and apparently hit the pilot well, for suddenly the machine turned on its left wing, came straight at me so that I could only just evade him, and then he fell down vertically when about 20 metres away from me. . . . I went after him like lightning. After 400 metres he flattened out again and received another burst from me, whereupon, suddenly, a colossal smoke cloud came from his right engine. When by chance I looked back, I noticed that because of a very strong eastern wind, I had been driven far over the lines, so that I had to leave him to his fate. I take it that he met the earth very fast.

'Back home I saw that he had hit me with a bullet through the right forerib, but until I got down it had all held together well.'

Thus we can see that while he admits to earlier fights, as I've concluded, he did not receive official confirmation, although he still deems this combat as a success. But as it was also one which was not officially confirmed, we must conclude too that these are his personal successes, ie: those he thinks crashed, but which he was unable to have confirmed. He must have confused his friends with these letters of 'victories' when offical communiqués were not giving him any credit.

The propaganda war was also hotting up. A British report read by the Germans on 28 January stated that the RFC had lost seven aircraft in air combat since 1 October 1915, eight more to ground fire, plus another missing; a total of 16. The Germans replied that the figure for the Western Front was actually, according to their records, 41 in air combat, 11 to ground fire and 11 more forced landed in German lines, presumably through mechanical problems. This total of 63, one assumes, included French machines.

Chapter Five

FEBRUARY – MARCH 1916

FLAK OR FIGHTER?

A German who was to become a consistently good fighter pilot as the war progressed almost gained his first victory on 1 February: Leutnant Josef Jacobs, flying with FA11. Jacobs was born in Kreuzkapelle, in the Rhineland, on 15 May 1894 and had learnt to fly in 1912, so it was natural for him to join the air service when war came. He joined FA11 in July 1915, flying two-seater LVGs but it was not until December that he had his first flight in a Fokker monoplane. By this time he had risen from lowly Flieger (private) to Vizefeldwebel (sergeant-major), and won the Iron Cross 2nd Class, the announcement of which surprised his mother, for she thought her son was firstly not in action, and secondly, not in the air service!

On 1 February he found a French Voisin and attacked, firing between 20 and 30 rounds at it before it disappeared into cloud. Keen to discover what had happened, he was delighted to learn upon landing that a Voisin had come down in the vicinity of Pierremond, near the location of his fight and he quickly drove to the spot. Upon inspection he found no trace of any bullet holes, and the French pilot – Sergent Hiriat (and observer Soldat Jean) from C28 (the machine had been a Caudron G4, not a Voisin) – had said he had lost his way and landed. In the end, credit for this victory went to anti-aircraft gunners. Five days later, Jacobs was commissioned.

FRANKL'S FOURTH VICTORY

Yet another Voisin was claimed by Frankl on 1 February, and again no recorded French loss can be traced. Only Jacobs' unconfirmed victory is noted, although KG2 is supposed to have claimed a two-seater at 1608 hours between Chaulnes and Prossaire, with its pilot killed and observer captured, but this appears merely to confuse the whole issue of this day's claims. However, according to AOK6, this Chaulnes machine fell on the 2nd, and in any event KG2 were not in this area of operations.

KEKS – AND A CHANGE IN RFC TACTICS

By this time, some Fokker pilots had been banded together to form fighter units, independent of operations with the various flieger-abteilungen, to become known as *Kampfeinsitzer Kommando*, abbreviated to Kek. These were created initially by the Bavarian *Inspektor* Major Friedrich Stempel, who was *Stabsoffizier der Flieger* (Staff Officer in charge of Aviation) to the German 6th Armee, itself commanded by Prince Rupprecht of Bavaria.

These units became the forerunner of the Jastas. One such Kek comprised those Fokkers based at Vaux. The task set for Kek pilots was to perform *Luftwachtdienst* (aerial guard duty).

The RFC, already on the defensive because of increased monoplane activity, had issued a directive in January, which was now taking effect in front line squadrons. It read:

> 'Until the Royal Flying Corps are in possession of a machine as good as or better than the German Fokker, it seems that a change in the tactics employed becomes necessary. It is hoped very shortly to obtain a machine which will be able to successfully engage the Fokkers at present in use by the Germans. In the meantime, it must be laid down as a hard and fast rule that a machine proceeding on reconnaissance must be escorted by at least three machines. These machines must fly in close formation and a reconnaissance should not be continued if any of the machines become detached. This should apply to both short and distant reconnaissances. Aeroplanes proceeding on photographic duty any considerable distance east of the lines should be similarly escorted. From recent experience it seems that the Germans are now employing their aeroplanes in groups of three or four, and these numbers are frequently encountered by our aeroplanes. Flying in close formation must be practised by all pilots.'

As we shall read, the Fokker pilots now began to engage small groups of RFC recce. machines, as the British squadrons followed the new directive, but still seemed more than capable of cutting out and downing a machine from the formation. The Germans also countered this by flying out in twos, threes or even in fours, which they could do more readily now that the Keks were forming.

VON ALTHAUS' THIRD VICTORY

Confusion over records continues to hinder accurate reporting on 2 February. Ernst Fr von Althaus was among this small band called Kek Vaux, and on 2 February he is believed to have brought down a Voisin near Biaches, south-west of Péronne. This machine came from VB108, with crewmen Caporal Arthur Jacquin, prisoner and Soldat Segaud, killed. Jacquin later managed to escape. With victories on 5th and 28th December, this made it three for von Althaus.

RUDOLF BERTHOLD'S FIRST VICTORY

A problem arises on this 2 February, as a Voisin was also credited to another Kek Vaux pilot, Rudolf Berthold, who had been born in Ditterswald, near Bamberg in northern Bavaria, on 24 March 1891. Learning to fly and receiving his pilot licence No. 538 on 26 September 1913, he had joined the air service at the beginning of the war, flying firstly as an observer on two-seaters with FA23 and later as a pilot.

On this day he engaged a Voisin which fell burning into a wood near Chaulnes. This machine too was noted as being downed by a Fokker, and Chaulnes, of course, is also south-west of Péronne.

With only one Voisin lost this date, who was it that actually downed the VB108 machine, Berthold or von Althaus? Indications are that it was Berthold, and that von Althaus shot down a Nieuport. A Nieuport two-seater was indeed lost this day, a machine from Escadrille N3, crewed by Lieutenant Rémy Grassel and Sergent Victor René Grivotte, who were both killed. It is however, known that they were shot down by a Fokker near Biaches, south-west of Péronne.

BERTHOLD GETS NUMBER TWO

Just three days later Rudolf Berthold scored again, this time a British machine from No. 13 Squadron. Second Lieutenants L J Pearson and Lieutenant E H E J Alexander, in BE2c 4091, were flying an escort mission on the morning of the 5th and Berthold's attack wounded Alexander and forced Pearson to land between Grévillers and Irles, near Bapaume, where both men were taken prisoner.

Upon his return from Germany, Leonard John Pearson reported that he and his observer had been escorting a recce. BE along with two other BEs. After being heavily 'archied' they had been attacked by a Fokker and not only had Alexander been wounded but both Lewis guns had been shot off their mountings. With two cylinders of his engine blown off too, the engine failed, leaving Pearson no alternative but to land.

Edmund Heathfield Eliott Joe Alexander also reported the action when he returned to England in 1918. Having taken off at around 07.30 he and Pearson had been the rear machine in the formation. Well over the enemy lines they had been attacked from behind by a Fokker monoplane, and Alexander was hit almost at once and then the engine had been knocked out and '. . . ceased to pull.' Pearson had tried to glide but from 6,000 feet it was insufficient height to do so and what made it worse was that Pearson had to 'stunt' quite a bit to avoid further attacks by the Fokker pilot.

* * *

This 5 February proved interesting in that three 9 Squadron BE2c machines, one piloted by Second Lieutenants C Faber and A E Wynn, had a combat with a Fokker east of Bapaume at around 09.10 hours, and another with two Fokkers and three Albatros two-seaters. Their combined fire started one Fokker smoking and they claimed it had been shot down. By 1918, Faber was a Sopwith Dolphin flight commander with 79 Squadron.

No.20 Squadron had been given the first prototype Martinsyde G.100 and with a report of a Fokker over Cassel, Captain J R Howett had been sent off to intercept it. At around noon he found a two-seater not a Fokker, but did not shoot it down. However, it is interesting to note that this new single-seat machine, which was really better suited as a bomber, as it later became, was thought able to engage and down one of the deadly Fokker Eindeckers.

Obviously RFC HQ were anxiously seeking something that could combat the monoplanes.

VIZEFELDWEBEL PREHN'S FIRST VICTORY

Alfred Prehn flew with FA62 alongside Boelcke and Immelmann. It had been very quiet in the Douai area, mainly due to the poor weather. Immelmann wrote that the English rarely came to Douai unless they were in formations of up to ten machines, and the French had not been over for a long time. However, Prehn was up and found a small formation of BE2s from 9 Squadron on the 10th. One was piloted by the same Second Lieutenant Faber (4132) who had been in combat with Fokkers on the 5th, but this time he had Second Lieutenant R A Way as his observer. The BE crews reported that they had encountered two Fokkers while on this escort duty, the three BE crews all reporting a scrap at around 11 am. Shot up over Roisel, Faber and Way were both wounded and headed down. Faber in fact fainted for a few moments, undoubtedly giving his observer a scare. They scraped over the lines amidst a good deal of rifle fire and flopped down behind the British trenches not far from Bertangles. Front line German observers saw them going down, their subsequent report confirming a victory for Prehn.

The wounded twosome reported that before they were wounded, the observer's return fire had been seen to hit one Fokker over Roisel. Another BE crew, Lieutenants R Egerton and B H Cox also thought they'd hit the first Fokker, which dived steeply and landed in a field.

Prehn later flew with FA5, and later still with Kek 3, then Jasta 10 and Jasta 11. He was to gain a second victory while with Kek 3 in June 1916. Leutnant Oskar Rousselle who later flew with Jasta 4, was credited with a victory on the 10th too, although a rather dubious one. Flying with Kek 1 he was credited with a balloon at 12.45 south east of Péronne. Strangely enough a German balloon, without an observer, broke away from its mooring and was carried into Allied lines near Vailly.

Oskar Rouselle's first operational unit had been FA32 on New Year's Day 1916, then moving to FA23 in mid-February. From here he was posted to Jasta 4 in July 1917, but he had to go into hospital in August 1917 following a wound on the 10th. In September he was with Idflieg then FEA12 until posted back to Jasta 4 in November. For most of 1918 he was adjutant of the Jasta until returning to Idflieg in August where he saw out the war.

LEFFERS' THIRD VICTORY

Flying his Fokker E (84/15) while still with FA32 (Kek Bertincourt), Gustav Leffers downed his third BE2c on 20 February near Aizecourt le Bas at 09.45. Second Lieutenant Frank A Garlick, 28, and Captain William Knox, 27, from 13 Squadron, did not survive the encounter. It had not been straightforward.

There were four BE machines and Leffers dived and opened fire on the rearmost aircraft, but then his engine stopped dead. Surrounded by return fire from the British aircraft, Leffers tried to re-start the motor, succeeded, then climbed back to engage once more. The rear BE came at him, but Leffers' fire struck home and the BE went into a steep dive and crashed.

The next day, 21 February 1916, the Battle of Verdun began. This was an important town for the French, not only strategically – its loss opened a road direct to Paris – but for their morale. They just had to defend it, and not lose it. The Germans knew this only too well and hoped that in defending it, the French army would bleed to death. It almost did, but so too did the attackers. The cost in lives during the long battle of Verdun was appalling and was to last almost the rest of 1916.

The German air commander had 21 Fokker and Pfalz monoplanes organised into three Kek units, one at Avillers, one at Jametz, the third at Cunel. Oswald Boelcke was now at Jametz, although he was still attached to FA62. However, just prior to the battle, Boelcke had been taken into hospital with stomach trouble and missed the opening of the offensive but he was soon back at Jametz and trying to get moved even nearer to the battle front at Verdun.

Over the next couple of days three French machines were downed over the battle area, one by FA67, another by FA71 and a third by KG2. With the former two, only pilot names are mentioned as victors on the 26th, but it is unclear if they were flying single-seaters or two-seaters. Oberleutnant Heinz Althoven of FA67 and Unteroffizier Kress of FA71 are the two named.

Christian Kress, born 14 November 1890, in Geroda, was to die under the guns of the French ace Georges Guynemer on 10 November 1916 flying with Jasta 6. It is known he was with Kek Metz prior to the Jasta formations, posted in on 23 July, and that he had two victories prior to going to one of the new Jastas, where he added two more prior to his own death. It appears, therefore, that he was an Eindecker pilot. If Kress was operating over Metz, his victory may well have been a machine from VB102, crewed by Caporal Marien Roche and Captain Jean le Grand, lost during a raid on Metz.

However, on the French side, Sous-lieutenant Jean Navarre claimed his fourth and fifth victories on 26 February, one a Fokker EIII. Both machines, the Fokker and a two-seater, were from KG1. There is a possibility that both, in fact, were two-seaters, but a French communiqué mentions a Fokker. The aircraft were reported down at Driene sur Meuse. Two dead Germans and another as a prisoner suggests a two-seater and a single-seater: the names given are Oberleutnant Heinrich Kempf as the prisoner, Leutnants Georg Heine and Alfons von Zeddelmann the two who lost their lives. Adding to the problem is that two are noted as being observers, Heine only as a pilot!

Jean Marie Dominique Navarre was a pre-war pilot aged 20. He made his name fighting over the Verdun front in 1916 and would accumulate a dozen victories but burnt himself out and spent the latter half of the war under medical care. He was destined to die in a crash in July 1919.

Mention above of a victory credit to Heinz Althoven may have confused his name with von Althaus who is supposed to have gained his third victory on this 26th day of February over a BE2c. There were no BEs lost this date, in fact no RFC losses at all are recorded for this day.

Another French claim over a Fokker came on the 28th, Lieutenant Vernin and Caporal Charpentier of Escadrille N68 being noted as downing one near Moyenvic, credited as a probable.

VIZEFELDWEBEL WÄSS' FIRST VICTORY

On the British front, two recent additions to the RFC's arsenal of aeroplanes had arrived in France, apart from, that is, the prototype Martinsyde G.100. 20 Squadron, who had this machine, now had as its main aeroplane type the FE2b, an update on the FE2a, the other new machine being the FE8, a single-seat 'pusher' scout. A prototype FE8 had gone to 5 Squadron in France in December 1915 where it was used quite extensively. One pilot to fly it was Captain F J Powell and he had a number of combats in it (7457). All these pusher-types, the VFB5, no longer at the front, the FE2a and 2b, then the FE8 and soon the DH2 scout, were classified collectively as either 'Vickers' by the Germans, or 'gitterrumpf' machines: 'lattice-tail' or 'lattice-hull', ie: they had no rear fuselage as with a tractor machine, merely open framework from the wing/gondola area, to the tailplane.

No.20 Squadron lost its first FE2b (6338) on 1916's extra February day – the 29th. While on a recce sortie near Menin, Second Lieutenants Lionel Arthur Newbold (Essex Regt) and H F Champion (Rifle Brigade) were attacked by a Fokker which shot them up severely, forcing them to make a landing inside German lines near Menin. Both men were captured and Vizefeldwebel Wäss of FA3 had his first victory. Champion was later to escape before many weeks had passed and got back to England. Once home, and a Captain, he made the following report:

'At 7 am on 29 February 1916 I left No.20 Squadron's aerodrome at Clairmarais to carry out a reconnaissance over the three enemy aerodromes at Gheluwe, Hallum and Moorseele. Lieutenant Newbold was pilot and I was observer, this being the first occasion we had flown together. Three machines escorted us. It began to rain soon after starting. One machine returned with engine trouble.

'We crossed the lines at Ypres at 6,000 feet, and soon after crossing, another machine dropped out; this only left Captain [C W E] Cole Hamilton to escort us. We passed over two aerodromes and were just nearing Moorseele when we were attacked by a Fokker which was driven off by our escort. We began to lose height owing to the fact that a cylinder water jacket had been destroyed.

'We were immediately attacked by another Fokker and an Aviatik. I fired a few rounds at the Fokker and then my gun jammed, probably owing to the rain having turned to ice in the gun. The engine then stopped and we were at 4,000 feet and to the east of Menin. Fire was opened on us from a brigade of infantry drilling to the south of Wevelghem. I destroyed my notes and maps and proceeded to throw parts of the gun over, also the drums. We landed in the next field to the infantry who at once took us prisoners.

'The petrol tanks and cylinder jackets were hit. We were taken to the Headquarters XIII Army Corps at Wevelghem.'

Their loss, of course, would have been prevented had they adhered strictly to orders. As we read above, RFC HQ had dictated that if any of the escorting machines dropped out, then the recce mission should be aborted. The trouble was the press-on nature of the RFC airmen made them take the risk, and it often back-fired.

Hillary Francis Champion came from Chislehurst, Kent, born 27 March 1894. A farming student at Eastbourne College, he had gone out to South Africa in 1913, working in Bloomfontein, in the Orange Free State. At the beginning of the war he had been with the 1st Kimberley Regiment of the South African Defence Force as an NCO. Coming to England he joined the 6th Rifle Brigade and had transferred into the RFC in November 1915. Joining 20 Squadron on 17 January 1916, he had been captured on 29 February and effected his escape on 27 April 1916.

By September he had been attached to 64 Training Squadron then took up various training posts, ending up by commanding No. 69 Training Squadron at the start of 1918 with the rank of Major. He received the Air Force Cross, gazetted 2 November 1918 and was Mentioned in Despatches on 29 August 1919. Demobbed in October 1919 he was repatriated to South Africa to resume his career.

* * *

At the end of February, it was reported that British and French losses during the month amounted to 20, 13 in combat, five from ground fire with two more having landed in German lines, cause unclear. The Germans admitted six of its aircraft as missing.

FOKKER FODDER

There is no doubt that the presence of Fokker monoplanes on the Western Front had a great effect on Allied airmen, but to some extent this was being overcome by March 1916. In saying this though, the battle was far from won, and the Eindecker pilots continued to inflict serious damage to men and aircraft. As my friend Trever Henshaw says in his information-packed book on RFC/RNAS/RAF casualties: *The Sky Their Battlefield*, Grub Street, 1995:

'March could be considered the beginning of the end of the Fokker's supremacy on the Western Front. It would see [too] British concern extending even to its Parliament, where Noel Pemberton Billing MP would articulate many people's fears by describing the BE2s and other products of the Royal Aircraft Factory as 'Fokker Fodder'. On the other hand, it would also witness the widening active use of British machines capable of defeating it.'

However, as far as many French and British aviators were concerned, the battles with the Fokkers did not seem to diminish that much and they continued to fight them for several more months. One observer to record a fight with a Fokker in a letter to his parents, was Second Lieutenant Graham Price flying with 6 Squadron (BE2c). Price had already had several encounters with German aircraft since November 1915.

One item of interest concerns a report by him and his pilot, Lieutenant Danby, on 20 January 1916. They had been sent out for artillery registration but with so many hostile aircraft about this morning, and having had three fights between 10 and 10.25 am: ". . . noticing several other hostile machines cruising about we thought it advisable to give up any endeavour to continue registration and proceed to carry out a policy of aggression."

Flying with Second Lieutenant G E H Fincham on 2 March they encountered a Fokker near Ypres. On the 5th Price wrote to his mother and father:

'I have just finished making up my log book for February and find I have made 22 flights – not bad considering the state of the weather. You will also be pleased to know that I have come out of my 13th fight, so everyone was more or less pessimistic about mine. I was pleased, therefore, to find myself safely on terra-firma after it. It took place over the trenches at only three thousand feet during the recent attack up here when we took 250 odd prisoners. We had been doing wireless work very low down owing to clouds and after an hour's work through the thick of the attack, a Fokker came up evidently sent specially to drive us off. Both of us were so busy taking notes of proceedings on the ground that the first we knew was the popping of a machine gun just behind us. The Hun had dived through the clouds just behind out tail. We turned round but he had gone out of range.

'He came again a few minutes later. This time we saw him and greeted him with a burst of machine-gun fire at 30 feet range. He hit us in two places and I think we hit him, but he was away again like a flash of greased lightning. He came again a third time and at the critical moment our gun jammed, so I fired a red light, which is a sort of S.O.S. call, and he went off just as one of our patrols came up to our assistance. He then made two more attempts to get at us, but the patrol drove him off each time. Talk about greased lightning! I have never seen anything so fast in all my life.

'Each time he made a dash he was only in reasonable range for about five seconds at a time and in ten was out of sight. I got the gun alright [un-jammed] after ten minutes work on it and we able to finish our job satisfactorily. It is very unusual for a Hun to attack one of our machines so low down and especially as we weren't even over the line but hovering about over the trenches. I bet the infantry enjoyed the proceedings.

'During the same affair (i.e. attack) we went along the German trenches at 1,000 feet and gave them some machine-gun fire. Don't suppose we hit anybody but it creates a moral effect, and especially bucks up our fellows.'

In Graham Price's next encounter – presumably his 14th air fight – the outcome was very different. On 9 March, again during artillery registration, he and Fincham were attacked by another Fokker near Ypres and 25-year-old George Fincham was severely wounded and died in the subsequent crash inside British lines along with his observer. It would seem, therefore, that his above letter was his last. He came from Sydenham, south London, and was 29.

Fincham had been the second and only surviving son of the late Lieutenant-Colonel G H Fincham AOD; his mother was also deceased. When war was declared he was an engineer in southern India but returned to join the colours. He had been made a flight commander before his death, but his captaincy had not yet been gazetted.

Price had first been a motor-bike despatch rider and had first gone to France in September 1914. He was granted a commission with the Royal Engineers in November 1915 and attached to the RFC.

* * *

Second Lieutenant B C Rice, an observer with No.2 Squadron RFC, made some notes on fighting the Fokker monoplanes and other types, which have survived in his papers now retained by the RAF Museum. Whether these were from something official, semi-official, or merely notes he and perhaps some of his squadron comrades put together is not clear. But they are of interest to this work:

NOTES ON COMBATS IN THE AIR

Attack on same level if possible. In BE2c use side mounting. Don't open fire over 500 yards; you don't carry enough cartridges to waste. Fire in bursts of not over ten [rounds]. Switch your gun quickly to back mounting as he passes, and fire remainder of drum.

(i) if Hun dives, replace gun on side bracket.
(ii) Put gun on front mounting, and dive for position under his tail.

Never follow a machine directly behind, he will rake you through and through.
Never let a machine get under your tail.
Never let a machine swoop down on you unawares from behind.

At first sound of a shot from behind bank to right, and left, with nose down before looking round even. It is with his first burst of fire that the Fokker scout gets his machine down or any other machine which uses a deflector propeller and fixed gun.

Tested 'tracer' bullets in 'Lewis' automatic. Find sighting best done independently of 'block'. Peep through above the block and use gun as a syringe. Very deadly.

If an E.A. scout presses his attack home and persists in following, go into a slow spiral loosing as little height as possible.

In studying these notes the reader is reminded that the observer in the BE2 was in the front cockpit and his Lewis gun was movable by lifting it from one position to another around his cockpit rim. Although not the best of positions for an observer, not least being surrounded by struts and wires which had to restrict his line of fire, he could at least fire forward, provided he aimed past the propeller blades. His pilot would, of course, fly in a direction slightly off direct pursuit to allow his observer to fire at an angle to miss the propeller. Rice's reference to the side mounting when in pursuit covers this, and the front mounting would be used to fire upwards as his pilot endeavoured to position the BE under the opponent's tail.

Bernard Curtis Rice, later Captain, had some air fighting experience. On 10 October 1915, while still a junior officer, he and his pilot, Lieutenant H W Medlicott met a Fokker over La Bassée and drove it off towards Lille. Another combat was fought in company with his pilot, Lieutenant A L Russell, on 11 November – a day 2 Squadron crews had no less than five combats with Fokkers, LVGs and Albatros two-seaters – and 29 December, in company with Second Lieutenant Keith D P Murray. In the New Year, he and Second Lieutenant W Allcock had a fight with an Albatros C-type on the 12th, retreating as three Fokkers came into view, followed by a scrap on the 23rd. In this fight – with another Albatros two-seater – Rice's fire stopped the engine of the German machine which began to plane down near Hulloch from 9,500 feet, but lack of fuel forced the BE team to retire.

Harold Medlicott and another observer were brought down on 10 November 1915 and taken prisoner. He was shot and killed trying to escape from prison camp on 21 May 1918.

Rice later became a pilot in April 1916, and then a flight commander with No.8 Squadron, still on BE2c machines, in the spring of 1917. On 24 April he and his observer, who rejoiced in the name of Second Lieutenant A C Heaven (which his pilots no doubt prayed he was not over keen to enter too soon), had a scrap with four German aircraft over Vis-en-Artois, and survived, although their BE was pretty much shot-up.

* * *

IMMELMANN'S NINTH VICTORY

Max Immelmann had had no luck since his last victory back on 12 January, nor for that matter had his friend Boelcke since the 14th. Immelmann was the first to score again, and to tie with Boelcke's score, by downing a Morane Parasol (5137) from 3 Squadron RFC at 10.35 on the morning of 2 March. Although still listed as being with FA62, Immelmann was now part of FAbW Kommando 3 – Fokker Abteilung West. Second Lieutenant Charles Walter Palmer and Herbert Frederick Birdwood were forced to land near Somain, Birdwood having been killed in the air. Palmer was wounded in one foot but not severely, although he then had to have it amputated. Blood poisoning set in from which he died on the 29th, officially of septicaemia. Birdwood had been the fourth nephew of General Sir George Birdwood to be killed in the war.

During the combat, Immelmann had been opposed by the Parasol's escort, a Morane N single-seater, flown by Sergeant T P H Bayetto. Immelmann was not alone as Bayetto discovered, for after seeing the first Fokker, he then found four more approaching. In extricating himself from this odds-against predicament, even claiming one of the Fokkers shot down, he escaped after his charge began to go down, and dashed for the lines and safety. Toné Bayetto, as a Captain, was killed in a crash in England in July 1918.

A significant action took place on the morning of 5 March which involved BEs of 9 Squadron. Five machines set out to fly a recce sortie and also to drop bombs on FA32's airfield at Bertincourt: brave or what! Not surprisingly Fokkers from the base's Kek quickly rose to oppose the intrusion and in the action which followed, Second Lieutenant C W Seedhouse, piloting 2099, was wounded. All four BEs made it home, although two others were shot about. One of the pilots was Lieutenant Henry E van Goethem (who would be killed flying on 11 July 1917) and he left us an account of the action which first started with AA fire as they crossed the lines, which put a fragment of a shell through his flying coat:

'We are now some five miles south-west of Bapaume. Looking towards it my eyes are attracted by something moving very fast over the ground. An effort of concentration and I am able to distinguish two Fokkers flying low, just rising, probably after us. They are black and venomous and have a sinister presence. My observer keeps them in sight without a break, while I get on with my business of photographing a hostile aerodrome south-east of Bapaume. This done, I hastily rejoin the formation and follow the leader in my appointed place.

'The Fokkers are now on our level and close behind us. A bank of cloud is blowing down from the lines some 20 miles away. The wind is north-west. We head towards this bank, while completing the railway observation, noting the rolling stock, etc.

'One of our machines at this point foolishly straggles; it is a criminal offence, for which the pilot paid in full later on. Both Fokkers, flying side by side, open fire in short bursts at 200 yards. None of our machines are answering, I notice. It is bitterly cold, and eight of our ten machine guns jam owing to frozen oil.

'My observer opens fire with tracer bullets, which can be seen to splatter all round the foremost Fokker, but as far as I can see do not hit him. Bullets cease to zip by.

'At this point I am able to turn round in my seat and take a snap of him just as he is diving off to attack the separated machine, piloted by Lt Seedhouse and manned by Lt H B H Cox, an observer. This machine, I can see, is making straight for home, and getting further and further away from us. The Fokkers do not return to us. They do not now approach within 300 yards and at that distance they do not even fire at us. I have to suppose they are just seeing us off the premises.'

As van Goethem remarked earlier in a narrative of his flying over France, these long reconnaissances were regarded as probably fatal for one of any group that flew out. At least they always expected a casualty, since the Fokkers had been introduced by the Germans, and the facts usually justified their expectations.

Seated in one of the Fokkers had been Leutnant Werner Lehmann and he noted how well the British machines kept close defensive formation – apart from the straggler! – and organised their defensive fire to maximum effect all the way back to the lines. In this way the Fokkers had been denied their prey, although as far as van Goethem was concerned they were happy not to come too close once the BE crews were alive to their presence.

Lehmann had concluded that: '. . . the British were no longer trying to get out of the way of the Fokkers, as they had done previously, but were using all their skill and energy to defend themselves.'

Certainly the RFC machines were now flying more and more in formations, even if only three or five machines, in order to help defend themselves. It was becoming more rare for the Fokker pilots to find single machines out alone too far over their side of the lines.

HANS BERR'S FIRST VICTORY

Oberleutnant Hans Berr was another who was about to make his name as a fighting pilot. From Braunschweig, born 20 May 1890, he had become a soldier early in life and at 18 he was a Leutnant with the 4th Magdeburg Reserve Regiment of Light Infantry. When the war began he was with the 7th Regiment but was wounded in action in September 1914, so joined the air service at the beginning of 1915. Flying as an observer before becoming a pilot, he later found himself assigned to a Fokker unit at Avillers and then Jametz.

On 8 March he fought an action which resulted in him being awarded his first air victory, recorded as a Nieuport. The French lost machines this day but it is not sure which was Berr's, or whether it came down on the French or German side of the lines. Three were claimed as downed inside German lines, five forced down on the French side. A Farman crew of MF5 also claimed a Fokker destroyed over Beauvallon.

Escadrille N3 had an observer wounded in a Nieuport two-seater – Sous-lieutenant Louis Pandevan – so he may have been involved with Berr, in which case he and his pilot got back, at least as far as the French side of the lines.

Amongst others downed was one by Leutnant Lothar Fr von Hausen and his observer, flying with KG2 who were credited with a Caudron G4, or possibly a Voisin, for his first victory. Von Hausen, from Leipzig, was the nephew of Generaloberst Max Fr von Hausen, commander of the German 3rd Army. He had attended the cadet school in Dresden, then joined his father's old 13th Jäger Battalion but was seriously wounded in September 1914. Transferring to the air service in the new year he finally arrived at Brieftauben-Abteilung-Metz in September 1915, which later became KG2, von Hausen flying with its Kampfstaffel 11. He was later to fly with Jasta 32 in early 1917, only to be another airman shot down by the French ace Georges Guynemer, on 15 July, and to die of wounds received.

Another was a Bréguet-Michelin machine, No.73, crewed by Lieutenant Charles Henri Marie Dutertre de Vaisseau, CO of the Escadre, taken prisoner, and Soldat René Paul Demont, who was killed. This went to Unteroffizier Kress of FA71 as his second victory, although whether he was flying a Fokker is unclear, but as mentioned earlier, it is thought he was operating with Kek Metz. If indeed this was Christian Kress, then he too was to fall to the guns of Georges Guynemer on 10 November 1916.

On the 9th FE2b No.6356 of 20 Squadron was shot down by a Fokker pilot from FA5. It came down on the road between Marguillies and Sainghin, near Haubourdin at 13.15. Both men were taken prisoner. Regrettably there is no apparent record of the German pilot's name. The FE was seen going down with steam coming from it, obviously the radiator having been holed, and it landed near Ligny, south west of Lille.

When Douglas Byron Gayford, the observer, returned home at the end of the war he confirmed being attacked by two monoplanes and that his Lewis gun had already jammed in a previous fight in which he claimed to have shot down an LVG and killed its crew. The FE was guarding a recce machine heading for Tournai, and defenceless; Gayford was wounded four times. Irritatingly, he does not mention the German pilot by name, as it seems he met him, for Gayford knew from this pilot that he had fired over 200 rounds at the FE. There is a bit of a time difference but this is probably due to bad record keeping by one side or the other.

Leo Roy Haywood, Gayford's pilot, confirmed being shot down by Fokkers whilst engaged on a recce and that his observer had been badly wounded. He himself was wounded in the right foot. He too confirmed bringing down a German machine then being brought down by a Fokker that got on their tail.

The British crew had shot down a machine from FA18 (Albatros CI 1833/15), who lost Leutnants Gerhardt Fr. von Gayl and Erwin Friedel over Lille, which is in the same area as the Fokker fight. Confirmation of this came from the German crew of a two-seater which came down in British lines on 12 March. The British crew must have been told this too whilst in captivity in order to report it upon their return from Germany.

A No. 1 Squadron Morane two-seater came off second-best in a fight with a two-seater crew from FA213 this day too.

BOELCKE REGAINS THE LEAD

Oswald Boelcke shot down his tenth hostile aeroplane on 12 March, a French Farman which crashed into French lines and was subsequently destroyed by German artillery fire. Boelcke was now flying from Sivry, where he had arrived on the 11th, Jametz being now far too far back from the front. Most fighters only took off upon the sighting of Allied aircraft arriving over the front, and from Jametz they could no longer see this happening through their long-range glasses and telescopes. He was now in charge of a small independent unit of just himself, one officer, an unteroffizier and 15 men. The rest of the Fokker pilots were still at Jametz.

This first action was against two French machines, of four he sighted, the duo sticking together to thwart their attacker. Finally he got behind one and gave it a telling burst. As it started to go down so both his guns jammed (some Fokkers were now carrying two machine guns), but he had found the mark. However, the French pilot managed to glide across the Meuse River to land just east of Marre. Front line observers saw one man run into a nearby village and return with a stretcher party that carried a second man away. Moments later the Farman was blown to pieces by gunfire. MF63 had two pilots wounded this date and another killed. Escadrille C61 also claimed a Fokker destoyed on the 12th, in German lines.

PARSCHAU'S THIRD VICTORY

The Germans claimed three victories this 12 March, number two going to Otto Parschau. All that is known is that it was a French aircraft downed in the Verdun battle area but it seems likely that it was a Nieuport from Escadrille N49, whose pilot, Adjudant Auguste Metairie, was wounded. My friend Frank Bailey, an acknowledged expert on French aviation in WW1, also believes Parshau's victim was Adjudant Metairie who came down in French lines. I would not argue with 'Bill's' deductions.

BOELCKE'S ELEVENTH

The same problem faces us with Oswald Boelcke's next victory, claimed on 13 March, a particularly active, and productive day for the Fokker pilots. His combat was timed at around 1 pm, east of Malancourt village, Verdun. Operating again from Sivry he shot down a Voisin into French lines, one of a formation of French aircraft heading towards Dun sur Meuse.

His first encounter was with a French fighter which he saw attack a German aircraft over Fort Douaumont, which he forced to retreat. Later he spotted the French formation and managed to pick off a straggler. Stung into action, the Voisin pilot made a hasty dive for the lines. Closing in for another attack, Boelcke was amazed to see the observer had climbed out onto the wing and whilst holding on to a strut was waving at him. Boelcke assumed his fire had damaged the controls necessitating this poor man to get out onto the wing to keep the machine on an even keel.

Being attacked by another of the Frenchmen, Boelcke had to leave the crippled aircraft but later he saw that it had crashed into French lines and could be seen quite plainly from the German trenches. VB107 had a pilot injured this date and a Bréguet crew of BM118 wounded, but that's the closest I can get. Other crewmen from GDE were injured but no reasons are given.

IMMELMANN GETS TWO MORE – NOS 10 AND 11

Up on the British Front Max Immelmann levelled the score by a double victory. The first came at 13.30 (German time), a Bristol C Scout (4678) flown by the CO of No. 4 Squadron, Major Victor Annesley Barrington-Kennett. He was up hoping to meet and engage German aircraft operating beyond the front lines and was just in the act of attacking one as two Fokkers came into view. On this outing Immelmann was flying in company with Leutnant Max Mulzer, but it was Immelmann who took no time in shooting down the Bristol which fell near Serre, close to the front lines. The British pilot did not survive the fall.

Barrington-Kennett had been in the Grenadier Guards prior to joining the RFC. Born in June 1887, the third son of Colonel B H Barrington-Kennett of Her Majesty's Bodyguard, they lived in Chelsea. Victor was educated at Eton and Balliol College, Oxford, and his interest in flight began with ballooning pre-war. He learnt to fly aeroplanes in 1912 and once war came, flew with No.1 Squadron. Two of his three brothers were also killed in the Great War.

That evening, Immelmann got his eleventh. This time it was a BE2c (4197) from No. 8 Squadron. He had flown off at 17.00 hours and forty minutes later engaged this BE which he found over Arras. There were four British machines altogether, Immelmann firing 300 rounds at the one crewed by Lieutenant Gilbert Dennis James Grune and Second Lieutenant Brian Edward Glover DCM. As the BE heeled over, Immelmann fired a further 200 rounds into the doomed machine, then watched as it crashed near Pelves.

Grune came from Brighton, Sussex and had been an engineering student and first saw duty with the artillery in 1914. Glover, at 21, was a year younger than his pilot but had already seen action with the Royal Engineers. He was also a Sussex lad, coming from Lewes, and he had been awarded the Distinguished Conduct Medal as a corporal, and the French *Médaille Militaire*. Gazetted a second lieutenant in late 1915 he was attached to the RFC as an observer.

BERTHOLD'S THIRD VICTORY

Rudolf Berthold added to the RFC's, and 8 Squadron's woes this day by shooting down the BE2c (4151) crewed by Second Lieutenant M A J Orde and 1AM P Shaw at 14.53. Orde was wounded, forced down near Bourlon, and both men taken prisoner. There were four or five British machines heading roughly towards Douai. By the time Immelmann had been ready to

take off, a call was received that two BEs had turned towards Cambrai.
However, in the air, and after a brief search, four BEs were seen and chased.
After the action, another 8 Squadron crew saw 4151 go down and also saw
two Fokkers land in the same field, one of three this crew said were in the
action. Michael Orde was repatriated in June 1918 and recalled:

> 'On a reconnaissance a Fokker monoplane got behind me and
> wounded me in the back and head, rendering me temporarily
> unconscious. A German Albatros followed us down and
> landed alongside us and the two occupants waited with us
> until more Germans came along, and then flew off.'

Unfortunately there is no clue as to who the benevolent two-seater
crew were, or whether they risked a landing to ensure the English crew did
not burn their aeroplane. Obviously they were not engaged in vital work if
they could take time out to land by Berthold's victims. As two Fokkers had
been seen to land, it may well be that the wounded Orde – understandably
not paying too much attention to detail – assumed the two airmen were
from a two-seat crew and may well have been Berthold and another Fokker
pilot.

Berthold wrote that he had two companions on this outing. Pilots with
the Kek units no longer operated singly but in twos and threes so as to
combat the larger RFC groups; tactics were changing. While this restricted
somewhat the period of cover they could provide because of their limited
numbers, it certainly enabled the leader to concentrate on attacking hostile
aircraft while being looked after by one or more other pilots, making sure
he was not attacked from behind. It was this system that was to be so
effective with the later Jastas, the leader usually making the initial attack
whilst protected from behind by his men.

Max Mulzer claimed a Morane this day too, but it was not confirmed and
the French do not record any losses this date. However, his time was
coming.

BERR'S SECOND KILL
While Boelcke was flying from Sivry, Hans Berr was still operating out of
Jametz, and on 14 March he downed his second victim, noted as being a
Caudron, north-west of Verdun. This too must have come down inside
French lines and the only loss that appears to fit is a Caudron G4 of GB1,
shot down in flames although this may also have been claimed by German
AA fire. However, the crew of Capitaine (and chef de battaillon) Alphonse
Jules Roisin, was taken prisoner, and Soldat Pierre Delphin Clement
Gousset, killed.

GUSTAV LEFFERS' FOURTH VICTORY
No. 15 Squadron lost Second Lieutenant J C Cunningham and 1AM J W
Newton on the 14th too, both being killed after their BE2c (4153) was shot
down at 13.20 at Achiet-le-Grand, near Gomecourt. Leffers, again in 84/15,
set their machine on fire. James Campbell Cunningham came from New

South Wales, Australia and was 21. John Newton was only 19 and came from Bakewell, Derbyshire.

Leffers fought the BE crew for several minutes, getting so close he later recorded seeing the pilot shake a raised fist at him. As the fight continued, both machines suddenly turned into each other. Leffers had the advantage with his forward gun, the BE's observer having nose, engine and propeller in his field of fire. Just as a collision seemed inevitable the German released his controls and the Fokker reared up, its wheels just brushing the top wing of the BE. The shaken BE crew made a sudden dash for the lines but Leffers was upon them quickly and this time his bullets hit home. The BE went straight down, crashed and burst into flames being totally consumed by the fire.

There were in fact several air fights with Fokkers this day. A No. 1 Squadron Morane LA was hit during a scrap with three Fokkers near La Clytte mid-morning, Captain R A Saunders MC (aged 21) being mortally wounded by a bullet in the stomach. One Fokker appeared to be hit in the fight, and while smoke was seen coming from it, it was not seen to go down. Saunders made a crash landing in British lines but died of his wound. A 20 Squadron FE2b was also shot up by a Fokker and the observer was wounded but the machine got home.

Reginald Arthur Saunders, from North London, was 21 years old, and had entered the British South Africa Company after leaving school. Commissioned into the London Regiment, he had transferred to the RFC in March 1915.

No. 13 Squadron had one of its BE2c machines badly hit by a Fokker and was forced to land near Le Touret, British side, with its observer dead, having been hit after his gun had been put out of action. There are no German claimants for these actions, but one German that did make a claim was Leutnant Hermann Göring, flying his AEG G (49/15) with FA(A)203. With Leutnant Graf von Schaesberg as observer, and gunner Boje, he attacked a French Caudron (1457) of Escadrille C6, whose crew of Sergent Gaston Eugene Delpech and Sous-lieutenant Georges Thevenin were reported missing.

HARTMUT BALDAMUS' FIRST VICTORY
Dresden-born Hartmut Baldamus, 10 August 1891, joined the air service at the start of the war and after pilot training went to FA20 in March 1915 as a gefreiter. Although he began flying two-seaters, by March 1916 he was flying Fokkers, and on the 15th, in a Fokker EIV, he shot down a French Caudron from Escadrille C28. The crew of MdL Jacques Decazes de Glucksberg and Sous-lieutenant François Lefebvre died in the burning wreck, which fell south-east of Beine, Champagne front. Another French crew reported seeing this team force a German aircraft to land in this fight, but one has to wonder if, in reality, they saw a victorious Fokker pilot merely land near his victim?

THE MÜLHAUSEN RAID AND UDET'S FIRST VICTORY
On 18 March 1916 the French mounted a major raid on the town of

Mülhausen, later reporting the composition of the force to be 13 80-hp Farmans, four 130-hp Farmans, three Bréguet-Michelins (one with a 37 mm cannon) and three Caudron G4s, total 23. Take-off from the airfield at Belfort was at 3 pm.

The Fokkers defending the German town were of the fighter detachment of FA68 based at Habsheim – Kek Habsheim – which had Eindeckers and Fokker DIIIs. The airfield, commanded by Hauptmann Walter Mackenthun, was just five kilometres east of the town. The Fokker DIII ('D' meaning doppeldecker – biplane) along with the earlier DII, had first come to the war front in 1916 and it was planned that they would gradually replace the Eindeckers. Other than being a biplane, its fuselage and tail resembled the monoplane design. Indeed the DII used the same 100-hp Oberursel engine, although the DIII had the 160-hp UIII 14-cylinder Oberursel. The DIII also carried two Spandau machine guns as standard. Kek Habsheim, led by Leutnant Otto Pfältzer, had four pilots, its CO, Feldwebel Karl Weingärtner, Unteroffizier Willy Glinkermann and Vizefeldwebel Ernst Udet.

One of the pilots to be warned of the approach of raiders, was Udet, but he was only told there were two French aircraft approaching. He had just received a new machine, a Fokker DIII (364/16), but this had been damaged during a landing the previous evening, so he took off at 16.16 pm – according to his action report dated the 19th – in a Fokker EIII, Nr. 105/16. Making contact with the raiders, he was astonished to find not two French machines, but 23! He dived into the middle of them and fired at a Farman, which burst into flames and went down. As it fell the observer jumped or fell out right in front of Udet, but the German could only think of one thing – victory number one! Udet then attacked a Caudron G4 and it limped away with one engine stopped. Udet's guns then jammed so he was unable to finish it off.

By this time other Habsheim aircraft had become airborne and were attacking. This author is unclear what they were flying. The Kek had a mix of DIIIs and Eindeckers, and it is inconceivable that all were flying biplanes. Three more bombers failed to return from the raid, and victories were claimed by Leutnant Pfältzer, Karl Weingärtner and Willy Glinkermann.

However, although four machines from MF29 (of Groupe de Bombardment 4) were lost, one is understood to have fallen after colliding with an AEG G (4/15) machine (FA48b, also based at Habsheim, lost a three-man crew over Napoleon Island, Habsheim). Udet's victim – a Farman 40 – crashed in the centre of Mülhausen, while Weingärtner's fell near Doller. Glinkermann saw his crash east of Rodern, just south of the airfield. As well as Udet's, one other bomber fell in flames. It is undestood that Pfältzer's claim was not upheld. When later he was with Jasta 15, its records noted that this pilot obtained his first confirmed victory on 12 October 1916.

The French claimed four German aircraft shot down and crashed during this action, three of them Fokkers, plus the AEG. Perhaps a trifle over-optimistic! Other than the AEG crew lost, one flieger is noted as killed at Mülhausen this date, unit unknown.

Udet, of course, would end the war with 62 victories, the highest scoring German pilot to survive the conflict. His second victory would not come until October 1916, by which time Kek Habsheim had become Jasta 15.

VON ALTHAUS' FOURTH VICTORY

Ernst von Althaus was credited with his fourth victory on 19 March, a Caudron G4 west of Lahons, operating with Kek Vaux. Its actual crash site was recorded as west of the road between Meharicourt and Lihons, and the rail line between Chaulnes and Rosières. If this was in French lines it is difficult to know who this was. Escadrille MF20 reported a casualty this date, with an observer killed, but the location is unclear. German AA gunners also claimed two French aircraft down, one in flames and another behind the French lines, as the flamer may also have been.

BOELCKE TAKES THE LEAD

The other known French loss on 19 March was a machine from Escadrille MF19, who lost Sergent Pierre Galiment and Lieutenant Jacques Marie Valentin Libman. They appear to have been the twelfth victory of Oswald Boelcke. He was sent up from Sivry as two Farmans were reported working over the front lines. At about 12.45 he spotted them above the west bank of the Meuse and then he saw bombs bursting below.

Boelcke closed in and saw one of the French machines begin to go for a German observation machine so attacked. Despite return fire from the French observer, Boelcke closed right in before firing, something he did regularly now. His fire took effect and one wing of the Farman broke off and then gradually the machine began to disintegrate, falling into the German trenches near Douaumont.

Later the German troops in this area sent some items from the crashed aeroplane to Sivry, including a machine gun and a camera. They also reported that the pilot had been hit several times and killed in the air.

Immelmann telephoned his friend and rival saying that he should refrain from shooting down any more aircraft until he had had time to catch up, and Boelcke, with a smile, said he would wait a week. In the event, Boelcke shot down another the next day, a day during which German pilots downed three hostile machines.

BOELCKE'S THIRTEENTH

On the 21st Boelcke shot down a Voisin from VB109 (No.V1417) near Fosses Wood, north-east of Samognieux, just inside French lines. Exploding AA shells guided him to his victim to the west of Ornes, which he identified as a Farman, which was in contact with a German two-seater. Boelcke went straight into the attack and his fire caused the French machine to explode – probably a hit in the fuel tank. It went down burning like a torch to crash into the wood, which was not far from Hill 344. The luckless crew were Lieutenant Jean Antonioli and Capitaine Félix Le Croart.

BRUNO LOERZER'S FIRST VICTORY

Another German pilot who was to make a name for himself in air fighting gained his first victory on this same day, Leutnant Bruno Loerzer, from Berlin. Born 22 January 1891 he had been an army cadet with Infantry Regiment Nr.112 before going to military school, being commissioned in January 1913. He began flying lessons before the war started and when it did begin he was sent to FA25 in October 1914. That same month a friend and fellow officer from the 112th joined him as his observer, Hermann Göring, with whom he was to have a life-long friendship and association. They flew together until June 1915. Eventually training as a single-seat pilot, Loerzer was sent to Kek Jametz.

Loerzer made his first claim on 21 March, a Voisin from VC111 in the same area as Boelcke's claim. In fact Boelcke mentioned another Fokker in the vicinity of his fight so this might have been him, going after another French machine nearby. It certainly fell near to Fosses Wood with its crew, Caporal Marcel Antoine Bornet and Matelot François Le Maout. It was found to be carrying a 37 mm cannon. There appears to be a claim by flak gunners for this Voisin but in any event, Loerzer was given a kill.

Bruno Loerzer would end the war as a fighter group leader, 44 victories and the *Pour le Mérite*. Friendship with Hermann Göring led him into the German Luftwaffe and in WW2 he held various commands.

PARSCHAU'S FOURTH

The third victory credited this same day was to KG1's Otto Parschau, a Voisin north of Verdun. However, the French only admitted to two losses in German lines, so this was possibly a machine that came down inside French lines. It was also Parschau's last victory for some months, for he was slightly wounded on 23 March over Ham, while attached to FA(A)271.

THE AIRCO DH2

The British fighter which was to help sound the death knell of the Fokker monoplane, the DH2 'pusher' scout, had been in France for some time, although only two had been attached to 5 and 11 Squadrons. This was really in similar vein to the first Fokkers being attached to two-seater units. These two DH2s and that FE8 prototype mentioned earlier, heralded the shape of things to come, and in February 1916 the first dedicated single-seat fighter squadron equipped with DH2 machines arrived in France. No. 24 Squadron was commanded by Major Lanoe Hawker VC DSO, and was based at Bertangles, near Amiens.

The very first DH2 that had been attached to 5 Squadron in July 1915 – No. 4732 – had been lost on 9 August. While the Germans rebuilt the machine, the significance of it was not apparent to them. This DH2 and the Fokker monoplane, had arrived at the front at about the same time, but it would be a year before the RFC pilots found that their pusher machine had the edge over the Fokker. It was not, as some suggest, a machine built specifically to combat the Fokkers, its design was not brought out until well into 1915, long after the early Fokker monoplanes were flying.

On 25 March 1916, one of the new production DH2 machines with 24 Squadron was lost due to a strong westerly wind which forced the British pilot to come down inside German lines and present them with another

DH2 machine, this one being totally undamaged.

This same 25 March saw a future ace, Leutnant Renatus Theiller claim his first victory, the first of an eventual 12. Born in Mülhausen on 13 September 1894 he was yet another pre-war pilot, having gained his licence, No.511, on 12 September 1913, the day before his 19th birthday. Serving with FA44 and then FA25 on two-seaters, his first victory was over a French Farman of MF35 near Caillot Wood. MdL René De Saint-Didier and Aspirant Robert Eugéne Frédéne Bel were both killed in the II Armée Verdun sector. However, it is not certain if Theiller was still flying a two-seater or a single-seater on this date; certainly no observer is mentioned.

The following day a Belgian Farman XX was shot down by Fokkers. This was a machine from Escadrille No.4 and its pilot, Lieutenant Pierre H Rigaux fell at La Panne and was killed. The only German pilot mentioned as having downed anything on this 26 March was Hans Karl Müller, serving with Kasta 11 of KG2, but they were at Verdun, so a long way from La Panne on the North Sea coast. All that is known of his victim was that it was supposed to be a French aircraft, and that some sources note this claim being unconfirmed. We shall meet Hans Karl Müller again as a pilot with Kek Avillers.

IMMELMANN'S TWELFTH AND THIRTEENTH

Max Immelmann closed the gap with Boelcke slightly on 29 March by shooting down Second Lieutenants F C Pinder and E A Halford of 23 Squadron. He got them late morning, their FE2b (6352) falling near Quéant, the pilot having been wounded in both arms. Both men were taken prisoner.

Immelmann had been sent up after six British machines had been reported heading in the direction of Douai, and he was followed by two other monoplanes. He found five enemy machines, spread out somewhat. Interestingly he later referred to them as the 'Farman' type; ie. pushers. In all he attacked three of the five and succeeded in bringing down 6352.

Once back at the airfield he telephoned to discover what had happened and was told his victims had come down at Bertincourt, not far from Bapaume, south of the Cambrai-Bapaume road. He and the Kek commander drove by car to the spot. He saw his fire had damaged the engine and wings, plus severing two control wires. The Canadian pilot, he found, was in the process of firing a signal flare that he was going to land, but just as he was about to do so, he was hit in the arms and so landed even more quickly. Also he discovered that the observer was in fact another pilot, having decided to fly as observer on this mission.

Getting home after the war, Edward Athelston Halford reported that they had been attacked by 'superior numbers' and shot down while on a recce mission. He also confirmed that Pinder had been wounded in both arms.

The next afternoon (30th), Immelmann drew level with Boelcke by downing a BE2c of 15 Squadron – No.4116 – whose crew were photographing the trench systems. He had left the ground at around 11 am and flying towards Bapaume as he could see nothing of interest in his own sector, he spotted three RFC machines and went after one. The BE pilot promptly turned west but Immelmann cut him off and attacked, exchanging fire with the observer. Suddenly the BE went down, and although, as he watched, Immelmann saw the machine level off briefly, it then crunched into the ground. He later heard that the pilot had been killed in the air, while the observer had died in the crash. Second Lieutenant Geoffrey Joseph Lightbourn Welsford had indeed been killed but Lieutenant Wayland Joyce had not, and survived as a prisoner.

Breaking off this action, Immelmann immediately went after another British machine but it was fast heading west. He chased it to the lines, firing as he closed the gap, and saw the aircraft start to descend in a steep glide west of Serre. However, he was satisfied with one victory for it had brought him level with his rival again. Immelmann would also be aware of the order not to cross the lines. This may have been a BE2c from 8 Squadron which had a combat with a Fokker near Villiers at 11.30 which as far as the British crew of Flight Sergeant T F B Carlisle and Lieutenant J A McKelvie were concerned, was inconclusive.

ANOTHER VICTORY FOR FA62, BUT WHOSE?

Not long after Immelmann returned to Douai he learnt '. . . with joy that another gentleman of our section [FA62] had also shot down an English machine – a Vickers biplane.' The Vickers in question was from 11 Squadron, an FB5 No. 5471, piloted by Second Lieutenant J S Castle with observer 2AM E R A Coleman, who were taken prisoner, on a photographic sortie. It seems that this machine was in combat with more than one German aircraft, either at one time or over a period during its flight, as it was claimed by several German airmen.

Obviously there is the FA62 pilot that Immelmann spoke of, who was either Oberleutnant Lieberts or Leutnant Max Mulzer, both of whom, records note, had scored a kill this date; or a two-seater crew of FA4b, Oberleutnants Wimmer and Kraft. Max Mulzer was certainly credited with a VFB5 on this day, north of Wancourt, but so was Oberleutnant Lieberts of the same unit.

Returning home at the end of the war, James Castle recorded that after they had taken their first photograph they were attacked by enemy aircraft but drove them off. When taking the second photo, they were attacked by two more from behind. His observer fired three bursts at one and it broke away, but then his aircraft erupted into flames at 8,600 feet. He dived, trailing smoke and flame while his observer threw maps, gun, ammunition and camera over the side. Castle's left leg and foot were badly burned before he managed to force land, resulting in a four-month stay in a German hospital, and hardly being able to walk for over a year.

In all probability, the two Fokkers were the same in both attacks, and were probably flown by Mulzer and Lieberts, with Mulzer winning the toss on who should receive credit. One has to wonder if the oberleutnant failed to pull rank, or because of his rank he let the more junior officer have it? However, there are two more Fokker pilots that may have been involved – see below.

The Vickers came down between Wancourt and Tilloy at about 11.07 German time, and initially the name of Lieberts was noted as the victor. There is another note that a claim was also raised by an unteroffizier of FA62, but Mulzer was a leutnant. According to another German report, a BE2c (from 8 Squadron – 2605) was shot down by a Fokker near Quesnoy Farm, south-east of Monchy au Bois. Yet another report also indicated that it had earlier been attacked by two Fokker pilots from FA62, and that two more Fokker pilots with FA32 had been involved – Leutnants Schmedes and Lehmann. If this is Werner Lehmann, then he was a former Fokker pilot with Kek Bertincourt, with three victories (dates unknown) by the time he went to Jasta 9 in September 1916, although he promptly died in a flying accident while at AFP3 on the 23rd of that month, crashing at Somme Py.

Of the BE crew, Lieutenant T C Wilson survived, wounded but a prisoner, while 1AM Arnold Walker was killed. It must be assumed that while there were several claims for these two aircraft, final credit seems to have been given to Mulzer and Lehmann.

From photos of the downed Vickers, it can be seen that most of the fabric has been burned away from the inner sections of both upper and lower wings, as well as the rudder and elevator, although the main structure appears more or less intact. The landing appears a good one too despite the flames.

In one of the photos (in this book) there seems to be at least three leather-clad airmen in the picture, denoting that either the victors were able to land nearby, or the landing site was not far from the Germans' airfield. Unfortunately two of the airmen's faces are turned away from the camera while the third, glancing at the cameraman, is not known to this author. Certainly it isn't Mulzer.

Burkhard Lehmann came from Halberstadt, born 20 March 1894 while Mulzer was a Bavarian, born 9 July 1893 in Kimratshofen. Lehmann had joined FA32 from AFP2 on 18 July 1915; he would be posted to FA(A)210 on 23 August 1916 but three days later went to the newly formed Jasta 1. Almost a year later he moved to Jasta 12 but was killed over Hendecourt on 5 August 1917.

Mulzer had graduated as an officer cadet in July 1914, and joined the 8th Cavalry Regiment in which he was commissioned in December. He then transferred to aviation and after serving with FA4b was attached to FA62's Fokker element in 1916. As he was to become well known and a *Pour le Mérite* winner by the summer, one must assume his list of victories is pretty accurate, and this shows his first *abschuss* was credited on 30 March. The only other possibility which might involve Lieberts is if he was an observer in a two-seater flown by Mulzer, although there is no suggestion that Mulzer was not flying a monoplane, or that Lieberts was not a pilot himself. If this had been the case, surely Immelmann in his letter home would have said 'gentlemen' rather than 'another gentleman'.

The French crew from Escadrille C64, Lieutenant René Doumer and Soldat Warnotte, claimed a Fokker shot down on the 30th near St Marie-à-

Py. The pilot is believed to have been Gefrieter Cäsar Becker, a 19-year old from Mülhausen, unit unknown, who was killed at St Souplet. This was the second successful combat by Doumer, who would later be a single-seat ace with Escadrille N76 – seven victories. He was the son of Paul Doumer, a senator and later President of the République, but would die in combat in April 1917.

On the last day of March, the Germans claimed four hostile aircraft shot down, all French. One 25 Squadron RFC FE2b was engaged with a Fokker over Gheluwe and its observer wounded in the leg, but no claim was made.

Two of the German claims were by two-seater crews, one from FA44 and one from FA60. The French losses were a Nieuport 11 from N57, the other a Farman from MF41. The other two appear to be victories claimed by monoplane pilots, Bruno Loerzer, his second victory (*luftsieg*), a French machine over the Verdun front whilst operating from Jametz, and a Nieuport 11 claimed by Unteroffizier Malz of FA39 flying a Pfalz monoplane. If Loerzer's claim was for a Farman, then MF41 lost a machine this date, its crew killed.

MALZ'S FIRST VICTORY
Josef Jacobs noted in his diary for 31 March a victory by fellow pilot Malz:

> 'Around noon [three French aircraft] appeared over Laon. Because of accurate AA fire two of the Frenchmen turned tail, the third, a Nieuport sesquiplane two-seater calmly flew in circles over the AFK division aerodrome and dropped bombs from a height of 200 m.
>
> 'Meanwhile all the Fokkers from Laon had taken off after the Nieuport which they chased, but it was a 80 hp Pfalz from F.Fl.Abt.39 flown by Kpl Malz on a defensive patrol who had the luck to down the French aircraft. The fight, which lasted about ½ minute, could be seen from Laon. The single-seat Pfalz came at the Nieuport from behind and from close range of eight metres fired 80 rounds. The Nieuport swung instantly, descended, appeared to flatten out, then had the left wing break off. Down went the Nieuport vertically and for a brief moment straightened out on one wing. Just before impact the observer jumped out and was still alive on his way to the hospital where he, a French officer, died. The NCO pilot, a corporal, must have been killed outright for his badly mutilated body showed a soft bullet wound behind the ear which happened before the Nieuport slammed into the ground.
>
> 'The Frenchmen had fought for their lives in the most courageous manner. The Pfalz was hit by eight well-aimed shots: one through the propeller, one in the nose and the others close to the pilot's seat. This is the first French aircraft shot down in the 7 Armee area.'

The Nieuport two-seater (454) went down near Laon inside German lines and was from Escadrille N12, crewed by Sergent Frédéric (Jacques) Quellennec and Lieutenant Jean Mourier, who were both killed. Malz was later a pilot with Jasta 12 as an offizierstellvertreter (warrant officer).

* * *

At the end of March, figures of claims and losses which appeared in the magazine *Flugsport* indicated that British and French losses totalled 44; 38 in combat, four to ground fire and two to mechanical reasons. Of these, 25 at least were downed inside German lines. German losses were admitted as seven in combat, three to ground fire and four to other reasons – total 14.

What had now been established on the German side by this time was the grouping of small numbers of monoplane fighters into Keks, even though several monoplanes were still being used by various flieger-abteilungen, while other Kek pilots, such as Boelcke, operated individually. However, as far as the Allied airmen were concerned, there were definitely more monoplanes about now, and more often than not, in twos and threes, rather than loners.

In his diary, Josef Jacobs noted that an announcement from the Feldflugchef stated that the German airmen on the Western Front were opposed by a total of 85 French and British airfields with an estimated 1,038 aircraft. Little wonder that the Germans were far more inclined to defend their part of the sky than attack the Allied side. Jacobs also noted that his unit – FA11 – had had its Fokker taken away and with other monoplanes it had been grouped into two fighting staffeln. These were Fokkerstaffel-Ost (east) commanded by Leutnant Eitel-Friedrich Rüdiger von Manteuffel, of FA26, and Fokkerstaffel-West (west), commanded by Oberleutnant Erich Hönemanns, of FA11, a future Jasta commander.

In a directive dated 21 March by von Borries of AOK (Armee Oberkommando – army headquarters), it admitted that monoplanes attached to two-seater units had mostly failed, certainly in the field of attacking hostile aircraft crossing into German air space. Therefore, from 1 April 1916 monoplanes would be assembled into the two units Jacobs mentions. Fokkerstaffel West, based at Le Faux Ferme, north-east of Coucy, were given four Fokkers from FA7, 11 and 39, while Fokkerstaffel East, at an airfield just west of St Erme, had five monoplanes taken from FA26 and 29. The two new units would be under the command of the Stabsoffizier der Flieger. On 1 April too, FA32's Kek at Cambrai had four Fokker EIIIs and one Pfalz EI monoplanes on strength. Things were now changing.

By this time, several Fokker pilots were starting to become disenchanted with the performance of their monoplanes, although they still had the edge of all but the fastest of the new Allied fighters. The EIII was still the mainstay, but the EIV was not giving a better performance. Boelcke complained about the EIV's rate of turn, being not so good as the EIII and that in a climb, above 10,000 feet, the EIV was inadequate. At that height the loss of speed was so great while in a climb that the Nieuports could escape without difficulty.

With the new biplane types promised, the Fokker monoplane pilots eagerly awaited their arrival, but they were still several months away. Despite this, they continued to inflict losses on the Allied aviators.

Chapter Six

April and May 1916

Berthold Claims his Fourth

Kek Vaux's commander, Oberleutnant Rudolf Berthold was given credit for his fourth victory on the first day of April 1916, a Farman down in French lines near Lihons. This may well have been a machine from Escadrille MF54, Sergent Louis Paoli and Lieutenant Alfred Braut, killed. Otherwise, there are two other possible candidates. One French aircraft that came down inside French lines was a Caudron G4 with only a pilot aboard, MdL Lucien Victor Prevost of MF2, killed in a fight with a German fighter. The machine had been converted as a single-seater for escort work. The other French loss was a Caudron of C43, seen in a fight with a Fokker before it blew up in the air, presumably with the loss of its crew, Adjutant Achille Degon and Sous-lieutenant Madelin, the latter possibly on attachment from C43.

The RFC had several skirmishes with German two-seaters, a crew of FA(A)213 claiming one victory, while flak fire forced another down in British lines. Otherwise, early April was dogged by bad weather keeping air actions to a minimum. At Douai, FA62 lost a tyro Fokker pilot, Gefreiter Albert Aschmann, in a flying accident on the 3rd.

What was significant was that on the 8th a Fokker EIII monoplane, serial number 210/16, came down intact inside Allied lines at Renescure, nine kilometres east of St Omer, the unwounded pilot being taken prisoner. The luckless pilot, described as a 24-year-old Gefreiter, had gone to Armeeflugpark Nr.6 at Valenciennes to collect a brand new machine for his unit, FA5. Taking off he was told to follow the railway line to Lille then head north-west to his airfield at Wasquehal. He had to land twice at German airfields to ask directions and finally, instead of following the canal north-east to Lille, followed the La Bassée canal to the west. He had no idea he had crossed the front lines until engine failure forced him down and the appearance of British soldiers ended his war flying.

The Fokker had a 9-cylinder 100-hp Gnôme engine and as soon as particulars were available from the intelligence people it was circulated to all RFC units. If the RFC had suspected an interrupter gear, then now, presumably, it was confirmed. This machine was later test-flown at both St Omer air base, and later at Upavon and today it can be seen in the London Science Museum. Much of the myth of the Fokker was laid to rest by RFC pilots flying it and testing it against a Morane in a mock air fight. It was found that the Morane had a distinct advantage over the German machine.

The secret was not speed, engine power or the height it could fly but climbing ability and manoeuvrability. These, plus the synchronised machine gun, were what made the Fokker so deadly. One thing was certain, the assumption of invinceability had gone.

* * *

On 9 April Oberleutnant Franz Josef Walz, a future *Pour le Mérite* winner, gained his first victory flying two-seaters with Kagohl I (*Kampfgeschwader der Oberstein Heeresleitung* – Fighting Squadron of the Army High Command). He commanded the 2nd Kasta (*Kampfstaffel* – fighting section) and would claim a total of seven victories by the spring of 1917, all on two-seaters, and then command Jasta 2 before going to Palestine as a squadron commander. He and his observer – Leutnant Gerlich – claimed a Caudron downed over Douaumont. The French list a machine from Escadrille C27 missing this day along with its crew, Sergent Gaston Henri Felix Guidicelli and Lieutenant Gaston Emile Marie Marchand.

Another famous two-seat pilot, Oberleutnant Georg Zeumer, also flying with KGI was credited with his first victory on the 11th, a French fighter north of Verdun, probably the loss sustained by N57 (No.653), Caporal André Aristide Bobba. Zeumer had been a pilot with FA4 in 1914 and was to gain four official victories with KGI, and like Walz, was to command Jasta 2 later, and was killed in action with it on 17 June 1917.

HÖHNDORF'S THIRD VICTORY
Walter Höhndorf claimed victory number three on 10 April, a Nieuport Scout from Escadrille N68, flown by Sous-lieutenant Marcel Thiberhein. Höhndorf had now left FA12 and while noted as being with Kek Vaux, is listed on this date as being with Fokker Staffel Falkenhausen.

Yet another intact Fokker EIII Eindecker was presented to the Allies on the 10th, Unteroffizier Roessier of FA22 running out of petrol and taken prisoner upon landing 196/16 intact on the wrong side of the trenches according to an interrogation report.

BERTHOLD MAKES IT FIVE
Bad weather further restricted operations until the 16th, and on this date Rudolf Berthold attacked and shot down a British BE2c (2097) of 9 Squadron. The crew of Second Lieutenants W S Earle and C W P Selby (Royal West Kent Regt) were directing artillery fire and fell in flames east of Maricourt. Earle was killed but Selby survived as a prisoner although wounded. The Germans noted the BE's fall as south of Maurepas, these two villages being just south of Combles. Wallace Sinclair Earle was a Canadian from Ontario, aged 27. He has no known grave.

Selby returned home in September 1917, having been released into Switzerland on Christmas Eve 1916, no doubt due to his injuries. Once back, he reported that Earle had been killed by the Fokker's first burst of fire but that he had fired back and wounded the German pilot in the leg. He knew this, and the pilot's name – Leutnant Berthold – because, he said, they were both in St Quentin hospital having their wounds attended to. This is the first indication this author has seen to Berthold being wounded, but presumably it was not a serious injury for he was flying again quite soon, being more seriously hurt in a crash on 25 April, as we shall read. Selby's report, dated 16 October 1917, read:

'On 16 April 1916 ordered by my Squadron Commander, Maj Burdett, 9 Squadron, to proceed over the line on artillery control, my pilot being Lieutenant Earle, a Canadian.

'I was informed that five other machines were also being sent out, three were to send wireless signals only on the enemy's side of the lines and the other three to send on our side. I was to be one of the former group.

'I proceeded over the lines at about 7,000 feet at 9.35 am and found that I should have to stay entirely across the lines to be successful in my artillery control. I began my signalling about 9.45 am, and after about ten minutes found that my target, an enemy battery in a wood, was practically impossible to see, also we were being very heavily shelled by hostile AA guns, who had accurately ranged on to us and were preventing successful observation. My pilot was trying to locate one of these AA batteries in order that I might change my target.

'Our machine was attacked by a Fokker at 10.05 am while the AA guns were still firing, the pilot of the enemy machine being a Lt Berthold. My pilot was killed by the first round fired, but the machine remained in control long enough to allow me to fire a drum, luckily hitting the attacking pilot in the leg. This I learnt when I was in the same hospital as him at St Quentin.

'When the machine began to get out of control, I climbed back to the pilot's seat and endeavoured to regain control, but found the rudder wires shot away. The machine then fell, controlled only by the elevators. I luckily managed to get clear, falling about 50 feet from the machine, thus escaping any fatal injuries.'

On this same date a 25 Squadron FE2b was damaged by AA fire over La Bassée but got home safely. Its observer was Corporal J H Waller who would feature in Max Immelmann's demise in June.

On the 17th one of Berthold's Kek Vaux pilots, Fritz Otto Bernert, a future ace, is supposed to have downed a French Nieuport, but there is no record of such a loss unless it came down inside French lines without causing its pilot any harm. Bernert had been wounded four times in the early part of the war whilst in the infantry. The last wound, a bayonet thrust to his left arm, severed the main nerve which left it almost useless. Unfit for soldiering, he transferred to the air service and later, as a Jasta pilot and leader, gained a total of 27 victories but died in the influenza epidemic in October 1918.

April 21 saw the death of a Fokker pilot, Leutant Werner Notzke of FA25 at Sivry, and a friend of Oswald Boelcke, and one who had been flying with him recently. He had been practice-firing at a ground target and hit a balloon cable, crashing to his death. He was the son of an army colonel. Replacing Notzke was von Althaus, who arrived with another Fokker pilot to fly with Boelcke, Leutnant von Hartmann, also in from Jametz.

IMMELMANN'S FOURTEENTH VICTORY
FA62's Fokkers were active on 23 April – Easter Sunday – and downed two 'pusher' machines. The first one was a Vickers Gunbus from 11 Squadron on a photo Op which took off at 08.45 and failed to return. This machine, crewed by Second Lieutenants William Charles Mortimer-Phelan and William Archibald Scott-Brown, were engaged by two Fokkers, flown by Immelmann and Mulzer. Unfortunately, the 11 Squadron crew had failed to meet up with its escort aircraft so had decided (again against orders) to push on anyway. Both Germans attacked and 120 rounds from Immelmann's guns badly damaged the FB5 and punctured the fuel tank. Forced to descend, Mortimer-Phelan put his machine down at Monchy-le-Preux, just east of Arras. Before capture they had time to set fire to their machine.

Mortimer-Phelan's brief report following his release from prison camp, noted that they were taking photos of German AA batteries at Fampaux, near Arras and nearby locations. The escorting VFB5 left them at some stage and then came the attack by two Fokkers piloted, he confirmed, by Immelmann and Mulzer. With his petrol tank riddled Mortimer-Phelan was forced to land near Pelves where he and Scott-Brown burnt the machine before being captured.

Scott-Brown said they were attacked from behind while taking photos and the first burst hit both engine and petrol tank. After landing they set fire to the aircraft, which was still burning as they were marched away, being almost completely destroyed. Quite apart from having most of their attention taken up by photography on such sorties, pusher crews had quite a blind-spot behind, with the engine, fuel tank and whirling propeller. If a German fighter pilot came in dead astern of a pusher, he had a good chance of taking the Allied crew by surprise and/or smashing something vital.

MULZER'S SECOND
At 11.30 Immelmann and Mulzer engaged an FE2b from 25 Squadron. Mulzer attacked first, followed by Immelmann, near Estaires. The pilot, Lieutenant W E Collison, on a 1st Army patrol over Fromelles, quickly turned for the lines as his observer, 2AM Geoffrey F Atwell, began to defend against the German machines. He was then fatally wounded in the front cockpit whilst changing a drum of ammunition on his Lewis gun. Collison said he also opened fire with his fixed gun but was then hit by AA fire – or was it another burst from the Fokker? – which compelled him to make a forced landing near Estaires, inside British lines.

There seems to be some confusion as to who got who in these actions.

Apparently when questioned, the captured 11 Squadron crew had said that the first Fokker attack had caused the major damage, and so credit might have gone to Mulzer, but all contemporary records indicate that it was Immelmann who was credited with the Gunbus. This leaves the damaged(?) FE as being credited to Mulzer, so there must have been some reason it was deemed to have fallen, or landed, inside Allied lines following Mulzer's attack. Whatever the circumstances, Immelmann had raised his score to 14, and Mulzer was no doubt happy with a second confirmed victory.

Rudolf Berthold had a bad crash on 25 April flying a Pfalz EIV monoplane, 803/15. He crashed on the airfield at Château Vaux and was badly injured. As we shall read later, this was the first of several injuries and wounds suffered by Berthold, who gained the title of 'The Iron Knight' in consequence, but again, probably post-war. The Pfalz monoplane did not possess as good a performance as the Fokker machine, and was, therefore, not so popular with pilots who flew it. Berthold's crash did nothing to improve matters.

There was also a big fight on the 25th between DH2s and Fokkers in the Bapaume area. BEs of 9 and 15 Squadrons were out on reconnaissance and they found evidence of a third line of defence the Germans were constructing behind the Somme front. Fokkers attacked in force. At least two Fokkers were driven down, one believed to have been flown by Immelmann, whose machine was shot up this day. Immelmann wrote:

'I had a nasty fight in the air today. I took off at about 11 am and met two English biplanes southward of Bapaume. I was about 700 metres higher and therefore came up with them very quickly and attacked one. He seemed to heel over after a few shots, but unfortunately I was mistaken. The two worked splendidly together in the course of the fight and put eleven shots into my machine. The petrol tank, the struts on the fuselage, the undercarriage and the propeller were hit. I could only save myself by a nose-dive of 1,000 metres. Then at last the two left me alone. It was not a nice business, but my machine will be serviceable again tomorrow.'

The two 24 Squadron RFC pilots were Lieutenants J O Andrews and N P Manfield.

Mulzer was in action again on the 26th, in company with Leutnant Österreicher and another pilot. Near Souchez at around 10.50 German time, they met and engaged an 18 Squadron FE2b (5232) piloted by Second Lieutenant J C Callaghan and Second Lieutenant James Mitchell, on a photo mission. The FE crew put up a spirited defence and managed to evade the three Fokker pilots, finally crossing the lines even though Callaghan, with his controls damaged, had his FE turn upside down before he made a landing near Château de la Haie. Callaghan had seen his observer hit in the head and after landing discovered Mitchell was dead.

In this instance, a victory was not allowed to any of the German pilots. While FA62 failed to achieve a victory, Callaghan and Mitchell were credited with a Fokker monoplane shot down in this action; possibly a consolation for Mitchell's loss. Joseph Creuss Callaghan would go on to win the MC with 18 Squadron; he died in action commanding 87 Squadron in July 1918. Mitchell was 33 years old and had previously been in the navy in 1898, and had served in China between 1900 and 1906. He then lived in Canada and when war came had joined the CEF.

BOELCKE MAKES IT FOURTEEN

Oswald Boelcke drew level again with Immelmann on 28 April by shooting down a French Caudron near Vaux during the morning. He had only just returned from a trip to Germany – a visit to the Oberursel engine factory at Frankfurt – and no sooner had he done so than two French aircraft were reported nearby. Driving to the airfield he took off but he was too late, observing one of the Frenchmen going down following a fight with a German two-seater.

Boelcke flew towards Verdun and spotted three French machines crossing the line and being attacked by another Fokker. However, the Fokker pilot got into difficulties and had to retreat. Boelcke went for one of the French aircraft, firing three times before it began to fall earthwards, later being reported down in a wood south-west of Vaux by front line troops. Escadrille C53 was in a fight with Fokkers this date, and claimed one Fokker shot down. Was this the second Fokker which broke off to go home? C53 had a pilot wounded – Sous-lieutenant Paul Fabre – but was this as a result of Boelcke's attack?

On the French front there was another action worth recording. I say this because if I recorded all the Fokker monoplanes that were claimed shot down by the British and the French, for which no obvious losses are found, this book would be longer than it need be. While German fatalities are pretty accurately reported, many wounded airmen are not, and pilots who force landed, with aircraft slightly damaged or destroyed, but who walked away also go largely un-mentioned. One has to wonder at the Allied airmen's reports of seeing German aircraft fall burning, for which no obvious loss is known. They were either seeing an Allied aircraft going down, or were embellishing their claims in order for the intelligence officers to look more favourably on their petition.

In a combat on the 28th, Brigadier Leon Vitalis flying as an observer with Escadrille N67, shot down a Fokker which fell between the lines, south of Hill 304, and within 200 metres of the French trenches near Froides. The pilot of this machine had just shot down Sous-lieutenant Jean Peretti of Escadrille N3 (previously N67). Peretti certainly died of wounds received this day (he had also claimed a Fokker monoplane shot down on 11 March 1916), but there is no German claimant – if the German survived – and no recorded loss (fatality) if he did not.

The victory over the EIII was credited to Vitalis (Marie Gaston Fulerand Leon) aged 26, as his first victory. A former Cuirassier cavalryman, he transferred to three-seater Caudron aircraft later that spring, going to Escadrille C46. With this unit he and his crew claimed a further six victories by April 1917. He later trained as a pilot and became an instructor.

OFFIZIERSTELLVERTRETER RÖHR'S TWO VICTORIES

One of the Fokker pilots with Fokkerstaffel West was Offizierstellvertreter Röhr, who would become a founder member of Jasta 12 later in the year. He was not only about to have his day, but his two days! On 29 April he attacked and brought down a Farman flown by MdL Jean Charrier and Sous-lieutenant Karl Favre of MF16, although it came down in French lines, the crew surviving, despite Charrier having been wounded. Then the following day he shot down a Nieuport XII two-seater (No.839) from Escadrille N3, crewed by Caporal Antoine Chassin and Adjudant Paul Hatin, who were both killed, falling in German lines near Salency, east of Noyon. Röhr received the Iron Cross and a commission. In 1915, Paul Hatin had flown many sorties with Caporal Georges Guynemer, long before the latter had started to become one of France's greatest fighter pilots.

A future ace who did not succeed in having a victory confirmed on this 30 April was Leutnant Friedrich Mallinckrodt, also flying now from Sivry. He claimed a French aircraft over the Verdun front but it was disallowed. He would survive the war with six victories, but only just. He was wounded five times; the last, on 30 April 1917, ended his operational flying.

Three Fokker pilots died this day too. Rittmeister Erich Graf von Holck was attached to FA(A)203, but before this he had been a pilot with FA69 on the Russian front, one of his observers being the future Red Baron, Manfred von Richthofen. Now a pilot, von Richthofen, flying with KG2 in France, saw a Fokker fall during a fight with some Caudrons, but only later did he learn that its pilot had been his friend von Holck. Credit for downing this Fokker went to Lieutenant Albert Louis Deullin of Escadrille N3, his fourth of an eventual 20 victories, which went down over Courriers Wood, near Douaumont at 11.00 hours. Deullin had claimed a Fokker monoplane on 31 March too, but in German lines.

Another Fokker loss was a machine of FA32 (Kek Bertincourt), flown by Leutnant Otto Schmedes, a 21-year-old Berliner, shot down, the Germans said, near Combles. This was the action reported by Second Lieutenant D M Tidmarsh of 24 Squadron, flying a DH2 (No.5965). He was escorting some FEs over Péronne and saw the Eindecker coming from the direction of Bapaume. He attacked it, and the Fokker pilot immediately dived, then appeared to get into difficulties and lose control at 1,000 feet. Tidmarsh saw it crash into some houses at Bapaume, the wings having separated. Tidmarsh said he was never nearer than 500 yards – and did not have the opportunity to open fire! This is odd, for the official German report noted that the flying wires had apparently been severed by machine-gun fire!

David Tidmarsh, from Limerick, claimed seven victories, firstly with 24 and later with 48 Squadron before being captured on 11 April 1917, having won the MC. He would also be involved in the death of Wilhelm Frankl three days before being brought down himself.

As if this was not enough, Vizefeldwebel Erich Kügler, a Fokker pilot with FA3b (or FA70) was lost over St Remy, the third casualty. If his birth date of 1877 is correct, he was 39 years of age, and came from Haynau. Whether this had anything to do with a claim by Lieutenant Jean Chaput flying with N31, over a Fokker E at 17.45 hours above Les Eparges, is uncertain. It was his third of an eventual 16 victories, mainly with Spa57. He would be killed in action on 6 May 1918. An Escadrille N3 pilot also claimed to have shot down two Fokkers mid-morning of the 30th, approximately in the same area as Tidmarsh's claim.

This was a bad few days for Eindecker pilots, for on the 29th Unteroffizier Georg Wilhelm Freiherr von Saalfeld had been killed in a fight with an FE crew from 25 Squadron over La Bassée, shortly after the noon hour. The Fokker was one of those attached to FA18 and the FE observer, Second Lieutenant R V Walker, got in a burst which resulted in the Fokker's wing crumpling up. The machine went down in a spinning nose dive into and behind the British lines. The FE's pilot was Second Lieutenant Lord Doune (Francis Douglas Stuart-Gray). For this and other exploits, Lord Doune received the MC, as did Robert Verschoyle Walker, formally of the 6th Connaught Rangers. Von Saalfeld was the son of Prince Ernst von Sachsen-Meiningen.

April 1916 ended with Germany admitting the loss of 22 aircraft, 14 in combat, four to ground fire and four to unknown causes. They claimed 36 Allied aeroplanes, 26 in combat (9 in German lines) and ten to ground fire.

BOELCKE'S FIFTEENTH AND VON ALTHAUS' FIFTH AND SIXTH
German summer time was announed for the night of 30 April/1 May. Allied summer time would begin on the night of 14/15 June, so with German time one hour ahead of British and French time already, on 1 May German time became two hours ahead of Allied time until 15 June.

This first May day saw another Fokker flieger killed. Unteroffizier Siegmund Antoschewski crashed at Montmedy, attached to Kest 1, while at the Armee Flugpark Nr.5.

During the evening of the first day of May, Oswald Boelcke was standing on Sivry airfield and saw a French aeroplane in the distance. Climbing aboard his Fokker he took off after it and following a brief encounter, shot it down within two minutes. This same day Ernst von Althaus brought down his fifth victory north of Feste St Michel. However, there is some doubt about the time, and conflicting reports suggest this may have been on 30 April – a Farman – confusion possibly due to the date of the communiqué announcing this victory.

A similar problem occurs with von Althaus' sixth victory, a French two-seater shot down over Caillette Wood, dates being given as both 2 and 3 May. Lack of French casualties for early May does not help to resolve the dates or the possible victims of any of these three victories. Boelcke describes a twisting dog-fight which suggests his opponent was a single-seater, but no French scouts were lost on 1 May. A report from the German 14th Reserve Division confirmed seeing the French machine crash vertically into wooded country south-west of Vaux. N48 had a pilot injured but it is unclear if this was war flying or otherwise.

FRANKL'S FIFTH VICTORY
There is no such problem with Wilhelm Frankl's fifth victory on 4 May, a day which also saw him promoted from Vizefeldwebel to Leutnant. A No.

Top left: Kurt Wintgens seated in a Fokker A-type possibly at Schwerin. Note there is no gun. Note too Wintgens' pince-nez glasses, held in place once in the air by his goggles.

Top right: Anthony Fokker seated in his M5K on 23 May 1915 whilst demonstrating his Eindecker, equipped with a machine gun, at the Crown Prince's Headquarters at Stenay.

Middle: BE2c 2008 of 8 Squadron, shot down by Hans-Joachim Buddecke, FA23, 19 September 1915 for his first victory. Note roundels on upper surfaces of the elevators.

Left: Oswald Boelcke with his former observer Heinz von Wuhlisch, FA62. Together they downed a Morane on 4 July 1915 prior to the arrival of the Fokker E-types.

Top: Eduard Böhme, flying with FA9, downed two Farmans on 25 September 1915, but was killed in a crash on 24 January 1916.

Middle left: Hans-Joachim Buddecke.

Middle right: Max Immelmann's fourth victory, BE2c of 16 Squadron, 10 October 1915.

Right: Immelmann seated in his Fokker, having landed to inspect victory No.5, an 11 Squadron Vickers FB5, 26 October 1915.

Top left: Close-up of Immelmann with the wing of the Vickers in the background. Note fore and aft gunsight.

Top right: Kurt von Crailsheim in an EII, 59/15, at Vrizy, October 1915.

Middle left: Kurt von Crailsheim, FA53, fatally injured in a flying accident on 30 December, died 4 January 1916.

Middle right: Erich Graf von Holck in an unarmed Fokker A-type 1915. He was killed in action in a Fokker of FA(A) 203 on 30 April 1916, by the French ace Albert Deullin.

Bottom: H-J Buddecke's third victory, 11 November 1915, another 8 Squadron BE2c, No. 1725.

Top left: Gustav Leffers standing by his first victory, BE2c 2049, 13 Squadron, 5 December 1915.

Top right: Max Immelmann's seventh victory, 15 December 1915, a Morane LA (5087) from 3 Squadron, near Raismes, Valenciennes.

Middle left: Oswald Boelcke standing in front of a 160 hp Fokker EIV.

Middle right: Boelcke in flight in an EIV.

Bottom: Otto Parschau (far right in group) standing with other airmen in front of his second victory, a BE2c of 12 Squadron (2074), shot down 19 December 1915.

Top left: The fuselage and tail from 2074 make a cross above the graves of Lieutenants N Gordon-Smith and D F Cunningham-Reid, 13 Squadron, 19 December 1915.

Top right: BE2c 2019 of 2 Squadron, brought down on 5 January 1916 by Leutnant Ernst Hess of FA62, for his first victory.

Bottom left: Ernst Hess, Kek Douai and Fokkerstaffel 'C'.

Bottom right: The victory cup – *Ehrenbecher* – awarded to airmen following their first victory.

Top left: French cannon-armed Voisin LA (No.991) forced down on 10 January 1916 by Vfw Wilhelm Frankl, for his first Fokker victory.

Top right: Ernst Fr. von Althaus by his Fokker Eindecker, Kek Vaux. Note head-rest and cover over the machine gun.

Middle left: Hans Berr in front of his Fokker, Kek Avillers.

Middle right: BE2c 4107 about to join 15 Squadron. It was shot down by Oblt Krug of FA5 on 19 January 1917, near Neuville. The other machine is a Morane Parasol.

(H S Clarke)

Bottom: Gustav Leffers shot down this 13 Squadron BE2c (2054) on 20 February 1916 for his third victory.

Top right: Morane BB (5137) 3 Squadron, forced down by Max Immelmann on 2 March 1916 for his ninth victory.

Middle: This well known picture of FA62 nevertheless shows several interesting faces. Left to right: Salffener, Meding, Max Mulzer (rear), Albert Österreicher, von Schilling, Oswald Boelcke, Max von Cossel, Hauptmann Hermann Kastner, Fromme, Max Immelmann, von Gusner, von Krause and Ernst Hess.

Top left: Vfw Wäss of FA3 forced this FE2b of 20 Squadron down on 29 February 1916 and landed beside it. The victorious pilot stands in the observer's cockpit showing he has been awarded 1st and 2nd Classes of the Iron Cross. This was his first victory. His name and the victory date have already been painted on the front of the FE.

Bottom: The 20 Squadron crew of Second Lieutenants L R Heywood and D P Gayford are driven away sullen and unhappy after being brought down by a Fokker on 9 March 1916. It is unfortunate that it has not been possible to identify who brought them down.

Top left: BE2c 4197, 8 Squadron, Immelmann's 11th victory, 13 March 1916.

Top right: Immelmann and Mulzer. Immelmann has the Blue Max and the Commander's Badge of the Saxon Military St Henry Order at his throat.

Middle left: Gustav Leffers shot down this 13 Squadron BE2c (4153) on 14 March 1916 for his fourth victory.

Bottom: Immelmann's 12th victory, FE2b 6352 of 23 Squadron, 29 March 1916. Here it is shown on display in Berlin along with other war booty, including Avro 504 No.874, brought down during a raid on Friedrichshafen on 21 November 1914.

Top left: Oswald Boelcke, Pour le Mérite and the ribbon of the Hohenzollern House Order and Iron Cross Second Class through his button hole. The Iron Cross First Class is pinned above his pilot's badge.

Top right: This 15 Squadron BE2c (4116) became Immelmann's 13th victory on 30 March 1916. The observer did his best to land it after his pilot had been fatally hit.

Middle right: Vickers FB5 (5471) 11 Squadron, brought down on fire and badly burnt, 30 March 1916. Although credited to Oblt Lieberts of FA62, several aircraft were involved in the action.

Bottom: VFB5 5471 again, with several German airmen inspecting the burnt wreck. One of them must be Oblt Lieberts, credited with this victory.

Top: Otto Parschau's Fokker EIII. Note the line of signal flares on the edge of the cockpit.

Middle left: Otto Parschau (left) with KG1 standing next to Hans von Keudell while he was still on two-seaters prior to becoming an ace with Jasta 1 in late 1916.

Middle right: Vfw Willy Glinkermann, Kek Habsheim, his Fokker being rigged and the gun being aligned. Note the weight balance hanging from the tail.

Bottom: BE2c of 9 Squadron (2097) shot down by Rudolf Berthold of Kek Vaux for his fifth victory, 16 April 1916.

Top left: Rudolf Berthold and his ground crew, Kek Vaux. The Fokker is an EIII, 411/15.

Top right: Another badly burned, and still smouldering, Vickers FB5 of 11 Squadron. This one – 5079 – was shot down by Immelmann and Mulzer but credited to Immelmann, 23 April 1916, for his 14th victory. *(N Forder)*

Left: FE2b No.6341, 25 Squadron, brought down by Vfw Adam Barth, FA18, 16 May, 1916 near Fournes. A gift aircraft, named *Zanzibar 1*, written on the port side, it also had *The Scotch Express* painted on the starboard side; it was captured intact. Barth landed nearby, as evidenced by the inset picture of his Eindecker with 'Sieger' (victor) written above it.

Middle: The inscription on the front of this Fokker says Fokker E 75/15; Ltn d.Res Protz. Hans Protz flew with FA70 and was killed on 12 May 1916, possibly by S/Lt Georges Pelletier d'Oisy of Escadrille MS12. Which of the two airmen is Protz is unknown.

Bottom: French two-seater Nieuport of Escadrille N68, shot down by Kurt Wintgens for his fourth victory, 20 May 1916. Note the absence of roundels on top wings and the red, white and blue banner/ flag painted on the fuselage.

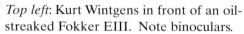

Top left: Kurt Wintgens in front of an oil-streaked Fokker EIII. Note binoculars.

Top right: FE 4909 of 25 Squadron being dismantled.

Middle: FE2b (4909) of 25 Squadron, involved in the final combat of Max Immelmann on 18 June 1916. *Baby Mine*, credited to Max Mulzer, is surrounded by troops and a couple of local youngsters.

Two painted bands on the nose denote a B Flight machine.

Bottom left: Max Mulzer, third from the right, with *Baby Mine*, now without undercarriage, back at the airfield with fellow pilots. 4909 became his fourth victory.

Bottom right: Hans Buddecke, centre, visiting KG1, with Hptm Ernst Fr. von Gersdorff, killed in action over Neuberg on 19 June 1916 with KG1, and Schulz.

Top: Kurt Wintgens brought down this 27 Squadron Martinsyde G102 (7471) on 30 July for his 12th victory. Note one prop blade has sheared off.

Middle left: Another view of 7471 from which one can clearly see the Lewis gun mounted on the top wing. These aircraft usually carried a second 'scatter' gun, mounted on the rear of the cockpit rim, set to fire backwards.

Middle right: Hartmut Baldamus, FA20, scored five Fokker victories.

Left: The bespectacled Kurt Wintgens, Pour le Mérite.

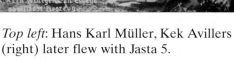

Top left: Hans Karl Müller, Kek Avillers (right) later flew with Jasta 5.

Top right: Hermann Pfeiffer, AOK 3, shot down four French Caudrons in the summer of 1916 prior to flying with Jasta 9.

Middle left: Pfeiffer, in flying helmet, by the wreckage of one of his Caudron victories.

Bottom left: Kurt Wintgens stands by his 13th victory, a 60 Squadron Morane BB, shot down on 3 August 1916. One of the unfortunate crew lies in the foreground, a tarpaulin pulled back for the benefit of the camera.

Bottom right: Wintgens, probably taken at the scene of his 13th victory crash site.

Top left: Fokker EIII 210/16 in flight at Upavon.

Top right: Wilhelm Frankl, Pour le Mérite.

Middle left: BE2d of 2 Squadron (5741) forced down by Wilhelm Frankl south-west of Bapaume on 9 August 1916, for his ninth victory. Out to attack a balloon, there is a gun fitted to the left of the pilot's cockpit, set to fire at an angle to miss the propeller blades. An observer was not carried on this sortie.

Bottom: Frankl, von Althaus and Alfred Lenz on 1 July 1916, probably in front of the FE2b of 22 Squadron (6365) shot down this date by Vfw Dittrich of Kek B for his first victory.

Top left: Ernst Fr. von Althaus, Pour le Mérite.

Top right: Max Mulzer, Pour le Mérite.

Bottom left: Walter Höhndorf, Pour le Mérite.

Bottom right: Otto Parschau, Pour le Mérite.

Top left: Gustav Leffers, Pour le Mérite.

Top right: Oswald Boelcke standing in the cockpit of his two-gunned Fokker EIV.

Middle right: Parschau in the cockpit of a Pfalz E-type. Note flare pistol by the cockpit.

Bottom: Kurt Student, AOK 3, with Fokker and mascot dog.

Top left: Kurt Student, CO Fokkerstaffel der III Armee 1916 with his EIV – two guns. Note gun sights, pilot's head rest and rear view mirror on strut.

Top right: Otto Kissenberth in an EII, 33/15, with FA9b.

Middle: Kek Ost, Avillers, summer 1916. Hans Berr stands third from right, while seated (l to r) are: Vfw Heinrich Bussing, Vfmstr Max Winkelmann, Vfw Hans Karl Müller, Paul Piechl, and an un-named flyer.

Right: Fokker monoplane in flight.

Top: The mangled remains of an FE2b, probably 4272 of 25 Squadron, which Max Mulzer shot down near Sallaumines, Lens, on 3 August 1916 for his tenth and final victory.

Bottom: Oblt Karl Albert, FA292 and FA5b, killed in a flying accident 22 September 1916. The machine is an EIV, 182/16.

Top: Ltn Werner Lehmann killed in a flying accident 23 September 1916.

Bottom left: Stefan Kirmaier, Kek Metz,

and later leader of Jasta 2. Killed in action 22 November 1916.

Bottom right: Rudolf Berthold, Pour le Mérite.

Top left: Hans Berr, Pour le Mérite.

Top right: Hans Berr in a Fokker monoplane, Verdun, 1916.

Middle right: Gustav Leffers with his captured Nieuport Scout. He is understood to have been shot down whilst flying this machine on 27 December 1916.

Bottom: The 'scourge' of the Allied airmen (l to r): Alfred Lenz (FA23), Karl Stehle (Kek 4), Walter Höhndorf, Hermann Margot (FA23), Hans Buddecke, Ltn Krawlewski, Rudolf Berthold, Otto Bernert, Ernst von Althaus, Hans Malchow (Kek Vaux), Wilhelm Frankl.

Top left: Bruno Loerzer, with Fokker EIII 20/15. Later a 44-victory ace with the Pour le Mérite.

Top right: Franz Walz, two-seater ace with Kasta 2. Pour le Mérite.

Bottom left: Willi Fahlbusch, two-seater pilot with Kasta 1.

Bottom right: Martin Zander, FA9b, two-seater pilot with FA9b and later CO of Jasta 1.

Top left: Albert Dossenbach and Hans Schilling of FA22 in 1916. Dossenbach who later became an equally successsful fighter pilot, was the first two-seater pilot to win the Pour le Mérite.

Top right: Von Althaus, fifth from the left, as CO of Jasta 10 in June 1917. Third from the left is Adam Barth who had flown with

FA13 as a Fokker E pilot.

Bottom left: Karl Odebrett flew Fokkers on the Russian Front before flying in France.

Bottom right: Emil Meinecke, seated on the engine of one kill, flew with Ottoman FA6. His early combats in a Fokker led to acedom.

Theo Croneiss also flew with FA6 in the Dardanelles and also became an ace.

7 Squadron BE2c flying an artillery observation sortie near Ploegsteert Wood in the early afternoon was spotted by the German pilot with Kek Vaux and attacked. His fire set the BE (4109) ablaze ending the lives of Second Lieutenants Edward Gurney Ryckman, a 19-year-old from Canada, and fellow-Canadian John Romeyn Dennistoun, aged 21, both of whom jumped to escape from the fiery mass before it hit the ground.

We have read how some German airmen were keen to inspect their victories, and with the majority of Allied machines falling inside German lines, this was often possible. It was not that difficult in the early days of the war but it could be dangerous. An interesting story that occurred on 4 May 1916 concerns the loss of a Royal Naval Air Service Caudron G4 (9118) shot down during a raid by 5 Wing RNAS upon the German base at Mariakerke in the early hours. Flight Sub-Lieutenant K L van Allen (Canadian) was its pilot and he died of wounds a few days later. However, according to an account in *Flugsport*, one of the men responsible for his loss was Flugzeugmeister Benno Schlütter, noted as a Fokker flieger. The next morning he walked out to inspect the wreck, not far from the trenches, tripped an electric land-mine and was killed.

French pilots claimed a Fokker down in the French front line trenches on the 4th, Sous-lieutenant Henri Guerin, an observer of MF221, assisted by Caporal Jean-Baptiste Pompet of MF41. On the 5th FA2b lost a Fokker pilot, Oberleutnant Hans Findt being downed over Petit Wasquehal, near Lille.

JACOBS' FIRST VICTORY

Josef Jacobs obtained his first of 47 victories on 12 May. Five days earlier he had been asked if he would care to join Fokkerstaffel West. His answer was immediately to pack up and leave FS11. He found the Fokker unit at Le Beaux Ferme, and discovered that it had three Fokkers, one Pfalz and a Morane Parasol.

On the evening of the 12th, he and others were having supper, but this was interrupted by the sound of AA fire. Running to the airfield, his Fokker (EIII 608/15) had already been rolled out of its shed and he immediately took off and headed for the AA explosions. He spotted a Caudron going towards Laon and despite the AA fire he closed in and after firing two bursts the Caudron went down and crashed by Bourguignon Wood, south-west of Laon.

Later he and his *staffelführer*, Hauptmann Kuhn, drove to the spot, to find troops and cavalry trying to find the crew who had escaped into the woods. However, the wreck was sufficient to claim the victory, although the AA people put in a counter claim. Upon inspection, the Caudron and one engine, clearly showed bullet holes rather than shell splinters, so the matter was quickly resolved. The machine was from Escadrille C30 and its pilot, Marechal-des-Logis (MdL-cavalry or artillery sergeant) Hulin, on a lone recce sortie, was later found and taken prisoner. He did not carry an observer on this flight, as Jacobs had suspected during the combat. It was also the first victory for Fokkerstaffel West. Jacobs' official report read:

'On 12 May 1916, towards 8.45 pm, an enemy aircraft was fired at by anti-aircraft guns in the area of Soissons-Laon.

'I started with my 100 hp Fokker E.III 608/15 and shortly afterwards met the enemy aircraft, a twin-engined Caudron, at 1,800 m near Pinon. Before the fight I fired a light-signal and opened fire on the Caudron when I was about 60-80 m away. A jam occurred after I fired 30 rounds, which I cleared.

'Meanwhile the Caudron flew towards the front and made a right-hand turn in the direction of Anizy-Eizy. Because I climbed during this time, I had the edge in speed and when I pushed my nose down to close in on the enemy machine, I fired 30-40 rounds in a turn from a distance of 80 m, whereupon the Caudron headed towards Bourguignon in a steep glide.

'Prevented from firing by a second gun jam, I tried by turning and spinning, to prevent the Caudron from getting away. Near the village of Bourguignon the Caudron was about 50 m from the ground and I thought he would land in a field of grass but he once again tried to escape over the valley. I rushed at the Caudron and fired more shots from 10 m; at once the enemy aircraft fell sideways.'

This same day the French credited Sous-lieutenant Georges Pelletier D'oisy of MS12, known to his friends as 'Pivolo', with a Fokker down near the French trenches near Vaux. There is no pilot loss noted although a Fokker pilot was killed at Charleville – Leutnant Hans Protz of FA70 – in an accident.

BARTH'S FIRST VICTORY

At noon on 16 May, Vizefeldwebel Adam Barth flying a Fokker EIII while with FA18, shot down an FE2b (6341) of 25 Squadron, on a photo sortie, east of Sainghin, near Fournes. Its crew, Captain Douglas Grinnell-Milne and Corporal D McMaster were both taken prisoner. In fact they were ganged-up upon by four Fokker pilots, two of whom, Unteroffiziers Hug and Walther of FA5 also put in claims, but Barth was given credit. Returning from PoW camp at the end of the war, Grinnell-Milne confirmed four Fokkers had got them, and a ruptured petrol tank had ended their struggle. He also observed one of the Fokkers to crash from his observer's return fire, close to the Lille-Douai railway line.

Adam Barth had started out as a gefreiter, and at one stage was with FA13. After service with FA18 he moved to Jasta 10 on 21 September 1916. He survived with this unit until killed in action on 30 January 1918 over Anneux. Barth was born on 31 March 1897, in Weinheim, Baden. He scored another victory with Jasta 10 and also had another unconfirmed. After his death, in an Albatros DV, he was awarded the Baden Silberne Militärische Karl-Friedrich Verdeinstmedaille, on 2 March 1918.

IMMELMANN'S FIFTEENTH

Immelmann levelled the score with Boelcke on 16 May by downing an 11 Squadron Bristol Scout (5301) that evening. The RFC pilot, Second Lieutenant Morden Maxwell Mowat was out on an offensive patrol and had attacked two LVG two-seaters, and German AA fire was trying to help deter the Canadian pilot. Immelmann was in the air testing a new Fokker and, seeing the exploding shells, headed for the action. Concentrating on the C-types, Mowat failed to see Immelmann until it was too late and he was fatally wounded by the German's fire. He crashed south of Drocourt, to the west of Douai, and died as German soldiers got him out of the wreck. One of the two-seater observers also claimed him, but bullets were found in Mowat's back, consistent with an attack from behind rather than from shots from the front that would have been fired from an observer's defensive position.

At this time Immelmann acknowledged in a letter home that his old Eindecker 13/15 was now on public display at the War Exhibition back in Germany.

A 13 Squadron BE2c (4105) was attacked by a Fokker on the 16th and its observer, Captain Gerald Blunt Lucas, killed. His pilot, Second Lieutenant F C A Wright, was wounded but got his machine down safely near Anzin. It does not appear to have been the subject of a Fokker claim. Lucas had been the youngest son of the late Lieutenent-Colonel C A deN Lucas, Indian Army.

The next day Boelcke and von Althaus had several scraps with Caudrons and Nieuport Scouts, but no victories were secured. At one stage there was a Caudron being pursued by von Althaus, a Nieuport chasing him, and Boelcke trying to close behind the Nieuport. Once this quartet went over the lines, the two Fokker pilots broke off and flew back.

Flieger-Abteilung 3b lost Vizefeldwebel Friedrich Schlindwein on the 17th, in the locality of Metz. 'Pivolo' D'oisy of MS12 downed another Fokker, his third victory, near Bezonvaux, but it is unclear if these two events are linked.

BOELCKE GETS TO SIXTEEN

The next evening Boelcke shot down a Caudron from Escadrille C56 near Ripont. The crew of MdL Hubert Cagninacci and Sous-lieutenant Louis Vivien were both killed. He managed a surprise attack after seeing bombs exploding on the ground. One engine began to smoke then burst into flames. As he watched the machine began to break up and burn even more fiercely before plunging into the French second line trenches. The next day, the 19th, was Boelcke's 25th birthday.

WINTGENS' FOURTH VICTORY

Kurt Wintgens had not scored a kill since the previous August with the exception of an unconfirmed claim on 24 January, due mainly to a period of ill-health, not the least of which was a bout of influenza at the end of January. On 20 May he was more successful, attacking and bringing down a Nieuport XII two-seater of Escadrille N68 south of Château Salins. Its crew were MdL Leon Cesar Léon Beauchamps and Sous-lieutenant Debacker. This day too, a 27 Squadron Martynside was shot down by the LVG CII crew of Leutnants Seibert and Karl Riegen, of FA5b, west of La Bassée, although observers reported the German machine to be a Roland two-seater.

It will be recalled that in chapter four it seemed that Wintgens was writing letters to his friend indicating successes that were not confirmed victories. Well, at least with this latest combat, he noted that it was Number Four. He wrote:

> 'My fourth was a 'Nieuport avion de chasse' of the latest built . . . . The machine had 80-100 hits and partly looked like a porcupine. The observer was riddled indeed, the pilot had the good fortune to emerge without heavy wounds, in spite of being hit five times; one of these under the left eye, the bullet leaving at the right eye. I had an interesting discussion with him in the hospital.
>
> 'My fifth the next day, was a twin-engined Caudron. Two Le Rhône engines, two tractor propellers, tailbooms, four rudders, about 20 m broad wings – quite a fellow! From 4,000 metres he was down vertically. After the 'landing' the engines were 1½ metres under the ground. The crate had automatically disintegrated and was spread out over several square kilometres. Yesterday the crew was buried with military honours; they had fought gamely to the end.'

Wintgens had remarked that the Nieuport did not carry the usual cockades on the upper wings, and an official photograph of the crash does show that there seems nothing more than what appears to be four lines of small white (?) dots running from leading to trailing edge on each wing, just about where the usual circular red, white and blue circles would be. On the fuselage sides is a red-white-and-blue pennant.

Meantime, on the 20th, Boelcke was in combat with a Farman – probably from MF72 – whose pilot was mortally wounded. Sous-lieutenant Bernard de Curel came down near Avocourt, on the French side. The claim was not upheld. Boelcke was to record:

> 'On 20 May I again went for a little hunting trip in the Champagne district, and attacked a Farman north of Verdun. I went for him behind his own lines and he immediately started to land. In spite of this, I followed him, because he was the only enemy machine in sight. I stuck to him and fired, but he would not fall.
>
> 'The pilot of a Farman machine is well protected by the motor, which is behind him. Though you can kill the observer, and riddle the engine and tanks, they are always able to escape by gliding. But in this case, I think I wounded the pilot also, because the machine made the typical lengthwise tilt that

shows it is out of control. But as the fight was too far behind the French front, I flew home.'

* * *

Two-seater pilot Oberleutnant Franz Walz of KGI/Kampfstaffel 2 claimed a RNAS Nieuport on the 21st which fell into the sea off Dunkirk during a raid on Mariakerke. However, the loss was a Sopwith 1½ Strutter (9384) whose pilot, Flight Commander T E Viney DSO of 5 Wing, was lost. This was Walz's second victory.

WINTGENS AND FRANKL BRING THEIR SCORES TO FIVE

The day after scoring his fourth victory, Kurt Wintgens downed number five in the Château Salins area, as he relates above. This time it was a Caudron G4 of Escadrille C43; Brigadier Vincent and Sous-lieutenant René Gauthier both died.

Not to be out-done, Wilhelm Frankl, on the British front, attacked and brought down a 20 Squadron FE2b (5206) near Houthem. Both crewmen – Second Lieutenant H L C Aked and Captain C E H James (B Flight) – survived as prisoners, and both were photographed with Frankl in front of their intact pusher.

Returning from his sojourn in prison camp at the war's end, Charles Ernest Hilton James reported that he had been on an escort mission to a recce machine. Attacked by two Fokkers his magneto had been hit and the engine soon cut out. He managed a forced landing in a field and was immediately surrounded by German infantry. Observer Henry Leslie Cautley Aked, upon his eventual return, made out the following report:

'At about 3 pm on 21 May, five machines left the aerodrome for a reconnaissance over the enemy's lines. The formation consisted of three machines, FE2bs, in front in a line, and on the same level, the recce machine being in the centre, and two BE2cs in rear and slightly higher. My machine, piloted by Captain Hilton James (Welsh Regt) was the right hand FE.

'We crossed the lines by Armentières, skirted to the west and north of Lille and did a left hand turn towards Courtrai. The recce machine drew ahead and allowed the formation to get a little scattered. Near Courtrai the formation did a complete left hand turn. By cutting across, Captain James managed to regain our position, which we had lost somewhat, owing to being slightly slower than the two other FEs. The other two FEs were again drawing ahead when we noticed a Fokker diving from the north-west at the right hand BE, which had lost height.

'We fired a Red light and turned to attack. The BE rushed passed towards Menin, as we turned. After firing a drum and a half, the gun jammed. Two other Fokkers had joined the first and fired from either flank. Captain James turned and headed for Menin. Immediately, the engine cut out. He switched to the service tank, but without result. We afterwards discovered that all the wires from the magneto had been severed. As soon as we turned, I used the rear gun, firing backwards over the top plane. Whilst changing drums the steel tubing supporting the gun and mounting was cut by a bullet and the whole [thing] crashed into the nacelle. We were now gliding for the lines. I remedied the gun that had jammed and realising the impossibility of reaching the lines, we turned several times in order to use the remaining gun from front mountings.

'The Fokker continued firing all the time from the rear, till at about 1,000 feet, an AA battery opened fire on us, cutting one of the tail booms and damaging the controls. Captain James managed to land in an open space at Bousebecque, near Menin, where German infantry were awaiting us. We were unable to burn the machine, having no ignition torch, whilst we were surrounded before being able to produce matches. I had thrown the guns out from a height of about 800 feet, after having disabled and partially stripped them.'

Frankl was awarded the Hohenzollern House Order, Knight's Cross with Swords after this victory, although it was not actually announced in the *Militär-Wochenblatt* until August.

A DOUBLE FOR BOELCKE MAKES IT EIGHTEEN

At about noon Boelcke was flying a barrage patrol above the Meuse River from where he spotted two Nieuports high above. Ignoring them and heading towards home he then saw two Caudrons and decided to attack one. However, one of the Nieuports saw this and dived to the rescue. Breaking off and heading north as if he had not seen the Nieuport, Boelcke let it close in before making a sudden turn at it. The Nieuport pilot raced for home but Boelcke closed up and attacked, sending the French machine down into French lines. Later reports from the front confirmed it had crashed on Mort Homme.

That evening he was up again and after two hours of fruitless search saw a French machine north of the Bois de Hesse. Pretending to fly away the French pilot thought he could make a surprise attack but again the German tactician turned the tables on his opponent. His attack set the French machine on fire and then it broke up in the air after an explosion. It fell into the wood below and was likewise confirmed by front line observers.

These would appear to be the machines lost by Escadrille N65, piloted by Adjutant Henri Brion and Sergent Georges Kirsch, both of whom were wounded.

In all seven Allied aircraft were claimed by the Germans this day, including one to AA fire credited to KFlak 44, commanded by Hauptmann Jancke, his gun crew's third victory.

MANTEUFFEL'S FIRST

Eitel-Friedrich Rüdiger von Manteuffel was born in Russia, at Capschjoken, on 12 March 1895. He had served in the 2nd Uhlan Regiment prior to transferring to aviation in 1915 and flew with FA26 before taking command of Fokkerstaffel-Ost towards the end of March 1916. On 21 May von Manteuffel was at Chauny were he was based, looking after FA11 in addition to his Fokker duties. Josef Jacobs had flown over in his Fokker for a visit and at the evening meal AA fire was heard which sent both men running to their machines. Once in the air they found a Caudron G4 and von Manteuffel, in a more powerful 160-hp Fokker EIV, made an attack. Jacobs, in his slower 100-hp EIII machine, then closed in as his leader broke away, and made two attacks on the Caudron which was already going down. One engine was running slowly now as the pilot made to land. The observer was also seen slumped over. Also in the action, flying a Fokker, was Dieter Collin, a future ace with Jastas 2, 22 and 56.

In the analysis, credit for the victory went to von Manteuffel, as it was assumed his faster machine and first attack had done the damage, forced the pilot to decide upon a landing, and the follow-up attacks by Jacobs had helped promote this decision. As it was, this was to be von Manteuffel's only victory of the war, but not the end of a career in aviation. He continued with several appointments, including Kest and Jasta commander, staff officer and instructor. In WW2 he had risen to Generalmajor in the Luftwaffe by 1944 and lived until 1984.

His victims had been Sergent Oliver Schneider, although Jacobs said the man insisted he had just become a commissioned officer, and Sous-lieutenant Danne of C43. The aircraft landed at Pont-l'Evêque, just south of Noyon at 21.30 hours, and Danne died of his wounds through loss of blood on the 22nd. Although the date of this action is sometimes noted as 22 May – no doubt due to the date that Danne died, not the day they were shot down – 21 May is correct.

While Jacobs might have been unhappy or unlucky, he was certainly not happy with the performance of the 100-hp Fokker. Not that the EIV was much of an inprovement, for while the 160-hp engine gave it more speed, the new engine had complications and it also made the interrupter gear timing difficult.

BALDAMUS' SECOND AND MULZER'S THIRD VICTORY

Hartmut Baldamus was still flying with FA20 and he gained his second confirmed kill on 24 May. This was a Farman of MF8 which went down over St Souplet, near Fichtelberg, in German lines. The crew comprised Lieutenant Jean Roux and Sous-lieutenant Masson.

At 11.20 on the morning of 31 May, Max Mulzer, Unteroffizier Heinemann and Max Immelmann engaged FE2b machines from 23 Squadron. Seven British aircraft had been reported and once in the air AA fire directed the trio to them. In the attack it seems as though Immelmann hit one FE which began to head for home. As Immelmann broke off to engage another FE which was engaging Heinemann, Mulzer pursued the first FE which eventually put down near the railway station at Inchy, west of Cambrai. This FE – 6345 – was piloted by Second Lieutenant A Cairne-Duff with observer Corporal G E Maxwell, both of whom were taken prisoner.

Meantime, Immelmann was firing at the other FE. Suddenly his aircraft shuddered and reared up; his synchronisation gear had malfunctioned and he had shot off one of his propeller blades. He immediately switched off the engine and as his remaining blade jerked to a halt, Immelmann began to glide earthwards. With some difficulty he landed near the Cambrai to Douai road.

The three Fokker pilots had certainly made a mark on 23 Squadron. Apart from Cairne-Duff's forced landing, Lieutenant Lindsay Carlton Powell, the observer to Second Lieutenant E F Allen, was killed in the air, hit during an attack during which the Fokker pilot was '. . . raining lead into the engine.' Powell had yelled for his pilot to go into a stall so he could get in a shot backwards over the top wing, but was then hit in the head. Was this Immelmann or Heinemann? Second Lieutenant A T Watson's machine was also shot up, and a 23 Squadron Martinsyde scout escorting the FEs saw one of the Fokkers appear to be hit and go into a nose-dive during an attack on Captain H Wyllie's machine. Wyllie also saw the Fokker go down and disappear.

With Immelmann seemingly out of the running, Mulzer was given credit for the downed FE, thereby gaining his fourth victory. By the logic applied to von Manteuffel's claim a few days earlier, one might have thought credit would have gone to Immelmann who seems to have made the initial attack which sent the FE heading down and west.

On his return from prison camp, George Edlow Maxwell, his rank given now as Second Lieutenant, told of the attack by three Fokkers and their engine being put out of action. His pilot was wounded in the arm and Maxwell himself was shot through the left leg several times which badly broke it.

* * *

In May, General Sir Henry Rawlinson held the conviction that the Fokkers were being matched by the DH2 machines who were now starting to escort and patrol parts of the British front in support of Corps and recce machines. He had based this too on the fact that the RFC's photographic machines had recently been able to photograph the whole of the German trench system in front of the 4th Army in mid-May. While it was no doubt true, as he wrote, that the DH2 was proving itself superior to the Fokker in speed, manoeuvrability, climb and fighting efficiency, one might have thought it was still very early days.

However, more help was on the way. The first flight of 70 Squadron arrived during the month, equipped with the new Sopwith 1½ Strutter two-seat fighting recce machines, fitted with an interrupter gear for the pilot as well as the swivel-mounted Lewis for the observer, who, unlike in the BE machines, was seated more sensibly in the rear cockpit.

Then at the end of the month, 32 and 60 Squadrons arrived, the former equipped with DH2s, the latter with Moranes, which while good, were not that good, although they had tested well against that captured Fokker in April. They would be re-equipped later with Nieuports, which No.1 Squadron was going to find, were a much better prospect for air fighting than Moranes.

On the German side there was also a new Fokker unit in being, for this month there was the first reference to AKN – Abwehr Kommando Nord. This in fact was the former detachment at Bertincourt. Hauptmann Mahnke at 2 Armee HQ decided to expand Kek Vaux (Bertincourt) which in the main had FA32 men: Leutnants Lehmann, Leffers and Vfw Dittrich, flying monoplanes EIII 400/15, EIII 161/16 and EV 411/15. A new arrival was Leutnant Hendrichs and EIII 238/15, posted in from FA59, plus pilots from FA1b, Leutnants Diemer, OffSt Max Müller, and Uffz Ehrentaller with Fokker EIIIs 414/15 and 211/16. In mid-June Gefr Hermann Keller and Fokker EIII 346/16 arrived too.

At about the same time, Kek Vaux also became known as Kek Süd (south). Another Kommando was also operating from Charleville. The Germans also recorded that they had accounted for 47 Allied planes during the month; 36 in combat, 9 to ground fire and two others forced to land. They in turn admitted losing 16.

Chapter Seven

JUNE 1916

Despite the anguish the RFC high command was having over the Fokker monoplane assaults on its aircraft and crews, it is surprising how few German pilots were actually inflicting hurt upon them. While several Fokkers were still attached to some flieger-abteilungen and others were being grouped – in small numbers – in Kek units, as we have seen in the previous chapters, it was only Boelcke and Immelmann who had produced high scores (18 and 15), with Frankl and Wintgens scoring just five each thus far. A relative few others had between one and four victories.

It is acknowledged that the sudden appearance of one, two or three Fokkers had a heart-stopping affect on British and French flyers, but there were far more combats than shoot downs. Looking at the air combats, there were just as many air fights with German two-seater machines, most of which were engaged on similar sorties to the British two-seaters. The appearance of fighting machines such as the Nieuport Scout, DH2 and FE2 was starting to make a difference, although many FE crews were no real match for a determined gaggle of Fokker pilots. The FE2b and later the 2d were to see considerable combat in the skies over France for most of 1917 before they were finally replaced by Bristol F2B Fighters, and relegated to night bombing. But by 1917, they had got their act together and by working in unison could generally fight their way out of trouble. In 1916, however, they were only flying in small groups of three or four, sometimes five or six. In 1917 it was almost always six or more, and with better aircraft flying fighter escort or patrols nearby; and the crews were more experienced.

It has to be remembered that in 1916 the sky was still fairly empty of aeroplanes compared to 1917 and 1918. And whatever year one is talking about, aircraft did not carry inter-aircraft radio, so all communication once airborne was by hand signals, wing waggling or signal flares. Anyone who has flown in cloudy skies over northern Europe will know that even these can be missed, or misinterpreted, always assuming too that the aircraft could be seen. Sun, haze, cloud, mist, rain, all helped to confuse even the most experienced aviators, let alone the embryo airmen recently out from England. Dumb, fat and happy is an American term still in the future, but it does express well some of the British airmen who arrived in France from training schools in Britain. They might be aware of the dangers but had no real idea how these were going to affect them the first time they found a German pilot on their tail, guns blazing.

Therefore in mid-1916, the Fokker monoplane danger was real enough but has to be taken in context. All air combat had its dangers, but the Fokker fired the imagination more than some of the other aircraft, being the first real German fighter. And no doubt German publicity which filtered through to the Allied side, telling the world of yet another victory by Boelcke or Immelmann, managed to concentrate the mind. If these two were doing well, so must be dozens of others. Yet in actual numbers, there were not dozens of others scoring. As time went on, however, the scores of the lesser aces obviously began to rise as 1916 progressed.

HÖHNDORF'S FOURTH VICTORY

Walter Höhndorf made it four on 2 June by downing a Caudron. Some records show this to have been from Escadrille C42, near Mörchingen. This machine came down in German lines with its crew, Lieutenant André Fernet and Lieutenant Marcel Brienne (a/c No. N2474). Confusion about this claim – especially the date – makes us question this victory, for this C42 crew are supposed to have been lost on the 1st. On the 2nd, a C4 aircraft flown by Sergent Guy Dussumier-Latour and Sous-lieutenant Henri Thévenin failed to return and if the 2nd is correct, they may have been the victims rather than the C42 pair.

Mention has been made earlier of the successful AA gun unit commanded by Hauptmann Jancke. At 12.47 pm on 3 June his KFlak 44 got their fourth victory, by shooting down the 7 Squadron BE2 (2750), piloted by Lieutenant R B Goodson, who was taken prisoner.

Vizefeldwebel Hermann Pfeiffer, a Fokker pilot with AOK 3 (3rd Army Fokkerstaffel) put in a claim for a French machine on the 8th but it does not appear to have received confirmation. This Bavarian's day would come too. Bad weather was preventing much flying over the Western Front, but on the 10th a British crew claimed a Fokker downed during a combat over Harbourdin. Second Lieutenant A A N D Pentland and his observer, Captain W H Waller (not Walker as sometimes quoted), were attacked in their 16 Squadron BE2c (4077), and Waller's return fire sent it down, Pentland seeing it crash into a field. In 1917-18, 'Jerry' Pentland, an Australian, would win the MC and DFC, ending the war with 23 victories in air combat.

FA62's Kek was detached from the main unit on 12 June, which was about to be transferred to the Eastern Front. Soon after this the Kek (Kek 3/Douai) was attached to FA5b, commanded by Oberleutnant Johann Moosmeir, a pilot who had learnt to fly in 1913.

* * *

British summer time began on 15 June, so German time was once again just one hour ahead of the Allied time. On 17 June the Fokkers got amongst the French.

WINTGENS AND HÖHNDORF SCORE THEIR SIXTH AND FIFTH VICTORIES

Kurt Wintgens shot down a Farman in flames into German lines in the vicinity of Bezange La Grande, south of Château Salins. The machine and

crew were from MF70, Lieutenant Brunel and Sous-lieutenant Pierre
Hemand. Wintgens wrote in a letter:

> 'It was a wonderful fight. It exploded marvellously. He was
> already behind the French lines when the pilot, who hung dead
> over the right side, apparently touched the rudder in some way.
> The machine turned and fell burning into the German lines,
> greeted by a thunderous hurrah from the whole of the front.
>   'A couple of hundred metres next to me, Höhndorf fought a
> Nieuport. The French thereupon wrote in their announcement:
> "In Lorraine, four of our machines gave battle to four Fokkers.
> Two of the latter fell down, one of them afire. One of our
> machines had to land."
>   'The one who fell in flames was supposed to be me. I had
> rather slid down somewhat, but as an old hand at stunt flying,
> had flattened out elegantly over the French lines. The flames
> mentioned were those of my opponent, whose landing took
> place at a negative angle.'

Walter Höhndorf claimed a Nieuport, downed in French lines but again lack
of French casualties hinders recognition, and having gone down behind the
French trenches, it could be merely a forced landing. However, two
Nieuport pilots were wounded this date and may have been involved with
the German ace. Sous-lieutenant Jean Navarre, the famous defender of
Verdun, with N67, was wounded in a fight, and Sergent Victor Chapman,
an American volunteer with the equally famous Lafayette Escadrille
(N124) also received a wound in combat.

The Lafayette pilots had been out on patrol with their French leader
Capitaine Georges Thenault, flying over the right bank of the River Meuse.
Spotting German aircraft over the opposite bank, Chapman, against orders
to cross the river, flew over to engage, several other pilots tagging along.
The fight was indecisive and while everyone returned to the airfield at
Behonne, Chapman landed at Vadelaincourt airfield to refuel and rearm.
Heading back to the front once more, Chapman engaged two Aviatik two-
seaters which were being escorted above by three Fokkers.

Chapman claimed one of the German machines down in flames but fire
from one of the Fokkers splattered his Nieuport, one bullet slicing through
his flying helmet, creasing his skull. Spinning down away from further
trouble, the Fokkers left him to his fate. Once at low level, the dazed
Chapman headed back to an airfield at Froidos, the home of N67, landed
and had his injury attended to before flying home. Kiffin Rockwell had
written to Chapman's brother Paul, of this fight:

> '[He] has been a little too courageous and got me into one of
> the mess-ups because I couldn't stand back and see him get it
> alone. He was attacking all the time, without paying much
> attention. He did the same thing this morning and wouldn't
> come home when the rest of us did. The result was that he
> attacked one German, when a Fokker which we think was

Boelcke, got full on Chapman's back, shot his machine to pieces and wounded Chapman in the head.'

As can be seen, the name of Boelcke was well known to the Allied airmen, and much like Baron von Richthofen later in the war, he was often associated with actions which resulted in someone being shot down, no matter what part of the front it happened. With von Richthofen, of course, any German aircraft with any red paint/dope on it had to be the Red Baron, whereas in reality, many German aircraft had areas painted red.

(The first serious wound to an American aviator occurred during a combat on Sunday 18 June. As might be expected, the pilot – Clyde Balsey – was a member of Escadrille N124, the *Lafayette*. He had engaged a two-seat Aviatik machine and was then surrounded by several more German aircraft. Although the types of the others are not mentioned, the word 'fighters' came into the report, so the presence of defending Fokkers cannot be ruled out. Balsey's gun jammed and then he was hit in the left leg, so severely that he lost all sensation in the limb and his Nieuport went into a spinning nose dive. He managed to right himself and still being pursued, raced low over the German trenches to crash-land in front of the French trenches. Rescued by French soldiers, his injuries put him out of the war.)

IMMELMANN FALLS AND MULZER GETS HIS FOURTH

The great Max Immelmann died on 18 June 1916, his luck finally running out. During the evening of this day he was to gain two more victories although his death prevented any credit being given.

Once again the Fokkers from Douai were to be up against the FEs of 25 Squadron in two separate engagements late in the day. Eight British aircraft crossed the lines near Arras and four Fokkers were sent off to intercept the intrusion. Immelmann attacked one FE, and wounded its pilot, forcing him to make a landing near Bucquoy, north-west of Bapaume. Both crewmen were wounded and taken prisoner, but the pilot, a Canadian, Lieutenant Clarence Elias Rogers, died later in the day. Sergeant H Taylor was taken to hospital, safe but a prisoner.

Having landed back at their base, the Fokkers had hardly been refuelled and rearmed before seven more FEs were reported heading over the lines. Mulzer, Prehn and Österreicher took off to intercept, followed soon afterwards by Immelmann and Heinemann. Immelmann was not flying his usual EIV machine, which had been holed by bullets in the earlier fight, and was up in an EIII (246/16). Reaching the area behind the front, the pair saw their comrades already engaged with the FEs and Immelmann headed in for an attack. His fire hit the machine flown by Lieutenant John R B Savage and his observer, 2AM T N U Robinson (4909) and both men were wounded, Savage fatally. The FE crashed near Lens where the wounded observer received further injuries but survived as a prisoner. [1]

---

[1] John Raymond Boscowen Savage, aged 17, was the son of Major A R B Savage RFA, and grandson of Colonel H J Savage, 91st Highlanders, who had fought in the Boer War. He was also the great-grandson of General Sir John Savage KCB, who had commanded the Marines at the Battle of the Nile.

Seeing Savage in trouble, the FE flown by Second Lieutenant G R McCubbin and observer Corporal J H Waller, (McCubbin from Cape Town, South Africa) dived to his aid, Waller opening fire as the Fokker came into range and flew across their nose. As far as the British pair were concerned, Waller had no sooner begun to fire, than the Fokker staggered, went down and began to break up. As they flew off, the pair were pleased they had scored against the Fokker but regretted they had been unable to save Savage and Robinson.

Immelmann's machine crashed near Sallaumines, having fallen from 2,000 metres. He died instantly. From that day on the controversy has raged as to exactly how he had been brought down. As far as McCubbin and Waller were concerned, their attack and Waller's fire had sealed the German's fate. (That is to say, once it became known who the German pilot had been.) Because the Fokker had been seen to break up, it was initially suspected that his machine had been hit by an AA shell, but later it was stated that the Fokker had lost a propeller blade due to the synchronisation gear malfunctioning, similar to what had occurred on 31 May. From this distance we shall never know for sure – perhaps Waller's fire had hit the propeller, or damaged the gun gear!? He had managed to get down on 31 May, surely a flyer of his experience would have shut his engine down immediately if he had shot off his own propeller. There is no indication that he had been hit himself, thus preventing him from doing so.

There is always the suspicion that 'higher authority' decided to follow the theory of the malfunctioning gear in order to give the impression Immelmann could not have been bested in air combat, although this wasn't done as other aces fell; but perhaps being the first . . .? The fact remained that one of the greatest and most well known fighter pilots in the German Air Service had fallen. McCubbin and Waller, once it was known who they claimed to have shot down, were decorated with the Distinguished Service Order and Distinguished Conduct Medal respectively, with Waller promoted to sergeant too.

Responding to correspondence with the Editor of the inter-war aviation magazine *Popular Flying*, in October 1935, McCubbin wrote from his home in the Transvaal:

'On the 18th of June 1916, a Lieutenant Savage with his observer, and myself with my observer, both of 25 Squadron, were sent up for the last patrol of the day merely to keep an eye on the line between La Bassée and east of Lens. At about 9.00 in the evening, we both saw three Fokkers at the back of Lens. Savage and I were quite a distance apart, but we signalled to each other that we were going to engage these Fokkers.

'Savage, whilst proceeding towards them suddenly signalled that he was returning. He was much nearer the Fokkers than I was, and they apparently noticed this as well, and one dived on him immediately. I was flying much higher than they were and immediately dived on the one that was by this time on Savage's tail, but did not open fire. The other two got on my tail, with the result that you had a string of machines all diving down.

'Savage's machine suddenly got out of control, as the Fokker had been firing at it, and Savage's machine went down. By this time I was very close to the Fokker and [the pilot] apparently realised we were on his tail, and he immediately started to do what I expect was the beginning of an "Immelmann" turn. As he started the turn we opened fire and the Fokker immediately got out of control and went down to earth.

'I then turned to see what the other two machines were doing, who had been firing at me, but found that they had turned and were making back to their own lines, which to my mind rather proved they knew that Immelmann was in the other machine.

'I went down fairly low to see what had happened to both Savage and the German machine, but as it was getting dark, I could see nothing, and although I flew around for some time I had to give it up and go back to my aerodrome and report the encounter.

'With regard to the German statement that Immelmann crashed because he shot his own prop off, it is quite on the cards that our bullets not only got him, but his prop as well, and that would be the reason for them trying to make this statement.'

And what of Immelmann's last two victories? Most so-called ace lists show Immelmann with 15, which tends to suggest his last two were not credited due to the fact he was unable to claim them. One might have thought that at least one could have been given to him, if not the last one, which, in any event, appears to have gone to Mulzer. It is not inconceivable that Mulzer saw the opportunity to claim the victory, as Immelmann would not be doing so. Savage and Robinson were flying 4909, which had 'Baby Mine' painted on the side of the gondola. Mulzer was later photographed with the wreck of this machine, a picture which leaves little doubt that he thought himself the victor.

Perhaps second after von Richthofen, the name of Immelmann tends to be remembered most by people recalling WW1 in the air. Perhaps because the name rolled off the tongue easily, or possibly because the name is recalled as being associated with a combat manoeuvre. History has preserved the 'Immelmann Turn' as being something that was invented and used by Max Immelmann in his Fokker Eindecker, and perhaps he did. Whilst sounding something really special and elaborate, it was merely a climb without putting on extra power, and as the stall came, the pilot kicked the rudder which made the aeroplane fall away to one side and dive. This had the effect of bringing the aeroplane back into action more quickly rather than, say, a climb, a roll off the top and then a turning dive to return to the same target. However, this assumes the target aircraft is not itself being put into some elaborate evasive manoeuvre by its pilot.

One has to bear in mind that pilots of the period under review did not make massive aerobatic manoeuvres in their aircraft in the way airmen did in 1917-18. Flying of any sort was still new in 1914-15 and even by 1916 most pilots were trained to do little more than fly straight and level, with easy-rate turns, climbs, banks and dives. There were few who either knew or dared to roll an aircraft, or put one into a loop. There would be little advantage in avoiding an attacking aircraft with some grand gesture of a manoeuvre if it had the chance of separating wings from fuselage!

Most of these early air battles were little more than straight forward diving attacks, or stalking attacks from behind, especially if the attacker felt the opposing pilot or crew was keeping less of a look-out around him in favour of making mental notes of what he could see on the ground. Most Allied airmen were flying recce missions, photographic missions, or watching for the fall of artillery shells.

If indeed Immelmann did invent this 'turn' he certainly did not use it every time he was in combat, only if the circumstances dictated it. And he would no doubt tell the other pilots about it and that it had a few interesting advantages, and they might try it – or they might not! In any event, if an Allied pilot or crew saw a Fokker pilot try this stall turn and dive, it could have been anyone, not necessarily Max Immelmann.

The next day, 19 June, the Fokker fraternity lost another pilot. Hauptmann Ernst Freiherr von Gersdorf, commander of KGI, was shot down over Neuburg in the German-occupied Lorraine sector, near Verdun, flying a monoplane. If his birth-date is correct, he was 38 years old, born Strasbourg, 25 May 1878. The French fighter pilot Jean Chaput gained his fifth victory this day, flying with Escadrille N57. Irritatingly the actual type claimed is not recorded. Chaput went on to score 21 victories before his own death in action on 6 May 1918.

There was another Fokker fight this day too. Sous-lieutenant Gaston de la Brunetière flying with N68, was surprised by a Fokker and was hit twice but claimed he then shot the monoplane down. He was then attacked by another Fokker and hit again but despite his wounds he managed to glide back across the French lines to safety.

* * *

By 20 June, AKN had a total of eight Fokker EIII machines plus one Pfalz EIV; Unteroffizier Leopold Reimann was assigned to AKN a few days later. This same 20 June a future fighter ace, Leutnant Albert Dietlen, while an observer with FA60, claimed his first victory along with his pilot, Unteroffizier Eugen Weiss. They claimed a French Nieuport down in French lines near the Bois de Ville, south-west of Grand Pré. The French admitted to losing two aircraft during the day, one claimed by a two-seat crew of FA25, the other may have been Dietlen's claim.

Dietlen later flew as a pilot with Jastas 23, 41 and 58, gaining a further eight victories before his death in April 1918. Weiss would also become a fighter pilot and may have claimed two more victories flying with Jasta 29 as a vizefeldwebel.

MULZER'S FIFTH VICTORY

Max Mulzer downed another FE2b on 22 June, and it was another machine from 25 Squadron. He timed the victory at 09.55, east of Hulloch near Loos. The pilot, Second Lieutenant J L P Armstrong was severely wounded but got his machine (5209) down, thus saving the life of his observer, Sergeant G Topliffe, who became a prisoner. John Armstrong died of his wounds later that day; he was 25.

From Dunmow, Armstrong had worked for Vickers Engineering in Sheffield upon leaving school and had joined the Army Service Corps when war came. Obviously news that he had been brought down by someone of note was recorded, for an obituary for him stated that: '. . . he was in combat with one of the enemy's foremost aviators, and received wounds to which he succumbed three hours later.'

SCHÜLCKE'S FIRST VICTORY AND HÖHNDORF'S SIXTH

Within five minutes of Mulzer's victory, Leutnant Schülcke (or Schülke), flying a Fokker with FA25, in support of the German 34th Infantry Division, claimed a French Nieuport, although this may have been confused with Walter Höhndorf's claim. He was credited with his sixth victory on 22 June, although there is reason to think his was a Caudron, but only because the type claimed was obscure, and he would be more likely to recognise a tractor Nieuport than confuse a Farman, Voisin or Caudron. His victory was noted as being near Lembach, and a Caudron (2484) of Escadrille C66 came down at this location. It was one of four French aircraft lost during a raid on Trier-Karlsruhe-Mülheim, and came down in flames. The crew of MdL Jacques Fernand Octave Bousguet and Caporal de Maulcon, fell west of Karlsruhe. Of course, there is no reason to suppose Höhndorf was so far away from his usual area of activity, so it might be prudent to look for another possible victim. The only other Caudron appearing in French casualty lists is a machine from Escadrille C34, which force-landed in French lines, crewed by Sous-lieutenants Edouard Goldschmidt and Grandperrin, both of whom were wounded.

Therefore, the Nieuport, a type XII two-seater of Escadrille N37 (1221), crewed by Caporal Leon-Jean-Marie Petit and Lieutenant Edmond Enos, may have been the machine claimed by Schülcke. But . . . .

HESS' SECOND

Ernst Hess was credited with his second victory this 22 June, a Nieuport XII over Lancom, while flying with Fokkerstaffel 'C'. In this confusing combat, Hess can also be noted as claiming this machine from N37. Certainly the French crew were engaged by three Fokkers.

HABER AND GLINKERMANN SCORE VICTORIES

Kurt Haber came from Beithen, Upper Silesia, born 4 July 1895 and in early 1916 he was a pilot with Bavarian FA6b. With his observer, Leutnant

Kühl, he had already been credited with two victories, on 29 February (a RNAS Voisin) and a two-seater west of Karlsruhe the next day. Now he was a Fokker pilot with FA68 and he engaged the French raid, shooting down a Farman F43, probably the machine lost by MF29 (1897), crewed by Sergent Marc Robert Auzanneau and Soldat Schmidt. Haber later became an ace before being killed in action.

Another Caudron downed was one of two machines lost by Escadrille C66, both coming down west of Karlsruhe. One would have fallen to Vizefeldwebel Willy Glinkermann, also FA68, his actually falling near Hügelsheim, his second victory. Who downed the other Caudron of C66 is not known. The two lost, whose crews were captured, were Nos. 1337 and 2470, Sergent René Marie Eugéne Seitz with Sous-lieutenant Léopold Mirabail, and Caporal Pierre Fournet with Capitaine Louis Faye. Glinkermann was later a Jasta pilot, flying with Jasta 15, and with this unit he would down two more French aircraft before his death in combat in May 1917.

The French raid was said to have resulted in the death of 48 civilians in Karlsruhe, including 30 children. Nine Allied aircraft were claimed on the 22nd. Four on the Germany raid, another east of Hulloch, one near Lancom, one near Merxheim and one south-west of Sennheim, plus one more near Ypres.

Another Fokker flieger was lost on the 22nd, Feldwebel (senior unteroffizier) Alois Hosp of FA3b who crashed at Vigneulles. This victory has been linked to the French ace Charles Nungesser as his tenth kill, but his claim was understood to be over a two-seater.

WINTGENS' SEVENTH VICTORY
Another American from the Escadrille *Lafayette* was downed in the early afternoon of 23 June. Victor Chapman, his head still bandaged from the 17th, had been about to fly to see Clyde Balsey in hospital and to take him some oranges but seeing his commanding officer, Capitaine Georges Thenault take off in company with Norman Prince and Raoul Lufbery, he decided to tag along. To the north-east of Douaumont they ran into five German aircraft and after a brief skirmish, the Nieuports flew back to the French lines.

However, Sergent Chapman did not break away and continued the action. In the vicinity a French Maurice Farman crew saw the fight, and saw too the Nieuport Scout being attacked by three fighters and beginning to fight them. They then saw the Nieuport start to go down out of control, the Frenchmen even seeing the pilot slumped forward just before the machine began to break up, falling six kilometres inside German lines. Wintgens claimed a Nieuport XVI (No.1334) shot down near Haumont, north of Verdun. (Just to confuse the issue, there is a suggestion that Wintgens' 7th victory was a Farman, downed at Blamont – in German lines. This machine of MF58 was crewed by pilot Adjudant Jacques Semelin and observer Sous-lieutenant Gallon who were killed. However, they were supposed to have collided with a Fokker, or perhaps some distant French observer thought they had.)

In truth, the collision was between a Fokker of FA32, flown by Gefreiter Hermann Keller and a Farman of MF58. Keller's machine fell near Bertincourt. He was 22, and came from Krefeld. More confusion here, as he is supposed to have died in a crash testing a Rumpler.

HÖHNDORF'S SEVENTH VICTORY

On the afternoon of the 25th, Walter Höhndorf shot down a Caudron (No.1202) of Escadrille C9, at Raucourt, north of Nomeny. It fell in flames, crashing near a tree-lined road along with its crew of Caporal Bresch and Sous-lieutenant Joseph Ransom. Both engines bored into the earth as the aircraft hit the ground.

Höhndorf had received the Hohenzollern Knight's Cross with Swords soon after his sixth victory three days earlier. He, along with Wintgens, also a recent recipient of the Hohenzollern Knight's Cross, was nearing the magic figure of eight victories, which at this time was the total required in order to be eligible to be nominated for the coveted *Pour le Mérite*. Boelcke and Immelmann had received theirs after their eighth victories and Buddecke had received his on 14 April, after seven confirmed and five unconfirmed victories.[2]

A Fokker pilot was killed on the 25th, Leutnant Erwin Tütschulte of FA23. He was reported to have been shot down over Grandcourt during a fight with a British FE2b, and both the wings of his monoplane tore away. There is no obvious claimant for this 25-year-old Berliner although it has been suggested 22 Squadron were involved but there are no reports to tie-up with.

At this time the leading German single-seater fighter pilots were:

Oswald Boelcke	18	Max Immelmann	15/16 +
Kurt Wintgens	7	Walter Höhndorf	7
Ernst von Althaus	6	Hans-Joachim Buddecke	6[3]
Wilhelm Frankl	6	Rudolf Berthold	5
Max Mulzer	5	Gustav Leffers	4
Otto Parschau	4		

If we compare these with the equally small number of Allied fighter (scout) pilots and their scores at this date, it gives an interesting picture:

Lanoe Hawker	7	Albert Ball	5
Charles G Bell	5		

---

[2] Hans-Joachim Buddecke we met in Chapter 4, flying with FA23. Having been posted as a Fokker pilot with FA6 in the Dardanelles, he had steadily added to his score against RFC and RNAS aircraft flying at Gallipoli. As well as the Blue Max, he had received the Hohenzollern Knight's Cross with Swords, the Saxon Military St Henry Order 4th Class, the Iron Cross 1st and 2nd Class and the Golden Liaket Medal and the Imtiaz Medals in gold and silver from the Turks. See also Chapter 11.

[3] Five victories on the Dardanelles front.

Jean Navarre	12	Charles Nungesser	10
Georges Guynemer	9	Jean Chaput	7
Eugene Gilbert	6	Maxime Lenoir	5
Edwards Pulpe	5[4]	André Chainat	4
Albert Deullin	4	Georges Pelletier D'oisy	4
Noel De Rochfort	3	Lucien Jailler	3

Of these 89 victories, only 12 are recorded as Fokkers.

As far as the German pilots listed above are concerned, virtually all of them were publicly known figures. And all of them had either received the Hohenzollern Knight's Cross, or were about to, a pre-requisite to the award of the *Pour le Mérite*.

This new dimension of air fighting had certainly flamed the imagination of the German people back home and these men had almost become, what 60 years later would be known as, 'pop-star' status. Postcards were on sale in all the big towns in Germany featuring these 'knights of the sky', and the various German states were eager and willing to heap awards, honours and decorations upon them. It must have been a heady experience.

MULZER'S SIXTH

Max Mulzer met up with 25 Squadron again on 26 June, just over a week after he and Immelmann had fought them on the evening which saw his friend's death. The FEs were out on a bomb raid, having left their base at around 7 am. Near Mazingarbe, the Douai Fokkers waded in and both sides claimed a victory. FE 5212 was shot up by Mulzer, wounding its pilot Lieutenant R C B Riley and mortally wounding his observer, Lieutenant Eric H Bird, a 22-year-old Londoner. Riley got them down on the British side, having been chased almost to Béthune, but Bird died the following day. The FE was wrecked.

Eric Hinckes Bird, aged 21, was the son of a doctor, and had been educated at Westminster School before passing into Sandhurst in 1913. Commissioned into the Royal Fusiliers just after war began he served for six months in the trenches before being invalided home. Joining the RFC he had arrived back in France only a fortnight before he died.

2AM Herbert Chadwick, observer to Second Lieutenant R Sherwell, in 6344, was hit and killed by another Fokker, four were seen in all, which Sherwell thought Chadwick had shot down before he was hit. Sherwell evaded further attacks and got back. A third FE, 6346, had McCubbin and Waller as its crew and they were shot about over Beuvray, but also survived.

The British squadron claimed two Fokkers as crashed, seen to do so by troops in the Loos Salient, but once again there are no fatalities in the German casualty list, so if crash they did, their pilots survived.

---

[4] One victory on the Russian front.

Heinemann's First Victory

Unteroffizier Heinemann had been in several air fights alongside Immelmann and Mulzer, and on 26 June, now with Kek 3, he finally scored his own individual success. Lieutenants H B Russell and J R Dennistoun had taken off in their FE2b (6348) as part of a 23 Squadron bomb raid at 08.50 but they had run into Fokkers to the east of Arras. Wolfgang Heinemann had attacked and his fire severely wounded James Robert Dennistoun, from New Zealand, whilst also wounding Russell, who then force landed by an embankment north of Athies. Both men were taken prisoner, but Dennistoun did not survive. He was 33.

James Dennistoun had been a justice of the peace in New Zealand, and had taken part in Captain Scott's Antarctic Expedition in 1910-11 and received the King's Antarctic Medal. After that he had gone into sheep farming and mountaineering, and was a member of the Alpine Club. One of his conquests had been Mitre Peak, in Milford Sound, which had been thought unclimbable. Joining the Irish Horse in 1914 he was in France the following year as an intelligence officer to an army division before transferring to the RFC. In his later report, Herbert Bainbrigge Russell (RFA) said that Dennistoun was hit three times in the stomach and died two months later (9 August) in a German hospital – mostly, he maintained, due to neglect. He also said of the action:

> 'I was employed on a bomb raid on Biache railway junction and owing to engine failure of first machine, was unable to go with the formation, and went over alone in a second machine. Bombs were thrown on the objective but on our return journey was attacked by three Fokkers and shot down in flames, myself being wounded in the right lung.'

In the event, the three other FEs had not continued with the raid once they reached the front lines. The leader thought the cloud too bad and decided to abort.

Boelcke Makes it Nineteen

Boelcke had been shocked at Immelmann's death and had flown north to Douai to visit his former friends there. Reluctant to fly back to Sivry he remained at Douai for a couple of days, and in one action with the other pilots, including Mulzer, he had sent a pusher across the British lines pouring smoke from its engine. Whether this was anything to do with the fight with 25 Squadron on 26 June is not known.

Returning finally to Sivry, Boelcke discovered he was to be taken away from front-line operations so as not to endanger the life of Germany's remaining fighter hero. Boelcke was upset by this and determined to fly as much as possible until the date of his posting. On the late evening of the 27th, despite very bad weather, he took off twice and on the second sortie met five French aircraft near Douaumont. As one came within range he attacked and although low over the French lines he pressed home his assault. It was almost dark and finally he lost sight of the Frenchman and so returned home.

Next day it was reported that a French machine had been shot down over the trenches and fallen into German lines. Boelcke telephoned for further information and as he was the only pilot flying at that time and place – due to the weather – he was credited with his 19th victory – a Nieuport.

Then he left Sivry and headed for Germany prior to travelling to the Balkans and to Turkey. He left the front as the highest scoring German fighter pilot, but he would be back and with his return came the birth of the Jagdstaffeln.

PARSHAU'S FIFTH VICTORY

Otto Parshau's next victory, which he claimed on 29 June, is noted as a French Voisin north of Péronne. Whilst no French losses are recorded, the RFC did lose Second Lieutenant K P McNamara of 24 Squadron, flying a DH2 Scout. Or to be accurate, they claimed Lt S K P Mckamare, which is near enough. Probably again, the confusion was due to the Germans calling all pushers a 'gitterrumpf'.

Second Lieutenant Kenneth Parnell McNamara has no known grave, his name merely listed on the Arras Memorial to the missing. He was last seen attacking four hostile aircraft and after a fight, spiralling down over Cléry with a fighter on his tail, and Cléry is just north-west of Péronne.

LORENZ'S FIRST VICTORY

NCO Heinrich Lorenz was a pilot with Parshau in KGI, and on the last day of June 1916 he was in combat and claimed a French Caudron for his first kill, down near St Quentin. Lorenz was a Saxon, born 30 January 1892 and had been an army cadet between 1902 to 1908. His first army assignment was to Infantry Regiment Nr.162 'Lubeck' but he transferred to the air service on 1 September 1915. He joined KGI in May 1916. He would later fly with FA(A)284 before being commissioned to join Jasta 1. Later still, as Staffelführer of Jasta 33 he would become an ace by June 1917.

On 30 June the French lost a Farman of MF7, noted as shot down by AA fire and had a Caporal pilot in Escadrille C4 injured. Otherwise, there are just two Nieuport casualties, one pilot missing and another wounded.

WINTGENS' EIGHTH

During a combat to the south-west of Château Salins, Kurt Wintgens shot down a Farman to reach the essential eight victories for his Blue Max. Unfortunately records of French losses this day are sparse, but it is possible it was this Farman mentioned above, the machine of MF7, crewed by Sergent Pierre Lamielle and Lieutenant Amédée Pluven.

Whatever or whoever, Wintgens was awarded the *Pour le Mérite* with effect from 1 July 1916, the fourth German airman to be so honoured. He was one month short of his 22nd birthday. Wintgens was one of several German pilots openly to wear spectacles and was often photographed in them. Obviously this did not hinder him for war service, nor did it prevent him from being a successful fighter pilot.

On the debit side of 30 June, Leutnant Leopold Reimann of FA32, was shot down flying an EIII (347/15) but survived, shaken but unharmed. Sous-lieutenant de la Brunetière of N68 claimed a Fokker this date.

DICTA BOELCKE

Before Boelcke left for Turkey, he had several meetings, one of which was with the chief of the air service, Oberstleutnant Hermann von der Lieth-Thomsen. He then spent a few days with the commander's staff officers during which Boelcke put on paper his ideas for the future of the fighter arm of the air service. He also wrote what was to become known as 'Dicta Boelcke' – his rules of air fighting:

1. Always try to secure an advantageous position before attacking. Climb before and during the approach in order to surprise the enemy from above, and dive on him swiftly from the rear when the moment to attack is at hand.
2. Try to place yourself between the sun and the enemy. This puts the glare of the sun in the enemy's eyes and makes it difficult to see you and impossible for him to shoot with any accuracy.
3. Do not fire the machine guns until the enemy is within range and you have him squarely within your sights.
4. Attack when the enemy least expects it or when he is pre-occupied with other duties such as observation, photography or bombing.
5. Never turn your back and try to run away from an enemy fighter. If you are surprised by an attack on your tail, turn and face the enemy with your guns.
6. Keep your eye on the enemy and do not let him deceive you with tricks. If your opponent appears damaged follow him down until he crashes to be sure he is not faking.
7. Foolish acts of bravery only bring death. The Jasta must fight as a unit with close teamwork between all pilots. The signal of its leaders must be obeyed.

These instructions were sent to all fighting units, although the words above are actually those issued to the new Jagdstaffeln in the autumn of 1916, because of the reference to Jastas in item 7. Considering air fighting was still relatively new, and fighter pilots were still learning their trade, all these fairly basic principles were to apply for many years to come. During WW2 the South African fighter leader Wing Commander A G 'Sailor' Malan DSO DFC was to write, and RAF Fighter Command issued, his rules of air fighting to all fighter squadrons, which in essence were very similar to Boelcke's.

The only one that later fighter pilots would and should not practise was item 6. Following down an enemy plane, either to ensure the pilot was not 'faking' – or to make sure of a kill – was absolutely forbidden. However, Boelcke can be forgiven for this item in the summer of 1916 because the air was still fairly empty of enemy aircraft; also, it was German tactics to have the leader attacking whilst being covered by his men. By the late autumn of that year, and for the next two years, pilots who did follow an opponent down, in whatever circumstances, became extremely vulnerable to attack from above, and new pilots to the front were told never to do it. It didn't always work and many new pilots were shot down ignoring the advice of their more experienced comrades.

Chapter Eight

THE BATTLE OF THE SOMME

1 JULY 1916

This massive battle which began with the now-famous 'walk' to the German trenches following a tremendous eight-day artillery bombardment under which it was believed, nothing could have survived, was to end with enormous casualties on both sides not only on the first day but the days and weeks following. 60,000 British casualties occurred on this first day alone. Virtually nothing was achieved. Look at that figure again – 60,000 in one day!

The Royal Flying Corps did have mastery of the air, of sorts, in that its pilots and observers could fly over the German positions at will to direct artillery, observe forward troop movements, photograph enemy positions, bomb supply areas behind the lines, and ward off any German fighters that tried to intervene. That is what RFC HQ believed, but in truth, the German fighters could still choose their moment of attack when favourable to them and even if they did not destroy RFC aircraft, their very presence interrupted these vital tasks, especially artillery directing, photography and contact patrols.

Nevertheless, the RFC felt it was winning, and the sheer numbers of aircraft which it could now put above a battle front, gave it an edge. Meantime, the German Fokker pilots, while out-numbered in many respects, could still dictate how and when to attack and being over their own lines, they were in less danger of falling into captivity, whereas British aviators, as always, were far more likely to come down on the wrong side of the lines in a crippled aeroplane, provided they didn't crash, or fall burning, after an engagement with the Fokkers.

During normal conditions on the Western Front, that is to say, when there is not a major battle in progress, it is far easier to tie-up who was shooting down who, mostly because with Allied aircraft falling in German-held territory, the captors were easily able either to identify bodies by their name-tags, or because the airmen were captured, or some identifying serial or engine number from a crashed or forced down aeroplane would be recorded, if not photographed. Where the normally meticulous German record-keeping failed was when men and aeroplanes fell into a battle area, or close enough to the fighting to make it more difficult to sift through the debris. Front line troops in the firing line, were, if they had the time and inclination, far more likely just to bury hurriedly any dead airmen that fell near to them without taking too much trouble in either recording any details from the bodies, or even the exact spot they were buried. This scenario no doubt featured on this First Day of the Somme, as we have several casualties, but little sound evidence of who brought who down.

Wilhelm Frankl and Ernst von Althaus are both mentioned in some German records as having brought down British aircraft this day, but neither have been credited with an official victory. Despite this, it seems that von Althaus flying with FA23/Kek Vaux, shot down a 13 Squadron BE2c (2648), killing its lone pilot, 18-years-old Lieutenant Christopher Monckton, while Frankl shot down another BE2c (4146) of 12 Squadron. Second Lieutenant Laurence Arthur Wingfield was also flying alone, because he was on a bomb raid to St Quentin. He was later to record:

> 'I had to go to St Quentin . . . to lay a couple of "eggs" on the railway station. The "eggs" to be carried were large ones, weighing 110 lbs each, full of TNT, and I had to carry two. That in a 2c meant that all superfluous weight had to be sacrificed. No observer could be carried, and even the weight of a machine gun would be an unjustifiable load. I ultimately decided to take a machine gun though it proved to be rather a disadvantage than otherwise. It was fixed in such a position that I could not readily use it, whilst its weight reduced my rate of climb. I had been informed that I was to be escorted all the way and back by a squadron of DH2s, but in fact, the escort failed to materialise.
>
> 'At the appointed time I started off; arrived at the line and awaited the escort. As it did not appear in sight I gave up waiting and proceeded over the line. The wind was south-west, about 30 mph. I arrived at St Quentin and dropped my bombs on the railway station. I observed a column of smoke arise to a great height. On the way home, I met a Fokker monoplane and that was the end of the story. It took the Fokker about 15 minutes to shoot me down, but I do not think there was at any time during the encounter much hope of my getting away from him.'

Wingfield was to spend the next 15 months as a guest of the Germans but finally escaped from Strohen prison camp on 4 October 1917 and was back in England on 12 October 1917, being awarded the MC. In 1918 he also received the Distinguished Flying Cross.

On the face of it, it is difficult to say exactly why these two Fokker pilots were not credited with victories. Perhaps it was just the confusion of the battle front.

DITTRICH'S FIRST VICTORY
A Fokker pilot who did apparently get a claim upheld was Vizefeldwebel Walter Dittrich of Kek Bertincourt (FA32). Soon after dawn 22 Squadron sent out FE2b machines and 6365 failed to return. Shot down over Cléry-

Longueval, Lieutenant J H Firstbrook, Canadian, was wounded and taken prisoner, while his observer, Lieutenant Reg Burgess died of wounds six days later in a German hospital.

Dittrich, who had had a long period as a two-seater pilot, would survive the war. In August he became an original member of Jasta 1 and gained one confirmed and one unconfirmed victories to add to his Fokker kill, before being wounded (losing two fingers) in June 1917. He later flew with Jasta 17 and ended the war as a Leutnant with FEA6, having been awarded the Saxon Silver St Henry Medal, the Saxon Gold St Henry Medal and the Saxon Albert Order, Knight 2nd Class with Swords.

Other RFC aircraft were lost this 1st July day too, but there is a distinct lack of information as to how they were lost. Another FE of 22 Squadron, Captain G W Webb and Lieutenant W O Tudor-Hart (6928) was brought down late morning, and in a letter from prison camp, Tudor-Hart said they were shot down by several German aircraft, although he did not mention the types. Webb was killed and Tudor-Hart had to crash-land the machine, and in his view the German pilots (presumably not finishing him off when obviously out of action) '. . . acted like sportsmen and gentlemen.' The victors possibly came from KGI.

Gilbert Watson Webb, 26, came from Belfast, one of four sons in the military. In 1915 he had been wounded with the Royal Irish Rifles, transferring to the RFC upon his release from hospital.

PARSCHAU'S SIXTH VICTORY
The following day Otto Parschau made it six with a two-seater victory on the French front. This was probably a Caudron CIV (2235) crewed by Sergent Lesire and Soldat Coat, of Escadrille C106. They came down south-west of Ham, near Noyon. There is a question of the exact date of this victory, some records show 1 July, and indeed, this French crew were lost on the 1st. If, however, the 2nd is the correct date, one would need to look at a crew of C64 who had a pilot wounded, or of C56 who recorded both crewmen injured.

MULZER'S SEVENTH – KIRMAIER'S FIRST
In one of those strange circumstances, it appears that two pilots were credited with the same aircraft shot down on 2 July. Max Mulzer was credited with a BE2c shot down (2654) which came from 9 Squadron, with Lieutenant I C MacDonnell and Second Lieutenant H A Williamson, who were both killed. Mulzer claimed them during a combat near Miraumont, while Kirmaier claimed, south of Bapaume. Miraumont is located west of Bapaume.

Ian MacDonnell, from Calgary, Alberta, was 21, Hugh Williamson, from Sale, Cheshire, was 29. Neither have known graves.

Stefan Kirmaier came from Lachen, born 28 July 1889 and before transferring to aviation had served with the 8th Infantry Regiment. Flying with FA(A) 203 he had then become a single-seater pilot with the unit's Kek Jametz, which was using FA23's airfield. However, it is possible that Kirmaier's victim was actually a French Nieuport XVII from Escadrille

N103 flown by MdL André Seigneurie, who was taken prisoner. Logically, because of the non-sharing rule, the Nieuport seems the more likely machine credited to Kirmaier. Two Fokkers were involved in the fight, but there is no reason to suppose Kirmaier was in the second one.

VON ALTHAUS' SEVENTH
Just to confuse the issue, Ernst von Althaus claimed a Nieuport this 2 July, although a location is not noted. It is possible that the N103 machine was his, but there is also the possibility that his victim was a Nieuport that came down on the French side without causing a casualty. The same, of course, goes for Kirmaier. [1]

GUTERMUTH'S FIRST VICTORY
Leutnant Hans Gutermuth of FA44 was credited with a balloon victory on 2 July over the Verdun sector. Gutermuth, a 22-year-old from Aachen who later flew with Jasta 5, was to be killed in action in February 1917 after gaining two victories with this unit. He was certainly a founder member of Jasta 5 after four days with Jasta 6. His period with FA44 had begun in November 1915, and later he moved to Kek Sivry. This is the first time we have encountered a balloon victory for a Fokker pilot. The balloon of the 27° Cie d'Aérostiers (II Armée) was shot down in flames this date, with observer Sergent Clément Volz wounded.

While it might seem that to destroy a balloon was not all that difficult, in fact they were extremely dangerous targets to attack. For one thing they were some distance behind their front line and were heavily defended by any number of guns on the ground. Why no attacks have been recorded upon them by the Fokker pilots until this time is partly due to the strict orders that monoplane pilots should not cross the lines into Allied territory.

An 11 Squadron FE2b was lost in the early afternoon, its crew taken prisoner after a combat with a German aircraft near Bapaume. They were later to report being shot down by three hostile aircraft near Vaulx whilst on a photo Op, but they were probably the victims of a Rumpler two-seater crew of FA23. In all the Germans claimed six victories this 2 July, four in German lines.

However, the Fokker fraternity lost Leutnant Werner Neuhaus on the 2nd, a pilot with FA(A)203. He came down between Damloup and Verdun following a collision with a French Nieuport flown by Sergent Marcel Garet of N23. By one of those strange quirks of fate, Neuhaus fell inside French lines, Garet inside the German lines.

HOWE'S VICTORY
Unteroffizier Hans Howe was a pilot with FA5b, and on 3 July, claimed a Morane shot down whilst flying a monoplane. He made his claim at 09.24 am, over Epinoy, near Carvin, the Morane N being A174 of 60 Squadron, flown by the unit's CO, Major F F Waldron, who was killed. Francis

---

[1] Ed Ferko thought von Althaus' claim was actually on 30 June, a Nieuport XI (1159) of N62, Lt François Mouronval, missing on the Somme front.

Fitzgerald 'Ferdy' Waldron was 29, the only son of Brigadier-General Waldron. A former cavalry officer (19th Hussars), he was one of the RFC's pioneer airmen, and became a pilot in 1912. Later he was an instructor at the Central Flying School.

This day, being a flying leader, he led the Squadron's A Flight on a patrol which ran into several two-seaters being covered by three Fokkers. In the fight which ensued Waldron's Morane was hit and was seen gliding down and it was thought that he had been wounded, and later died of his wounds whilst in German hands. However, photographs of his machine, standing on its nose, show the body of its pilot lying nearby. Hans Howe also flew with Kek 3 and later Jastas 10 and 11 as a feldwebel.

Oberleutnant Franz Walz gained his third two-seater victory on 3 July, south of Péronne. Although he and his observer claimed a Bristol Scout, it was in fact a BE2c of 16 Squadron (5746), again with a lone pilot, New Zealander Second Lieutenant S H Ellis, who was wounded and taken prisoner. The Kasta 2/KGI observer was named as Oberleutnant Gerlich.

RICHARD'S FIRST VICTORY, PARSCHAU'S SEVENTH
Otto Parschau shot down a balloon on the 3rd, over La Neuville, while Leutnant Richard of Fokkerstaffel East claimed a Caudron GIV of either Escadrille C30 or C11, near Amifontaine, between Grandcourt and Thiepval. Its pilot, Sergent Charles Hardoin was killed, Sergent L M Schwander, the observer, was wounded. The C11 crew consisted of Sous-lieutenant François Ciccoli and Lieutenant Eugène Angot. (Frank Bailey favours the C11 crew.) Angot later effected an escape from prison camp in August 1918.

Richard was possibly Werner Richard, later with Ober-Ost, and still with it in mid-1917 when this become Jasta 81. Born on 14 February 1895, at Spremberg, he was killed during a test flight at Ost Jastaschule, near Wathram-Riga, on 8 September 1917.

STUDENT'S FIRST VICTORY
Bad weather restricted flying above the Somme battlefield over the next several days and few combats were reported. But on the 6th, AOK 3 claimed a French Nieuport XI Scout (No.1324) flown by Lieutenant Jean Raty of Escadrille N38 near Péronne, wounded and taken prisoner. The victorious pilot was Kurt Student, a 26-year-old Brandenburger. Commissioned in 1911 he later volunteered for flight training and saw action on the Eastern Front with FA17. Promoted to Oberleutnant he had gained one unconfirmed victory over the Galician front before flying Fokkers in France from the autumn of 1915. He had taken command of 3rd Armee's Fokkerstaffel on 1 June 1916.

MULZER'S EIGHTH
Max Mulzer reached the yard-stick eighth victory on 8 July. Once again he was flying near Bapaume and encountered a BE2c, this time of No. 4 Squadron (5765) on a photo Op, crewed by Lieutenant Eric C Jowett, from Melbourne, Australia, and Corporal L R G Johnstone. Mulzer's fire sent the

BE down to crash on the outskirts of Miraumont, west of Bapaume, Jowett losing his battle for life the next day, although his observer survived as a prisoner. Jowett, aged 24, was studying at Cambridge when war was declared and he immediately joined the Northumberland Fusiliers.

Mulzer was now awarded the *Pour le Mérite*, the fifth German pilot so honoured, and went on leave. The date the award was announced, the 9th, was one of the Fokker pilots' best days.

LEFFERS' FIFTH VICTORY

During the morning of the 9th, Gustav Leffers of AKN gained victory number five by downing one of two 11 Squadron FE2b 'pushers'. As far as can be established he shot down 6952 crewed by Second Lieutenants D H Macintyre and H Floyd who had taken off at 06.05 and fell to the Fokker pilot at 07.40 German time near Bucquoy, Bapaume. Macintyre was wounded in the leg and hand and taken into captivity, while 20-year-old Hayden Floyd from County Down, died of injuries on the 11th at Fabreuil.

Returning from Germany post-war, David Hamilton Macintyre confirmed he had been shot down by a Fokker. All his controls had been shot away, and both petrol tanks holed. Along with six other 11 Squadron FEs he had taken off at 04.30 am to bomb Douai aerodrome. His engine gave trouble and at 05.30 he was forced to return. With his engine now fixed, Macintyre took off again to try and catch the others but they had long since returned from Douai and he found them patrolling between Souchy and Gommecourt.

Macintyre, still with his bombs, decided to drop them on the railway station at Bapaume but then saw a better target to the south-west. After bombing he turned to join up with the other FEs but saw a Fokker coming from the south and turned to face it. Floyd fired, but the Fokker was quickly behind them, and as Floyd reached for the rear-firing Lewis gun he was hit and fell unconscious. Another burst from the Fokker's guns did the damage and Macintyre side-slipped to the ground and crashed.

PARSCHAU GETS TO EIGHT

The all-important eighth victory for Otto Parschau was another balloon that morning just north of Grévillers. It came amidst cheers from German positions as the balloon crew had been directing artillery fire on their trenches. The balloon was of the 55° Cie d'Aérostiers, its observer, Adjudant M Mallet being killed. The following day Parschau was awarded the Blue Max to add to his Knight's Cross of the Royal Hohenzollern House Order, awarded following his first balloon kill on the 3rd.

MÜLLER GETS A BALLOON

Leutnant Hans Karl Müller, previously with Kasta 11, and now with Kek Avillers, was also credited with a balloon on the 9th for his second victory, or first if his victory of 26 March 1916 was in fact unconfirmed. He had left Kagohl 2 on 28 June, reassigned to Kek Avillers to fly Fokker monoplanes. His balloon was brought down over the Verdun sector and credence to this being his first confirmed kill comes with the award of the *Ehrenbecher* on the 14th with an accompanying document signed by Oberstleutnant Hermann von der Lieth-Thomsen, Chef des Feldflugwesens (Chief of the Field Flying Sections). Lieth-Thomsen became Chief of the General Staff to the Commanding General of the Air Forces later in 1916, Ernst von Hoeppner.

Also on the 9th, Parschau was posted to command AKN (*Abwehrkommando-Nord*) together with another KGI Fokker pilot, Leutnant Werner Schramm. AKN, which had now become an autonomous unit, was also operating with two Halberstadt DII biplanes, among the first of the biplanes that would soon supercede the monoplanes.

West of Neuville, Oberleutnant Walz and his observer, Oberleutnant Gerlich of Kasta 2 downed another aircraft, bringing Walz's score to four. The other successful two-seater crew of this period, Leutnants Willi Fahlbusch and Hans Rosencrantz of KGI also scored a victory. They shot down an RE7 pilot of 21 Squadron, Second Lieutenant C V Hewson, who was killed. He was seen engaged with seven German aircraft and fell over Marcoing that afternoon. Charles Hewson, from Gore Bay, Ontario, was 22.

Other fights on the 9th concerned the loss of a Martinsyde G100 of 27 Squadron, whose pilot, Second Lieutenant R W Nicholl, became a prisoner of war. He came down near Masnières at 07.35 German time whilst engaged on a dawn bomb raid in aircraft 7301. Nothing is known for certain but one report mentions two Fokker monoplanes were involved. After the war Robert Nicholl said a bullet from one of six hostile aircraft hit his petrol tank and engine which forced him to fall out of formation with the five other G100s and he had to land near Cambrai. At 09.14 am, a Vickers was reported going down in flames near Courcelles following an attack by Uffz Walther of FA5, but other details are sparse.

On the Germans' debit side, Flight Sub-Lieutenant R S Dallas, a future RNAS/RAF fighter ace, was in a battle with a Fokker monoplane which he claimed as shot down near Mariakerke aerodrome mid-afternoon. He was with 1 Naval Wing and flying a Nieuport 11, and this EIII was his fifth accredited victory. The next day, the 10th, von Althaus of Kek Vaux was slightly wounded and put out of action for a few days.

On 11 July, Stefan Kirmaier of Kek Jametz is reported to have scored his second victory by destroying a kite balloon. With continuing bad weather, the next successful combat came on the 15th, Franz Walz and his observer downing a French Caudron west of the Somme, believed to be 2149 of Escadrille C106 (Caporal Pichard and Sergent Pierre Tabateau). It was Walz's fifth victory.

HÖHNDORF'S EIGHTH

On 20 July a German communiqué recorded that Walter Höhndorf had succeeded in downing his eighth hostile aeroplane on 15 July and had been awarded the *Pour le Mérite*. This victory was over a French Nieuport XVI (1392) piloted by MdL Georges Abel Nautre of Escadrille N62, who was captured. It apparently came down near Athies, south of Péronne. Höhndorf became Blue Max-winner number six.

WINTGENS AND HÖHNDORF TIE WITH NINE

Kurt Wintgens was now officially with Kek Vaux and he brought his score to nine on 19 July. He engaged and shot down a Sopwith 1½ Strutter of No. 70 Squadron (RNAS serial 9653, now A386) in the Cambrai area. Both airmen in the Strutter, Lieutenant Henry Rathbone Hele-Shaw, 20, and Second Lieutenant Robert Claude Oakes, 18, were killed. It is just possible that Wintgens may have, by now, started to fly one of the new Halberstadt DII biplanes.

Hele-Shaw was only 20, the son of a doctor from south-west London. He had been at Marlborough College and had just received an open scholarship to Cambridge when war came. After learning to fly he was retained as a ferry pilot due to his age but finally joined a squadron in France. Wounded in action he resumed flying upon recovery and then went missing. His grave was found in April 1917 following capture of previously German-held territory. Oakes was only 19, the son of a colonel, from Bury St Edmunds. He had been educated at Wellington College and Woolwich and his older brother, a captain in the Yorkshire Regiment, had been killed at Neuve Chapelle in March 1915.

On the same day Walter Höhndorf was also credited with his ninth victory, in the Péronne area. This appears to have been a Farman of Escadrille F207, crewed by Lieutenant Lucien Rousselet and Sous-lieutenant André Frémont.

Further north, a patrol of 25 Squadron FEs and 32 Squadron DH2s, were in action with Fokkers around 06.30 and one was seen to go down and lose a wing. One DH2 flown by an Australian, Second Lieutenant John Godlee, attacked a Fokker but was in turn fired on by another and crashed west of the lines near Noeux Les Mines, south of Béthune, and died on the 22nd. His Squadron thought he may have downed one of the Fokkers but it seems it was in fact shot down by the FE crew of Second Lieutenant N W W Webb and Lieutenant J A Mann (in 5245). The Fokker crashed by or on the airfield at Provin. The German pilot was Vizefeldwebel Otto Dapper from the Kek of FA18, a 25-year-old from Meissen, who was killed.

Noel William Ward Webb, a 19-year-old from Margate, Kent, had been with 25 Squadron for just four days, but had now achieved his first victory. With this unit he would go on to score five victories and win the MC. In 1917 he would return to France as a Camel pilot with 70 Squadron, and run his score to 14, gaining a Bar to his MC, before being shot down and killed by Werner Voss on 16 August.

John Anderson Mann came from Glasgow and had transferred from the Scottish Rifles to become an observer. He too had won the MC. This was his fourth and last victory, being killed in action on 9 August 1916, shot down by Max Mulzer!

On the 20th a 9 Squadron BE2c crew, Lieutenant B T Coller and Second Lieutenant T E Gordon-Scaife, were on an artillery observation (Art Obs) job in the Combles-Flers area and got into a fight with a Fokker. Gordon-Scaife hit it with a burst of gunfire and it went down smoking and burst into flames, to crash near Bazentine-le-Petit. This was around 08.30 and the Fokker had been chasing a DH2. Was this the huge fight with several

Fokkers and LVG two-seaters, which involved 24 Squadron's DH2s? In all three Fokkers were claimed as destroyed. A Jametz pilot of FA203 was also lost this day, the missing named as Flieger Johann Steinmann, who came from Osterfeld, aged 22.

During the 20th, AOK 2 was reinforced by the arrival from KGI of Oberleutnant Karl von Grieffenhagen. This east Prussian, born 1 January 1889 was a former dragoon officer, and had flown as an observer before learning to fly. He would later serve in Jasta 1 and command Jasta 18. He scored two victories with the latter unit in early 1917.

On this same day, the 20th, we have another problem loss for the RFC. Second Lieutenants D S C Macaskie and C I Sandys-Thomas, flying in a 23 Squadron FE2b (6351) failed to re-cross the trenches and were taken prisoner. They were last seen low over Péronne, having left at 18.15. Macaskie was later repatriated, and arrived in Switzerland on Christmas Eve 1916. Eventually being sent back to England, it was only then that the reason for their loss became known. In his report dated 4 October 1917, he said:

'Took off from Izel le Hameau at about 6 pm on 20 July, accompanied by five other machines of the type FE2b, for the purpose of dropping bombs on the town of Bapaume and then to proceed on a reconnaissance flight over Cambrai.

'The Flight fell into formation at 9,000 feet above the aerodrome, at about 7 pm, and proceeded to cross the lines to the north of Gommecourt. At this period my machine was leading on the left, and in order to regain my [correct] position in the formation, I did a complete left hand turn, which brought my machine a few hundred yards in the rear of the Flight. Then, as I was receiving the "back wash" from the other machines, I turned slightly to the right, with the idea of catching up the Flight quicker.

'A few minutes later, as we arrived over Bapaume, my machine was attacked from the rear by a Fokker monoplane. My observer fired off at him with the rear Lewis gun over the top plane, but was unfortunately unsuccessful owing to the German taking up a position which placed the top plane of my machine between himself and my observer's gun.

'The German continued to fire into my machine for about 20 seconds, from his position at the right of my tail boom, making a large hole in the bottom of the top petrol tank, puncturing the main pressure tank and hitting myself through the right knee joint and right forearm, in such a manner that I was unable to move my right leg below the knee, and the fingers of my right hand. The German had dived underneath my machine and I did not see him again.

'I then endeavoured to turn round to reach the lines, but after a minute, the engine stopped, presumably through lack of fuel, and I commenced to glide down, first slowly, at the machine's usual gliding angle, then, as I was beginning to feel very faint from loss of blood, I increased the speed to about 80 mph.

'On nearing the ground we crossed some German trenches at a height of about 150 feet, from which we were heavily fired at, my observer being hit through the right thigh.

'I managed to land in a field about 200 yards from a German communication trench, from which the Germans continued to fire at us. We alighted with difficulty as I was unable to walk, and lay on the ground in front of the machine. After lying on the ground for a few minutes, under rifle fire from the trench, and being unable to discern any shell hole or other sort of cover near at hand, my observer proceeded towards the German trench, from which came five or six Germans of the 81st Regiment. Two of them carried me to their trench where they dressed my wounds. My observer being able to walk, was led away at once, while I was placed in an officer's dug out, where I remained all night, as owing to the bombardment of our guns [the Somme battle was raging], I was informed it was impossible to remove stretcher cases. They also informed me I had landed opposite the town of Albert, but I am unable to verify this.

'The next night I was moved to the rear and was sent to the hospital at St Quentin, which I reached on the afternoon of the 22 July, where I found my observer who had preceded me. On the 25th we were sent off to Germany to the camp at Ohrdruf, in Saxony, and arrived at our destination on the 27th.

'On 12 August, after various operations on my knee, it was decided, by the German doctor, Dr. Stern, that an amputation was necessary, which he performed on this date.'

This is a case where no Fokker pilot put in a claim for a victory, and as in all probability, neither Macaskie nor Sandys-Thomas volunteered the information that it had been a Fokker attack which had led them to force land, no credit was given. More than likely it was the troops of the German 81st Regiment that thought they had brought them down.

As Macaskie says, the Fokker rapidly disappeared after its pilot had done the damage, so we can assume that either he was inexperienced, running low on fuel, or, just possibly, his machine had taken hits from the FE's observer. One feels certain that in any other circumstances the Fokker pilot would have stuck around once the FE began to lose height, ready to secure a victory.

ÖSTERREICHER'S SECOND VICTORY?
Kek 3's Leutnant Österreicher flew to the Arras-Cambrai areas following a call that British aircraft were again active over the front, on the morning of 21 July. At 09.30 he spotted several BE2c machines and went for them, along with Wolfgang Heinemann. The BEs were from 12 Squadron, out to

bomb the railway bridge at Aubigny-au-Bac in order to stem the flow of German reinforcements getting to the Somme battle zone. They were escorted by 23 Squadron's FEs.

Österreicher attacked one BE – none carried observers owing to the bomb loads – and its pilot, Second Lieutenant R M Wilson-Browne, felt the impact of bullets on his machine (2100). Trying to evade his attacker, more bullets raked his aircraft as a second Fokker came up behind him and opened fire. Hit and badly wounded, Wilson-Browne headed down to a crash-landing.

Meantime, the escorting FEs were in a fight with at least four Fokkers and one or two appeared to be driven down. Vizefeldwebel Wolfgang Heinemann, Immelmann's old sparing partner, was reported killed on the 21st over Harcourt.

WINTGENS SCORES NUMBERS 10 AND 11

Kurt Wintgens was in the second Fokker to attack Wilson-Browne. Whatever damage Österreicher had inflicted was compounded by Wintgens' fire, which also wounded the Englishman. Wintgens later filed a claim for a Bristol, No.2100, and was credited with this, his 10th kill. Österreicher got nothing.

On the afternoon of 21 July, Wintgens scored his second victory of the day. 60 Squadron mounted an offensive patrol (OP) at 17.30 and in a fight with German aircraft lost a Morane N (A128) flown by Captain N A Browning-Paterson over Achiet-le-Petit, near Combles. His victor was Kurt Wintgens.

Rowland Murray Wilson-Browne, from Warwickshire, was 19, and came from Sutton Coldfield. He died of his injuries later that day. During his school days at King Edward's High School, Birmingham, he had been an outstanding gymnast and sportsman, winning the gymnastic open championship three years in succession. He trained with the school OTC and as a member of the Dolobran Athletic Club, won several prizes, and was also well known with the Sutton Coldfield Cricket and Swimming Clubs. Leaving school he had been employed in the aeronautical department of the Daimler Works. He had joined his squadron in May 1916.

Mortally wounded in the air fight, Wilson-Browne was taken to the German Nr.5 Corps Dressing Station, and after his death, was buried in the Vis-en-Artois Communal Cemetery, although the exact location was subsequently lost.

Captain Norman Alexander Browning-Paterson, from London, was 22, fell in flames and has no known grave. Browning-Paterson had gone to France in August 1914 and had taken part in the retreat from Mons, and been Mentioned in Viscount Sir John French's Despatches (Commander BEF). He had been an observer prior to pilot training, and had become a flight commander at the end of June 1916.

HÖHNDORF'S TENTH VICTORY

Wintgens and Höhndorf were having almost the same sort of contest that had gone on between Immelmann and Boelcke earlier in the year. No sooner had one scored than the other scored also.

Walter Höhndorf claimed a Nieuport south of Bapaume on the 21st (sometimes attributed to the 22nd) but with no RFC losses this, it must be assumed, was a French machine that fell – came down – inside French lines, but seen by front line troops to 'go down'. Two Nieuport casualties are recorded: Lieutenant Henri Dagonet of N37 who died of wounds, and Lieutenant Albert Deullin of N3, wounded.

Albert Louis Deullin from Épernay, born 24 August 1890, was a former dragoon, and was commissioned in December 1914. He transferred to aviation in April 1915 and flew Farmans before becoming a fighter pilot. Once flying with Escadrille N3 he had gained his fifth victory in June despite being wounded in April, and now he had been wounded again. He would end the war with 20 victories commanding Spa73.

VON ALTHAUS' EIGHTH VICTORY

This 21 July also saw Ernst von Althaus achieve his eighth victory, and the award of the *Pour le Mérite*. He claimed a French machine down over Roye which was, presumably, the Farman of Escadrille F16 crewed by the unit's CO, Capitaine Comte Marcel Dubois, and Sous-lieutenant Georges Gounon, which came down in German lines this date.

In all, the Germans claimed seven victories on the 21st, four south of Bapaume, one south-east of Arras, one west of Combles and one near Roye. The RFC lost one aircraft to AA fire.

The day was marred for the Germans by losses suffered by the Fokker pilots. Apart from the actions mentioned above, and particularly the fight with 23 Squadron, there were two other major engagements during the day between aircraft. During an OP by 24 Squadron led by Captain J O Andrews, five Rolands and five Fokkers were fought near Roisel. One Fokker went down near Allaines. In another scrap, a Fokker was seen to go down vertically after being attacked by Lieutenant R H C Usher of 27 Squadron.

In another fight between a 3 Squadron Morane Parasol, FEs of 22 and DH2s of 24 Squadron, a Fokker was seen to fall 7,000 feet to crash near Warlencourt with two more being forced to land near Le Transloy. Another still was seen to go down out of control into Combles, while yet another was seen to crash near Beaulencourt. In all on the 21st, six German aircraft were thought to have been brought down and three more driven down.

German losses were severe. Vizefeldwebel Wolfgang Heinemann of FA62 had been killed over Harcourt as mentioned earlier. But the severest blow was the loss of Otto Parschau. Wounded in the chest and head during combat over Grévillers he got down but later died of his injuries. Leutnant Werner Schramm, also with FA32, was likewise shot down and killed in the same action, falling over Combles. It was the greatest number of Fokker pilots lost in one day.

Charles Nungesser has again been associated with Parschau's fall, but the area is wrong and so is the aircraft type – he claimed an Aviatik (two-seater?). John Oliver Andrews of 24 Squadron was credited with a Fokker destroyed, the first of 12 victories he would achieve in WW1, winning the

DSO MC and Bar. His career in the RAF would raise him to Air Vice-Marshal. He died in May 1989. The Fokker he sent down was also attacked by Lieutenant Pither as it fell. He saw it crash-land with a smashed undercarriage and then he fired at a group of men that had rushed to the wreck, scattering them. As Parschau survived the crash only to die later, it seems possible this was Parschau, and that Andrews was his victor. Parschau and Schramm were later buried in the same grave at St Quentin.

STÖBER'S FIRST VICTORY, AND HABER'S FOURTH

Vizefeldwebel Hugo Stöber, flying with Kek Ensisheim (FA8), and assisted by Vizefeldwebel Heldmann of FA48, brought down a Farman (1899) on 22 July. The French mounted a raid upon Mülheim and nearby villages on this day by Groupe de Bombardment 4's, – six Farmans and six Bréguet-Michelins, escorted by Nieuport Scouts from Escadrilles N49 and N51. Escadrilles MF29 and MF123 each lost one Farman.

MF123 lost MdL René Weise and gunner Soldat Aviez to Stöber, in 1899 which came down near Mühlhausen, while MF29 lost a Nieuport XII (1282) crewed by Adjudant Collin and gunner Soldat Pauli. This latter crew went down to Leutnant Kurt Haber of FA6, falling near Hirzfelden, for his fourth victory. Despite some indications that Haber's kill came on the 21st, the 22nd seems more correct due to the location of the air fight.

Vizefeldwebel Heldmann was, presumably, Alois Heldmann, a 20-year-old from Cologne, who, after serving in the infantry had flown on the Serbian, Montenegrin and Bulgarian fronts with FA59 before being posted to France. He was later commissioned and became a successful fighter ace with Jasta 10, in 1917-18.

At least four fighters were claimed by French crews over Mülhouse, no doubt four crews claiming the same falling machine. Two crews reported the machine to be a Fokker, another just a fighter, the fourth merely an enemy aircraft. Vizefeldwebel Kurt Schörf, flying with FA(A)216 was shot down over St Georg, Ensisheim, near Mülhouse, and killed.

MULZER GETS HIS NINTH AND BALDAMUS SCORES A DOUBLE

Max Mulzer was also credited with a victory east of Hulloch, north of Lens, on this 22 July for his ninth victory, but again little is known about it. Bad weather prevented too much flying and the only British casualty was a Sopwith 1½ Strutter of 70 Squadron being shot-up in combat during a recce of Cambrai and being forced to make a landing inside British lines near Albert which is far too south to be the same action.

Hartmut Baldamus, still flying with FA20, claimed two victories on 24 July, his third and fourth. Nothing is known of the first but the second is recorded as a Caudron G4, downed north-west of Verdun. Caudron No.2236 of Escadrille C6 was lost along with its crew this date, Caporal René Blanc and Sous-lieutenant Bayard.

The French had two Nieuport Scout pilots wounded on the 24th, one from N31, the other from N57. The latter was the ace Jean Chaput, who had scored his eighth victory the previous day. He would end his war on 6 May 1918, and at his death he had 16 victories.

HARTL'S AND LEHMANN'S FIRST VICTORIES
Leutnant Hans Hartl was a Fokker pilot with FA9b and he was credited with his first victory on 25 July, claimed as a BE2c. Flying on an artillery patrol, 9 Squadron lost a crew to combat over Delville Wood this day, with the death of Second Lieutenants James Alfred Brown and Fritz Bowyer. Neither have any known grave.

Leutnant Werner Lehmann of AOK 3 was also credited with a victory the next day, the 26th, near Beine, east of Reims. This is assumed to be Caudron 1527 from Escadrille C39, who lost MdL André Waldmann and Sous-lieutenant Félix Giacomelli this date.

HOPPE'S FIRST VICTORY
Mid-morning of 29 July, Unteroffizier Paul Hoppe, flying with the Fokkerstaffel attached to the 34th Infantry Division, attacked and shot down a Farman of Escadrille F2 near Hill 285, south of Boureville. It fell in flames with its crew of MdL Albert Divry and Sous-lieutenant Henry Santrot. Hoppe, who came from Braunschweig, born 9 February 1895, later flew with Jasta 5, which was formed from the Fokker unit known as Kek Avillers. He was killed in a crash at Noyelles on 6 April 1917 following a collision with his Staffelführer, Hans Berr. He had added two more victories to his tally by the date of his death.

Leutnant(?) Winkelmann is also listed as claiming a Farman this date but with no further details it is difficult to be certain of this. Another Farman was lost on this day, a machine of Escadrille F29 (MF.2118) crewed by Sous-lieutenant Boisson and Brigadier Vermillet on a bombing raid that came down east of Sonnheim (Cernay). This may have been Winkelmann's victim but also possible is that it was the fifth victory of Hartmut Baldamus (see above). All three French machines came down in the same vicinity, so one of the claims is false. Max Winkelmann later flew with Jasta 5 but became a prisoner of war after being shot down by British AA fire on 26 January 1917, although his rank is given as Vizeflugmeister (aviation chief petty officer).

Meanwhile, Oberleutnant Franz Walz of KGI was credited with his sixth victory on the 29th, over the Somme area. 27 Squadron RFC was in combat with hostile aircraft and had two Martinsydes damaged and pilots wounded, but none lost.

STÖBER'S SECOND
Hans Stöber of Kek Ensisheim downed his second enemy aeroplane on 30 July, just over a week after his first. The Farman from MF29 went down in French lines, the crew escaping unhurt. The location is given as Sennheim, north-west of Mülhausen, right on the border between French and German lines. This was during yet another raid upon Mülheim by aircraft of GB4 together with three Sopwiths from 3 Wing RNAS.

GÖRING'S FIRST FIGHTER KILL
Hermann Göring had progressed onto Fokkers following his first two victories as a two-seater pilot and was now flying monoplanes and

Halberstadt D-types with FA(A)203's Kek Jametz, following a period with Kek Stenay. It is believed he was flying a Halberstadt biplane on this day. Encountering five Caudrons at 10.30 am north-west of Nancy he claimed one shot down over La Côte, just west of the Moselle River. French records do not indicate any Caudrons lost this date, although Escadrille C10 had Sergent pilot Girard-Varet wounded in combat. If it came down in French lines it may have been the machine seen to force land, fired upon by German artillery and apparently destroyed. There must have been some evidence to support the claim for it was confirmed the very next day as his third kill.

HÖHNDORF'S ELEVENTH VICTORY, WINTGENS' TWELFTH
Although sometimes noted as 31 July, Walter Höhndorf downed his eleventh victory on the 30th. Still operating with Kek Vaux, Höhndorf and Wintgens went up to intercept a formation of eight Martinsyde G100s of 27 Squadron, out to bomb Epehy during the afternoon. Both men claimed a victory, Höhndorf's going down near Sapignies, north of Bapaume, Wintgens' east of Péronne.

Martinsyde 7304 was flown by Lieutenant E R Farmer, who was taken prisoner, while 7471 was piloted by Second Lieutenant L N Graham who was wounded and then captured.

Getting home from prison camp, the two men reported the events of the 30th. Eric Rowland Farmer recalled being attacked by two German scouts which came in between him and the escort machines and opened fire. The fuel tanks of his G100 were both shot through and he had rapidly to look for a landing site. He crashed on landing and managed to set his machine on fire before being surrounded by soldiers.

Leslie Norris Graham remembered being briefed at around mid-day for the bomb raid on the railway at Epehy Station, four aircraft with bombs, three as escort. They crossed the lines at 12,000 feet and then came down to 8,000. Graham, the rear aircraft of the diamond-four, heard gunfire. He looked round, expecting to see one of the escort pilots testing his gun but saw instead a German aircraft diving on his tail, and a second German appear below him and starting to fire.

Graham turned to engage but was immediately covered in oil and petrol, then hit in the face and neck by fragments from an explosive bullet. He switched to the auxiliary tank and jettisoned his bombs but found he had no control over the aircraft which had started to go down in a slow spin. As he hit the ground he noticed another aircraft also going down.

These victories came at around 16.30 German time and an hour later Captain L S Charles and Lieutenant C Williams in a 60 Squadron Morane biplane (5193) were brought down and killed near St Quentin after a fight with five German aircraft. Another crew were also shot about and wounded but they got home. Unfortunately there is no indication as to whom 60 Squadron were fighting.

On the German side Oberleutnant Franz Walz was severely wounded on the 30th, thus ending his successful period as a two-seat pilot with KGI. Later in the year he was to receive the Knight's Cross of Hohenzollern

House Order and later still would become a Jasta commander. He gained one further victory in 1917, his seventh, and then served in Palestine. In 1918 he received the *Pour le Mérite* having at that time flown more than 500 missions, so this was in recognition of his long service rather than for a specific victory tally.

A BE2c crew of 4 Squadron on a photo sortie were attacked by two Fokkers and three LVGs between Courcelette and Martinpuich, one of the Germans being seen to go down in a sudden and steep dive.

Thus ended the July fighting, which had seen some intensive actions by German fighters on certain days during the latter part. Claims against Allied aircraft during the month totalled 81. Of these 59 were in combat, 15 to ground fire, six for other reasons and one lost during a spy-dropping mission. The Germans admitted the loss of 19 aircraft, 17 in combat, one to ground fire, and one missing.

Chapter Nine

AUGUST, AND THE COMING OF THE JASTAS

The first day of August 1916. Exactly a year since Max Immelmann brought down his first Allied aeroplane; it was also Kurt Wintgens' 22nd birthday. Immelmann had been dead more than six weeks and the German Air Service now had eight fighter pilots holding the *Pour le Mérite*. Oswald Boelcke was still the leading scorer with 19 victories although he continued to be serving in Turkey and Bulgaria. But his name had not been forgotten.

Despite being taken from the Western Front following on from Immelmann's fall, Boelcke's active and tactical mind had been working on the theory that fighters would be far more successful if totally segregated from the various flieger-abteilung they were attached to. The Kek units had been working well but there were few of them and the number of pilots and aircraft of each Kek was also minuscule. Boelcke's view was that each fighting unit should be independent of any flieger-abteilung allegiance and be used as fighting units attached to the various Army commands. The number of aircraft in each unit should also be higher and more standardized; certainly eight to ten, and ideally as many as 12-14, each led by either an experienced fighter pilot or, if present protocol demanded it, a long serving, ranking commander, but one who had a flying background.

His talks with various high ranking officers and finally a report on his beliefs as to how a fighter arm should develop, finally met with approval and on 10 August 1916, Feldflugchef Oberst Hermann von der Lieth-Thomsen, seeing the merit in Boelcke's ideas, ordered the formation of the first Jagdstaffeln.

The first twelve Jagdstaffeln, abbreviated and thereafter known more familiarly as Jastas, were formed over the next few weeks. This is not to say that everything happened immediately, or even quickly. The German Air Service was still being hard pressed over the Somme battlefields, and each of the first Jastas had to be formed either around existing units, such as the Keks, or from a cadre of men in a flying unit behind the front, such as an aircraft park.

Quite often an increase in establishment turned a Kek into a Jasta, whereas some were formed from a group of pilots such as those at Flieger Ersatz Abteilung (FEA) 5, at Braunschweig, Germany, which became Jasta 3. But while this change was slowly happening, Kek units continued to operate independently with their Fokkers. New aircraft were promised, such as the Halberstadt DII and Fokker DI biplanes, which had already reached the front, albeit in only a handful of cases, while the promised

Albatros DI and DII biplane fighters had yet to be seen at all. By the end of August 1916, the new Jasta units could only muster 25 Halberstadt DIIs, perhaps two Albatros D-types, and 35 Fokker D-types plus 124 'ageing' Fokker and Pfalz monoplanes.

STUDENT'S SECOND VICTORY
It was still a Fokker monoplane that started the scoring in August 1916. Oberleutnant Kurt Student commanding AOK 3 caught Caudron No. 2059 of Escadrille C4 over Blitzberg and shot it down near Marvaux, along with its crew of Caporal Broussard and Caporal C Fouché.

On 2 August the Germans claimed four aircraft shot down. One of these fell to AA fire, and another to a Marine crew. A third was engaged by a Fokker but it was also claimed by, and then credited to Hauptmann Jancke and his experienced KFlak 44, whose fifth victory this was for his gun crew – a 5 Squadron BE2c which came down near Boesinghe, putting its pilot, Captain C W Snook in a PoW camp.

Coming home from Germany in late 1918, Charles William Snook recorded that while leading a formation to bomb the Zeppelin sheds at Brussels, his propeller had been hit by AA fire and he was then engaged by two Fokkers while he was trying to fly back. He claimed that he put one out of action but that machine-gun fire from the other hit his engine which stopped.

WINTGENS' THIRTEENTH VICTORY AND FRANKL'S SEVENTH
The fourth claim was made by Kurt Wintgens, a Morane Parasol, shot down during the afternoon south-east of Péronne. In fact it was a Morane BB biplane (5177) of 60 Squadron, which was seen falling near Pouilly from the British side. Its Canadian pilot, Lieutenant John Anthony Ninian Ormsby, 22, survived badly wounded but died on the 5th, while his observer, Second Lieutenant Henry Joseph Newton, 19, was killed outright.

Wilhelm Frankl was also credited with the destruction of a Morane at this time, and while sometimes he is linked with the machine of Ormsby and Newton, his claim must have been over the other Morane BB of 60 Squadron (5181) lost this same afternoon. Frankl reported his victim to have fallen at Beaumetz, a location also to the south-east of Péronne, and also not far from Pouilly. The crew of Second Lieutenant Lyonel Latimer Clark, aged 18, and Sergeant Alexander Walker, 22, from Lanark, Scotland, both died. 60 Squadron had been out on a raid upon Estrées.

No. 23 Squadron claimed a Fokker destroyed during an evening photographic sortie near Douai, and another forced down, out of four monoplanes that attacked them.

MULZER'S TENTH, MÜLLER'S THIRD AND PFEIFFER'S FIRST
Max Mulzer got into double figures on 3 August with Kek 3, downing a FE2b (4272) near Sallaumines, Lens, at 07.30 German time. This was a machine from Douai's main rival, 25 Squadron, who lost Second Lieutenant Ken Mathewson, a 22-year-old Canadian, and Private Eric Merril Des Brisay, from Vancouver, aged 23.

Vizefeldwebel Hans Müller's – Kek Avillers – third kill went down to crash on 3 August in the Verdun area at 09.08 am. There were two Nieuports lost this day by the French, one with the tail number N1442, flown by MdL Debrod, the other N833, with Sergent Jean Maffert on board. Both were N103 pilots. This would be Müller's last victory with a Kek, for he was soon to join the new Jasta 5, formed from the Kek, with which he would bring his score to nine by December 1916 before being badly wounded. He would be commissioned in 1917.

Vizefeldwebel Hermann Pfeiffer with AOK 3, finally scored his first victory on 6 August. He attacked and shot down a French Caudron (1467) in his Fokker monoplane, which crashed at Aubérive, along with its crew of Sous-lieutenant Verdie and Lieutenant Escolle, with Escadrille C56.

STUDENT GETS HIS THIRD

At 10.30 on 8 August, Kurt Student shot down a Nieuport north of St Souplet to gain his third victory, and his last for AOK 3. This was a two-seater of N38, whose crew got down alright despite a forced landing, although the observer had been wounded. Their names were Lieutenant Hubert de Fels and Sous-lieutenant Emile Deviterne.

In this same fight, Student's AOK 3 lost Leutnant Benno Berneis in combat. Two locations for his fall are noted as St Souplet and Dontrien. He was 33 years old and came from Furth, shot down by Sous-lieutenant Marcel Burguin of Escadrille N38 who claimed a Fokker shot down in flames into the German side of the lines.

Student too would soon be joining a Jasta – Jasta 9 – with which he would bring his score to six by the end of 1917, as its commander. He would win the Knight's Cross of the Hohenzollern House Order, and the Saxon Albert Order, Knight 2nd Class. In WW2 he commanded the German airborne assault forces, and planned the attacks on 10 May 1940 over Holland and the invasion of Crete in 1941.

FRANKL'S EIGHTH AND NINTH

There is something of a mystery about Wilhelm Frankl's next two victories. First of all the date. They have been noted as being claimed on the 9th and the 10th, but the 9th seems to be the actual day; probably past confusion with a different communiqué date announcing the victories.

Then there is the victim types. Firstly a Voisin, secondly, just an enemy aircraft, without reference to times (not totally unusual for this early period in the war) or locations. As there was no RFC flying of note on the 10th, due to bad weather, RFC losses on the 9th disclose little to help other than a 2 Squadron BE2d (5471) failing to return from a test and height sortie during the afternoon. That the pilot, Captain E W Leggatt, was later reported as a prisoner indicates that he went over the lines. Frankl's victory elsewhere shows the time to have been 12.25 (German time), south-west of Bapaume, clearly too early for Leggatt who did not take off until 14.40 British time.

When Captain Edward Wilmer Leggatt was repatriated, arriving in England on 16 August 1918, he gave a different story to that of a test flight:

'Went out with the intention of shooting a hostile kite balloon. Dived from 12,000 feet, emptied two drums of Buckingham tracers into balloon without effect; balloon pulled down. Followed it to 1,200 feet, left balloon, attacked by Fokker and a Nieuport (with black crosses). Machine gun jammed. Fokker shot away left rudder controls. Came down spinning – landed safely, unwounded.'

Saying that he carried Buckingham ammunition indicates that he was on a balloon strafing sortie, as this was not generally allowed to be carried unless specifically going for the enemy's balloon lines. It was designed to ignite and the Geneva Convention forbade its use against aeroplanes. However, it was a bold pilot who attacked balloons in a BE2d.

His interesting observation concerning the Nieuport either means he mistook the machine for one of the new Albatros Scouts, or indeed it was a captured Nieuport, perhaps even the ones known to be used by Gustav Leffers and Kurt Student.

An FE2b of 25 Squadron, likewise missing, did not take off until 15.05 British time but was credited to Mulzer, and a Sopwith two-seater of 70 Squadron was thought to have been brought down by AA fire, although this was also seen being chased down by a German machine. Time given for this loss by the Germans was 12.25.

There are French losses this date. Escadrille N15 lost a two-seat Nieuport with its crew taken prisoner, while N48 also lost a two-seater Nieuport (but see Klever's victory below), both crewmen wounded and captured. The only Voisin-type was a Caudron of C13, its pilot wounded on the II Armée front. They reported being hit by flak fire. The Germans claimed five Allied aircraft this day, three admitted by the RFC and two by the French. Whatever occurred, Frankl still clearly claimed – and was credited – with two kills which brought his score to nine, and brought him the *Pour le Mérite*. Because of this prestigious award, one must assume there was a firm basis on which to credit him with these victories. An educated guess would be a Nieuport, and the Caudron in French lines.

MULZER'S ELEVENTH?
The mystery of the 9 August claims continues. The 6 Armee Flugmeldbucher indicates Lieutenants C J Hart and J A Mann MC both being killed, having been shot down by Max Mulzer near Coulotte, by the Don to Givenchy road, at 18.00 hours German time. Clifford John Hart, a 30-year-old Londoner, (noted as Captain at his death) and John Anderson Mann, a 21-year-old Glaswegian, are both buried at Fleurbaix. The mystery, of course, is that Mulzer does not appear to have been credited with a victory on the 9th, or any victory after his tenth kill on 3 August!

KLEVER'S FIRST VICTORY
A pilot named Klever was credited with a victory on the 9th. This was (presumably) Leutnant Josef Klever, who had joined Kek Avillers (Falkenhausen) from FA67, and who later served with Jasta 14. The victory

is listed as the Nieuport XII (1520 of Escadrille N48) downed near Saarburg, where its crew of Sergent Raymond Boudou and Lieutenant Roland de Blomac, were taken prisoner. Their actual place of capture is given as by the Forêt de Blamont, near Ciery.

On 12 August Leutnant Hans Kopp with Kek 3 (FA5b) crashed near the railway station at Sallaumines near Lens. This appears to be a result of a fight between Martinsyde Elephants of 27 Squadron, returning from a bomb raid on the railway and factories at Blanc Misseron, east of Valenciennes. On the way back two Fokkers attempted to attack the Martinsydes but were driven off, one Fokker being claimed shot down by Lieutenant P A Wright. Kopp came from Munich and was 25.

Percival Albert Wright gave his address as Harrow, north London, but came from Fort Francis, Ontario, Canada. Joining the RFC in April 1916, he arrived at 27 Squadron on 5 August. Thus he had only been with this unit for a week by the time he shot down Kopp. Percy Wright was wounded on 3 September following an AA hit on his machine which forced him to land inside British lines. He was killed in a flying accident at No.5 Reserve Squadron in England on 20 December 1916, aged 29.

The two-seater crew of Albert Dossenbach and Hans Schilling of FA22, scored their third victory (although sometimes noted as their fifth) on 13 August, a 19 Squadron BE12 (6549) piloted by Second Lieutenant G L Clifford-Geen, who became a prisoner of war. Geen later recorded that he had been fighting five German aircraft but that his timing gear '. . . went wrong . . .', and he was shot down. Geen also said he was with 41 Squadron, and had come down near Friencourt, near Bapaume.

The BE12 was in reality a BE2c, adapted as a single-seater fighter by covering over the observer's forward cockpit and either mounting a Lewis machine gun on the top wing, set to fire over the propeller arc, or a synchronised Vickers gun firing through the blades, although this was off-set to the port side of the fuselage because of the BE's large air scoop on the cowling. As a fighter it was not much of a success; this was the first BE12 lost in action, and was in service with both 19 and 21 Squadrons.

* * *

Mid-August 1916 saw a lull in air-fighting, because of the poor summer weather! In fact the Germans made only one claim on the Western Front between 14 and 19 August – six days. The next combat was on the 20th by a Kek Vaux pilot, Leutnant Hans Klein, who would end the war as a 22-victory ace and *Pour le Mérite*-winner. Stettin-born Klein had previously been with the infantry, then joined the air service and finally reached Kek Vaux in the summer of 1916. On this day he attacked the BE2 (2613) of 2 Squadron, flown by two Canadians, Second Lieutenants R T Griffin and H H Whitehead. Both men were wounded and taken prisoner, but Herbert Whitehead later died of his injuries.

Back in England after the war, Robert Thomas Griffin confirmed being brought down by AA fire and two Fokkers during a bomb raid, and he was wounded. So this was obviously a case of a shared victory which had to be awarded to just one victor and Klein lost the toss. Klein was denied this victory as it was disputed by a counter-claim by KFlak 38 and arbitration gave the victory to the gunners. Three days later AA fire brought down another BE2 of 10 Squadron and a French Caudron.

Kek Bertincourt pilots, along with those of other Fokker monoplane units, were also starting to appreciate how improved Allied aeroplanes were matching their prowess in the air. Bad weather or not, lack of recent success was demonstrating the Fokker's loss of superiority. Kek-B's success was certainly trailing off and with Hauptmann Schregal, who had taken over from Otto Parschau as Staffelführer, things were about to change. On 23 August the Kek's 14 pilots and support personnel were attached to FA(A) 210 at Sains-lez-Marquion, to the west of Cambrai, and very shortly afterwards, it was disbanded to become Jasta 1.

Also at Bertincourt, Jasta 2 was formed on 10 August under the command of Hauptmann Oswald Boelcke. He had returned from his sojourn to the Balkans and had been allowed back into a combat unit by being given command of this unit. He had also been allowed to pick many of its pilots from men he had known in France, or had met while on the Eastern Front. One of these was Leutnant Manfred von Richthofen, who would become the German ace-of-aces, as well as the top scoring fighter pilot of all the fighting nations in WW1. Another was Erwin Böhme. Two other Kek pilots were chosen, Hans Imelmann (note the different spelling to Max Immelmann) a 19-year-old from Hannover, and 23-year-old Leopold Rudolf Reimann from Kek Bertincourt, after an initial spell with Jasta 1. All three would become aces.

These new Jagdstaffeln did not have new aeroplanes. Indeed, Jasta 2 initially had no aircraft at all. Jasta 1 had the Fokkers of Kek-B, and in one of them, Jasta 1 scored its first success on 24 August.

REIMANN'S FIRST VICTORY AND PFEIFFER'S SECOND

Offizierstellvertreter Leopold Reimann – although also known as Rudolf, his second name – shot down a Sopwith 1½ Strutter of 70 Squadron (A879) on the 24th at 18.30 east of Metz-en-Couture for Jasta 1's first victory. Two 70 Squadron machines were hit by AA fire and then attacked by fighters. As one fell to the ground, this was credited to Reimann, although he is just as likely to have attacked the other Strutter, flown by Lieutenants A M Vaucour and his observer A J Bott.

Bunny Vaucour would become an ace on Strutters and Camels with 70 and 45 Squadrons, commanding the latter in 1918 and be killed with it over Italy having won the MC and DFC. Alan Bott MC and Bar would also become an ace, scoring victories as an observer and later as a pilot in Palestine with 111 Squadron, before being taken prisoner.

Vaucour and Bott's machine was hit by a hot piece of AA shell which set the fuselage fabric on fire, which Bott had then to tear away with his hands. No sooner had he sorted this out than a fighter was upon them and they only just made it across the trenches. Then their engine failed and they had to force land south of Carnoy, but got down safely.

The other crew, undoubtedly credited to Reimann, were Captain Robert

Gerald Hopwood, 31, from London, and Gunner Charles Rapley Pearce, a Canadian, both of whom were killed. Neither have any known grave.

Hermann Pfeiffer claimed his second kill by downing another Caudron G4 over Pont-Faverger, flying a Fokker EIII of AOK 3. This machine came from Escadrille C64 (1309) flown by Sergent Jouanny and Aspirant Florentin, who were both made guests of the Germans.

BERTHOLD GETS HIS SIXTH PLUS AN UNCONFIRMED

Rudolf Berthold, still flying with Kek Vaux, brought his score to six with a victory over a Nieuport Scout of N37 (N1552) north of Péronne at 19.00 hours German time. The French pilot is named as Caporal Henri Danguenger, who was killed. Another Nieuport Scout, from Escadrille N48 (1472) was also shot down this evening, its pilot, Adjudant André Gros, also being killed over Roisel. If Berthold was involved in both of these, he only received acknowledgement of one victory, so the other must have fallen unseen inside French lines.

In all on 24 August, four Allied aircraft were claimed north of the Somme, three others over the French sectors. Apart from those mentioned above, the others were all victims of AA fire, two Caudrons, a Farman and a Nieuport two-seater.

ZANDER'S THIRD VICTORY

The next day, Hauptmann Martin Zander of Jasta 1 brought down an FE2b (4285) of 22 Squadron for his third victory, Lieutenants R D Walker and C Smith being captured near Gueudecourt. A second FE was shot-up during this fight with two Fokkers. This second crew thought its defensive fire had hit one of the monoplanes, but Jasta 1 did not record any losses. Charles Smith noted on his return from Germany that while escorting a photo machine they were attacked by three aircraft on their way back and the FE's fuel tank was riddled. Forced to land they were immediately surrounded by German soldiers.

Ronald Draycott Walker, when he got home, noted that their formation had been split up by AA fire and he and Smith were then attacked by three German fighters which shot holes in his fuel tank and engine.

Second Lieutenant A M Vaucour, who along with Alan Bott had had a narrow escape on the 24th, had another close call on the 25th. In the same 1½ Strutter – A890 – its burnt fabric repaired overnight, attacks by enemy aircraft killed his observer (not Bott on this occasion), then AA fire holed his fuel tank, forcing him to land inside British lines.

Another future ace to appear in a German communiqué for 25 August 1916 was Vizefeldwebel (later Leutnant) Rudolf Windisch. Windisch made a name for himself with Boelcke and Immelmann's old FA62 but not before it had moved to the Eastern Front in June 1916. He and his observer, Leutnant Maximilian von Cossell attacked and shot down a Russian balloon on the 25th, and later in the year Windisch flew behind the enemy lines, landed, and dropped off von Cossell who then proceeded to blow up a railway bridge. Next day Windisch returned to the landing spot and picked up von Cossell and flew him home. For these feats both men were decorated. Windisch added a further 21 victories to his name flying with Jasta 32 and 66, winning the *Pour le Mérite* before being lost in action in May 1918.

HANS MÜLLER'S FOURTH VICTORY

Jasta 5 was formed on 21 August from Kek Avillers commanded by Hans Berr, at Béchamp, on the Verdun front. Although it had Halberstadt biplanes, it also carried over its Fokker monoplanes, and it is believed Müller was in one of these on the 26th, the day he downed a French Voisin to gain his fourth victory. This may have been an aircraft (Caudron) from Escadrille C53, Sergent Mars and Sous-lieutenant Humbert, missing this date. In any event it was Jasta 5's first victory.

The main feature of the day, however, was the loss of five pilots from 19 Squadron in their BE12 machines, on a bomb raid on railway targets in Havrincourt Wood. Bad weather was their main downfall, a heavy storm forcing most down to death or captivity. At least one pilot, Captain I H D Henderson (a future ace) was engaged by LVG aircraft without positive results, although a crew from FA57 claimed a victory near Biefvillers that evening. Whether it was Henderson or merely one of the other crashed BE12s that was credited, is unclear.

At least one of the BE12 pilots, upon his return from prison camp, reported having been overcome not by the weather, but by German aircraft. Second Lieutenant Arthur Wilfred Reynall, one of the escorts, said four German machines attacked him near Bapaume, putting his aircraft completely out of control (6532). While uninjured when he crashed, he was stunned.

BETHGE'S FIRST VICTORY

Oberleutnant Hans Bethge, from Berlin, born 6 December 1890, had earlier flown with BAO, which became KGI, and then going to Kek Bertincourt. Now as Jasta 1, the former Kek pilots were starting to claim victories, Bethge claiming his first ever kill on 29 August, possibly still operating in a Fokker. His victim was a 15 Squadron BE2c (4187) on an ArtObs patrol, being brought down near Auchonvillers at 12.05 German time, which was just inside British lines. Both men, Lieutenants Robert Burleigh, 23, and Reginald Charles Harry, were killed; their crashed machine was shelled by German artillery for good measure.

* * *

LEFFERS' SIXTH KILL

On the last day of August the Germans were able to claim eight victories. These were seven Allied machines down, plus one balloon. Four of them were Martinsydes from 27 Squadron bombing targets in Havrincourt Wood, which had the misfortune to run into Jasta 1's fighters. The German pilots shot down three, while a fourth was engaged and brought down by the two-seater crew of Willi Fahlbusch and Hans Rosencrantz of KGI.

The three successful Jasta 1 pilots were Gustav Leffers, Hans Bethge and

Leutnant Hans von Keudell. Leffers' kill was his sixth, Bethge's his second, and von Keudell's first. According to some sources it was Fahlbusch's and Rosencrantz's fifth victory. A note of caution, however, comes while reading the German communiqué for 4 September 1916. As there had been no communiqués for 2 and 3 September, the 4th stated that in the Somme area 13 Allied aeroplanes had been shot down and four on the French sectors. In these actions, Boelcke had scored his 20th victory, while Leffers, Fahlbusch/Rosencrantz had important parts in these successes.

Another of the claims was for a 23 Squadron FE by a FA32 two-seater Rumpler crew, south of Haplincourt. Hans Müller of Jasta 5 got the balloon, which brought his score to five, the second victory for his Jasta.

It is not known for certain if any of the Jasta 1 pilots were flying Fokkers, but it is interesting that each victor was either an ace or would soon be one. Leffers, of course needs no introduction, and Bethge we met in this chapter. Von Keudell's star was just starting to ascend and by mid-February 1917, this 24-year-old Berliner and former Uhlan officer had a dozen victories with Jasta 1 and 27, before being killed in action leading the latter unit on 15 February.

Gustav Leffers was now just two victories away from his *Pour le Mérite*, while Bethge, with 20 victories by early 1918, was nominated for this award but his subsequent death in action precluded its approval.

Two other victories claimed during the month of August was a balloon by Sivry's Hans Gutermuth (his second victory), date unknown, but possibly 31 August, and a victory credited to Leutnant Walter Kypke of Kek Avillers, date unknown. Kypke would score nine victories by mid-1918 not only in home defence but as the staffelführer of Jasta 47.

During September, the Germans recorded that the August 1916 claims against Allied aircraft had been 78. Of these, 31 RFC, and 18 French had fallen in German lines, 28 shot down in Allied lines, with another forced to land in Allied lines. German losses were confirmed as 17.

Chapter Ten

FOKKER FINALÉ

From now on it is difficult to record with any certainty which aircraft were being used in the Jastas and what pilots were flying. During this transitional period from Keks to Jastas, and while other Fokker units still operated, there was a total mix of machines.

Fokker monoplanes were still in evidence, and it is inconceivable that these would not be flown if there was nothing else available, although Halberstadt DIIs were arriving as well as Fokker D-type biplanes and Albatros Scouts.

An 18 Squadron FE2b was shot up in combat with a Fokker Eindecker on 1 September, wounding the pilot, but it was not lost.

PFEIFFER GETS HIS THIRD, DINKEL HIS FIRST

Fokkers were, of course, still operating with AOK 3, and on 2 September, Hermann Pfeiffer and Leutnant Friedrich Dinkel engaged several Caudrons and each shot down one. The former's victim came down near St Souplet, the latter's at Aubérive, which was in French lines, but it was finished off by German artillery fire. The French lost a Caudron G4 (1574) from Escadrille C64, together with its crew of Capitaine Berthin and Sergent Ramponi, so we might assume the crew down in French lines escaped injury before the shelling began.

The French had a Nieuport XVII of N23 downed south of Aubérive, with the loss of Sous-lieutenant Marcel Burguin, and is only mentioned because of the same location as Dinkel's action, on the chance the aircraft type was noted incorrectly.

Thirty-year-old Dinkel was a Würrtemberger and former infantry officer. Transferring to the air service in the summer of 1915 he had been with AOK 3 since May 1916, under Kurt Student. When AOK 3 became the nucleus of Jasta 9 in October, with Student still in command, Dinkel moved to it as well and was decorated with the Würrtemberg Gold Military Merit Medal, the first Jasta pilot to win the honour.

LEFFERS' SEVENTH VICTORY

To confuse everyone still further, not to mention the RFC airmen of 1916, it was not uncommon for German aviators to fly captured Allied aeroplanes, suitably marked with the black iron cross of the German nation. This was mentioned in the previous chapter.

At this time Gustav Leffers had begun flying a captured Nieuport 11, fitted with a synchronised Spandau machine gun. He was not unique in this. Kurt Student flew another Nieuport 11, the one he had brought down on 6 July, from Escadrille N38. On 3 September Leffers attacked a 23 Squadron FE2b (6934) whose crew became prisoners, at 08.00 near Mory.

Interestingly, Frank Douglas Home Sams, the FE pilot, recorded the action upon his return home at the end of the war. He said he and his observer, Corporal Summers, were flying at the rear of a seven-aircraft formation and upon turning for home they were attacked by five hostile aircraft. The first burst from a captured Nieuport destroyed their propeller and Summers was wounded in five places. Sams dived and lost height and tried to glide for the lines but they were too far and he had to put down into a corn field, still pursued by two aircraft. What is interesting too is that Sams identified his attacker as flying a 'captured Nieuport'.

WIELAND'S FIRST VICTORY
On the 6th a Fokker pilot with FA6b, Leutnant Philipp Wieland, another Würrtemberger from Ulm, shot down a BE2e of 42 Squadron RFC, the unit's first loss since arriving in France. The BE (7078) came down north of Frélinghien, north-east of Armentières at 07.30 German time, its pilot, Second Lieutenant Cyril Llewellyn Seymour Thomas, aged 19, not surviving. Wieland later took command of Jasta 27 following von Keudell's death but the appointment was not a success and he was relieved shortly after being wounded. However, he commanded other Jasta units, and survived the war with this, his single victory in air combat. Nevertheless, he was awarded the Knight's Cross of the Würrtemberg Military Merit Order and also became Knight 2nd Class with Swords of the Friedrich Order three days before the Armistice.

Otto Bernert gained his second victory this 6 September, which was the first claim by the new Jasta 4. Jasta 4, formed on 25 August from Kek Vaux, was commanded by the former Kek commander, Rudolf Berthold, and based at Roupy on the Somme. No sooner had the formation been instigated than Berthold handed over command to Hans-Joachim Buddecke.

It will be recalled that Buddecke had been flying Fokkers with FA23 in the autumn of 1915 but had then been sent out to the Gallipoli front to fly fighters with Ottoman FA6, where he had been very successful. To his three Western Front victories, he had added four more confirmed kills and at least seven more unconfirmed. Despite not having the required eight victories, he had been awarded the *Pour le Mérite* on 14 April 1916, as already mentioned. All his victories with the Turks had been Farman types around the Dardanelles, mostly flown by British Royal Naval Air Service units.

Bernert claimed a Caudron for the Jasta's first victory, in Allied lines near Dompierre, which is south-east of an area covering Bray-Cappy. There is no report of any French losses this date although C28 and C11 had pilots wounded. A second victory was claimed at 18.55, an FE2b, by the Staffelführer, Buddecke, and although in some records this turned out to be his eighth confirmed victory, other records show it as an unconfirmed claim. Again the locations differ, the unconfirmed claim is the same as

Bernert's – Dompierre – the confirmed claim noted as Chaulnes. Dompierre is south-east of Bray, while Chaulnes is some distance due south of Dompierre. The only FE lost was a 25 Squadron machine shot down in flames during a combat with a Fokker into the German side of the lines in the late afternoon, its crew both killed – in fact the pilot was seen to jump from the flaming aeroplane. This aircraft was on a patrol in the Loos-en-Gohelle area, north of Arras, which is way far too far away to be anything to do with Buddecke, unless Chaulnes is an incorrectly given location.

The FE – 5238 – was supposed to have been downed by one of three Fokkers which attacked it south of a village called St Laurent, and which came from Kek 3 at 06.20 German time, but no names are recorded, and the time is way off again from Buddecke's 18.50. (Unless, of course, Buddecke's time was in fact 06.50, ie: 6.50 in the morning, and not 6.50 in the evening! But then Buddecke was with Jasta 4, not Kek 3.)

Unhappily, 6 September seems to be one of those days where nothing ties up nicely and one is left with a number of imponderables.

LEHMANN'S LAST VICTORY

Leutnant Werner Lehmann was credited with three combat victories while with FA32 and Kek Nord. The last occurred on 7 September, south-east of Reims between Fort de la Pompelle and Cliquot Mühle. The aircraft fell in flames but there is no obvious French loss. Von Keudell and Wilhelm Frankl both claimed victories for their respective Jastas on this date – both Nieuports – and the French also had a Nieuport pilot wounded. The latter was the ace Sergent André Chainat of Escadrille N3, who claimed a probable victory in this his last combat. The Frenchman was flying a Spad VII, another new fighter to the war front. Keudell may have shot down a pilot from N38, Frankl, Sergent Bordes from N73.

Lehmann was assigned to the new Jasta 9 which was to be formed on 28 September at Vouziers, taking men like Lehmann from the former Fokkerstaffel there – AOK 3. He became the embryo unit's first casualty as it was beginning to form with Albatros DIIs, being killed in a crash at the Army Flug-park at Somme-Py on the 23rd.

* * *

Several well known pilots scored victories in early September 1916, but were probably not flying Fokker monoplanes. Oswald Boelcke with his Jasta 2 had the strange situation of having no aeroplanes for his pilots. The Jasta had just a couple of machines – Fokker DIII biplanes – but Boelcke flying one of them (352/16) had shot down his twentieth victory on 2 September and another on the 8th, and his twenty-second on the 9th, which was a 24 Squadron DH2.

Wilhelm Frankl got his tenth on the 7th, the French Nieuport Scout from N73, north-east of Combles. Keudell claimed a N38 machine this same day. Otto Bernert gained another for Jasta 4 on the 11th, while Wintgens scored a double on the 14th, his fourteenth and fifteenth, the same day as Boelcke also got a double, numbers 23 and 24, one being yet another DH2.

WINTGENS' SIXTEENTH VICTORY

We know for certain that Kurt Wintgens was flying a Fokker on 15 September because the downed pilot, Second Lieutenant Colin Elphinston, in a 21 Squadron BE12 (6583) flying an Offensive Patrol, reported the fact when he arrived home from prison camp in 1918. He said the control wires to his rudder were shot away at the same time as he was wounded. Falling out of control he managed a sort of crash-landing at La Orel, near Manancourt, and went into 'the bag'.

By the end of September, these aces had increased their scores even further. Boelcke's score had risen to 29, Frankl's to 13, Höhndorf's to 12, Wintgens' to 19, Buddecke's to ten, and Berthold's to eight. Berthold in fact was the next man to receive the *Pour le Mérite*, on 12 October, the tenth fighter pilot to be so honoured. Leffers, still with seven victories at the end of September, gained his eighth on 7 October and with it came the Blue Max on 5 November.

One pilot to gain his first victory during September 1916 was Manfred von Richthofen of Jasta 2, on the 17th. By the end of the month he had scored three, and was sure he was on the way to claiming his own Blue Max. Yet Fokker monoplane victories were still being scored in these twilight days of the Eindecker.

VIERECK'S FIRST KILL

Vizefeldwebel Wilhelm Viereck had been a pilot with FA5b prior to going to Kek 3. He had been involved in a combat with a BE2 on 8 September but this was only noted as 'zlg' in German records, which stood for 'zur landung gezwungen' – forced to land. It is difficult to understand what these were, for although it appears obvious – an opponent forced to land in its own territory – we have seen so often other pilots forcing Allied pilots to do the same, but somehow being awarded a confirmed victory. One would assume that after 'landing' the aeroplane was later seen to be shelled into matchwood by artillery fire, but we know that was not always the case. Obviously the Germans had a system, but how it was administered, and how sometimes victories awarded and sometimes not, remains a confusing issue. Perhaps it was simply a downed machine that appeared later to have survived the landing and any shelling.

Nevertheless, Viereck's victory for 16 September was upheld and he was flying a Fokker monoplane of Kek 3. The Battle of Flers-Courcelette had begun the previous day, the third phase of the Somme offensive, attacking a section of the front between Morval and Le Sars. RFC casualties had leapt on the first day, mostly to ground fire, although Wintgens and Boelcke had both scored in air combats. Viereck's victim was a 2 Squadron BE2c (4495) that took off to bomb Douai, without an observer in lieu of bombs and was seen shot down by a Fokker. The Canadian pilot, Second Lieutenant D Cushing, became a prisoner of war, lucky to survive at all. The German pilot would shortly become a member of Jasta 10.

Jastas 1 and 2 were in the thick of the fighting on the 17th, in their biplanes, and aces such as Wintgens, Höhndorf, Boelcke and Frankl all scored. And so did Reimann of Jasta 2, while two other pilots of this unit opened their account against the British – Erwin Böhme and Manfred von Richthofen.

With the arrival of the Jastas, the Fokker Eindecker era on the Western Front was almost at an end. Dossenbach and Schilling of FA22 got their fifth, or sixth, shortly after mid-day on 24 September, a BE12 of 19 Squadron over Havrincourt. Its pilot, Second Lieutenant George Edwards fell out or jumped, from his burning machine. A Londoner, he was 28. Dossenbach must obviously have witnessed this most terrible of deaths. As fate would have it, he himself would suffer an identical end.

This aggressive two-seater crew scored again two days later, the 26th, downing a Sopwith 1½ Strutter of 70 Squadron (A1916) near Bapaume mid-morning, actually crashing on the Ervillers-St Leger road. Second Lieutenant Frederick StJ F N Echlin (from Guernsey) and 1AM Arthur Grundy both died.

Dossenbach and Schilling were obviously on form as the next day came another victory, this time an FE2b (4839) of 25 Squadron. On this occasion, however, the opposition bit back, and although the FE came down inside British lines, the observer's return fire hit the two-seater which also came down on fire, both men receiving injuries from the flames. The British crew, Second Lieutenant V W Harrison and Sergeant L S Court, were not injured. The fight had been above Tourmignies and although this was Harrison's first victory, it was his observer's sixth!

Leslie Simpson Court had previously been successful with three other pilots and his first four victories had been claimed against Fokkers during June and July 1916! Nor was this the first time he had been shot down, AA fire bringing down his FE back on 5 August. Court went on to claim eight victories by November and the following year he received the French Médaille Militaire.

On the 22nd a Fokker pilot was lost in the locality of Sailly, south-west of Douai, flying an EIV. Oberleutnant Karl Albert (or Abert), from Selb, a month past his 26th birthday, was operating with FA5b – Kek 3. He had previously been with FA292 on two-seaters. He fell between Sailly and Douai during a combat with British aircraft and was killed. Two claims for Fokkers were made this day in this general area, one by Captain D O Mulholland flying an FE8 (6384) of 40 Squadron, the unit's first victory, the other by an FE2b crew of 25 Squadron. As Mulholland recorded that the Fokker was attacking an FE and went down in a spinning nose dive, it is highly probable that the Fokker was the same machine claimed by the FE men. Time – 0820.

The FE crew was Sergeant T Mottershead and Second Lieutenant C Street (in 6998). They had just bombed an ammunition train at Somain railway station, east of Douai, and were climbing away to return home as the Fokker dived on them. In the fight which followed Tom Mottershead manoeuvred his pusher in order for his observer to get in an accurate burst at their antagonist. Hit by this return fire, the Fokker nosed over and fell to the ground – in a spinning nose dive – and was seen to crash. For this and previous actions Mottershead received the DCM. Shortly afterwards he was posted to 20 Squadron and on 7 January 1917 fought an action which resulted in him being awarded a posthumous Victoria Cross.

VICTORIES EIGHTEEN AND NINETEEN FOR WINTGENS

Despite the new biplanes arriving on the equally new Jasta units, Kurt Wintgens may possibly have continued with a Fokker monoplane for his last victories. On 24 September he is credited in some records as having downed two 19 Squadron BE12s, although Dossenbach and Schilling got one of the two BE12 losses this date. Wintgens' second victory was in fact a Martynside from 27 Squadron. We know this for certain because its pilot, Second Lieutenant E N Wingfield, reported upon his return from prison camp in 1918 that he had been shot down by a Leutnant Wintgens.

The problem is he only noted being shot down by a Fokker at Ribécourt. This, of course, could have been either a Fokker monoplane or biplane, but on the assumption that Ernest Wingfield probably didn't know or appreciate that there was such an aeroplane as a Fokker biplane, but undoubtedly knew all about Fokker Eindeckers, it is not difficult to assume his mention of a Fokker meant a monoplane. One can also assume, therefore, that the earlier BE12 victory was also scored in his Eindecker.

PFEIFFER SCORES NUMBER FOUR

Another Fokker victory came on the 26th, Vizefeldwebel Hermann Pfeiffer of AOK 3 claiming a French Caudron over Binarville. This was probably the G4 (2208) from Escadrille C6 which had Lieutenants Maurice Jean Munier and André Dellon missing this date. This would be his final Fokker victory; he was about to go to Jasta 9.

This was just about the final victory claim by a monoplane pilot, although possibly Vizefeldwebel Schürz of FA19 got one on 25 September, and Vizefeldwebel (later Leutnant) Karl Oberländer with FA71 got another on 26 October. Schürz claimed a Caudron G4 on the II Armée front which was a machine from Escadrille C4 crewed by Lieutenant Louis Genevois and Sergent Emile Cabella, who were both wounded.

Oberländer certainly shot down a Nieuport XVII on 26 October north of Verdun for his first victory, with five more coming with Jasta 30 in 1917-18. Unfortunately there are no French Nieuport losses recorded for this date.

Most of the new Jasta units had now been or were being equipped with biplanes, Fokker DII, Halberstadt DII, and Albatros DII. Any remaining Fokkers were kept for a short while just for practise flying, the others sent back to Germany for the training schools, but they too soon disappeared.

The day of the monoplane had ended, the era of the biplane fighters was about to begin. The impact of the new biplanes could already be seen by the successes of Zander's Jasta 1 and Boelcke's Jasta 2, whose fledgling pilots were already creating havoc amongst the British and French aviators, and would continue to do so into the spring of 1917. Zander himself scored three victories between August and October 1916 which brought his score to five once added to his victories on two-seaters.

WINTGENS IS KILLED

If Kurt Wintgens was going to die it was perhaps appropriate that he should do so just as the ascendency of the Fokker Eindecker was ending. On 25

September, flying a Fokker EIV, Wintgens, flying in company with Walter Höhndorf, got into an air battle with the French ace Alfred Heurtaux of Escadrille Spa3, flying one of the new Spad VII fighters. The action took place above Villers-Carbonnel at 10.00 that morning, and diving out of the sun, the Frenchman put a burst into the Fokker's fuel tank which caught fire and caused the monoplane to explode. Heurtaux returned to his airfield in the certain knowledge that he had gained his eighth victory. If the story is correct, Wintgens was going to the aid of a German two-seater of FA23. The pilot in the C-type was a future fighter ace, Leutnant Josef Veltjens.

Alfred Marie Joseph Heurtaux came from Nantes, born 20 May 1893 and he attended the French military school at St Cyr in 1912, then assigned to the 4th Regiment of Hussars that October. Commissioned in August 1914 with the 9th Regiment he received three citations in the early part of the war before requesting a transfer to flying. His first squadron was MS38 but he then moved to Escadrille N3, assuming command on 16 June, at which date he had yet to bring down a German aeroplane. He began scoring in July and by the end of 1916 he had achieved 16 victories and been made a Chevalier de la Légion d'Honneur. Severely wounded in May 1917, upon recovery he resumed command of his escadrille, and became an Officer of the Legion of Honour for his 21 WW1 combat victories.

MULZER FALLS
As if the loss of Wintgens was not enough of a blow for the German fighter arm, the very next day saw the death of the handsome Max von Mulzer. He was still, no doubt, getting used to his new status as a 'ritter' and a 'von' following his achievements with Kek 3. On the 26th he took off to test-fly an Albatros DI (4424/16) at the Armee Flugpark 6, Valenciennes, and crashed. He was 23.

The French were never any good at detailing aircraft types in their records, and as often as not only recorded actions against EA – enemy aircraft. And if a type was noted, it still left a query sometimes, such as the first victory of Sergent Georges Madon of N38, north of Reims (Pomacle) on 28 September. The records merely report a victory over a Fokker but whether a monoplane or biplane is uncertain. His victim was Leutnant Hans-Werner Kühn, from Breslau, flying with KG4 who reportedly fell over Gouzeaucourt, near Péronne, and was killed.

In fact Madon's first three victories were all 'Fokkers' but victories two and three came in November 1916, by which time the Fokker biplanes were being more widely used. Madon was to score a total of 41 and with the rank of Capitaine survived the war, only to die in a plane crash on 11 November 1924 – celebrating the fifth anniversary of the Armistice!

* * *

Perhaps a sign of things to come occurred on 12 October 1916. Former Eindecker pilots Leutnants Otto Kissenberth and Ludwig Hanstein had both flown monoplanes with FA9b but both had recently been given Fokker DII biplanes to fly. Neither man had had the opportunity to score victories with the monoplanes, a fact which changed dramatically this October day.

The French mounted one of their large raids, this time against the Mauser factory at Oberndorf, a small town some 50 miles south-west of Stuttgart, supported by aircraft of the British RNAS. The raiders needed to pass close by the German airfield at Colmar, which was the base of the Bavarian FA9 with its attached Kek Ensisheim. As far as can be ascertained, the French/British force consisted of the following aircraft this autumn afternoon:

6 Farmans of Esc MF29   5 Farmans of Esc MF123
7 Bréguet Vs of Esc BM120   2 Bréguet Vs of 3 Wing RNAS
13 Sopwith Strutters, 3 Wing RNAS 4 Nieuport Scouts, Esc N124

4 Caudrons of Esc C61 on a diversionary raid against Lörrach.

Kek Ensisheim sent off its fighters to intercept. After the battle it was discovered that no less then ten Allied aeroplanes had been shot down – three by Otto Kissenberth. Another had been downed by Hanstein, and one each by Leutnant Hans Hartl and Vizefeldwebel Ludwig Hilz. In each case apart from Hartl, these were first victories, Hartl having scored a Fokker monoplane victory back on 25 July.

Kissenberth's amazing three victories were a RNAS Bréguet V, a Farman from MF123 and a Bréguet V of BM120, while Hanstein had downed a Sopwith (9660), Hartl and Hilz Bréguet Vs. The other 3 Wing Bréguet had fallen to ground fire. Meantime, aircraft of Jasta 15 had also become involved and Leutnant Otto Pfältzer downed a French Bréguet (his own second victory), while a certain Vizefeldwebel Ernst Udet had got another, the second of his eventual 62 victories. Leutnant Kurt Haber also downed a Bréguet which was not only Jasta 15's first victory, but his own fifth, and last. Kissenberth would go on to score 20 victories and win the Blue Max in 1918. Hanstein was killed in March 1918 with a victory score of 16.

One of the escorting Nieuport Scouts of the American Lafayette Escadrille (N124) had also been lost as the raid was coming to an end. The pilot, Norman Prince, had landed, refuelled, and taken off again to help shepherd the survivors back. Coming home in the twilight he hit a high tension cable, crashed, and succumbed to his injuries three days later.

One RNAS crew claimed a two-seater shot down and forced to land, and an Unteroffizier August Buchner of FA6b was severely wounded this date.

THE DEATH OF BOELCKE

The man who really put air combat on the map in WW1 and whose ideas helped to create the fighter units within the Imperial German Air Service, Oswald Boelcke, died on 28 October 1916.

Tragically his death was the result of a mid-air collision with one of his own people, Erwin Böhme, during an air fight with DH2s of 24 Squadron. Both pilots were going for a British machine and Böhme's wheels struck a glancing blow on the top wing of his leader's biplane. Neither man could see the other because of their upper and lower wings obstructing the view

– something that would not have happened so readily with the Fokker monoplane, at least, not with the pilot below another machine whose upward vision was not obscured by a top wing.

Boelcke began to go down, shedding bits of his shattered top wing and finally plunged to the ground near Bapaume. Considering it was only late 1916, with the war continuing for another two years, only a handful of German fighter pilots scored more victories than Oswald Boelcke's 40. A considerable achievement.

While his last 21 victories had all been scored in biplanes, Halberstadt and Albatros D-types, he had nevertheless, along with Immelmann, Wintgens, Parschau, von Mulzer, Höhndorf, Buddecke, Frankl, Leffers, von Althaus and Berthold, held sway over the British and French air forces on the Western Front between August 1915 and July 1916.

The German fighter pilots during this period, and those who followed during the far more bitter years of 1917 and 1918, imposed heavy casualties on the Allied air forces but could never hope to overcome the sheer numbers that continued to be pitted against them. The British Empire was too large and too full of men willing to put their lives on the line, in the air as well as on the ground, for there to be any hope of success for the German Empire. And when finally the United States of America came into the conflict, the end was in sight for those honest enough to see it.

To fly daily across the trenches into German-held territory, in flimsy aeroplanes very prone to fire and damage, without armour, with engines having only degrees of reliability, and with no means of escape should fire break out, or control surfaces/wings tear away whilst hundreds if not thousands of feet above the earth, took a certain kind of human being. Especially, in the early days, knowing the enemy had superior aeroplanes and fire power. The younger generation today might call them mad, but that older generation who grew up with a backbone of duty, called the Allied pilots brave, heroic, daring.

There is a significant passage in the book *Per Ardua*, by Hilary St George Saunders (Oxford University Press, 1944), which records the rise of British air power between 1911 and 1939, but which covers mainly the air war of 1914-18. While it refers to the dreadful month of April 1917, it is still relevant to the 1915-16 period. Saunders talks of the losses and the reasons for them, noting the chief cause as:

> '. . . the implacable determination of the Royal Flying Corps to pursue the offensive no matter what cost. Every one of its pilots was well aware that to practise the doctrine of attack day in, day out, meant losses, and if the enemy were as skilled and resolute as, for example Leutnant Werner Voss and his pilots [in 1917 Ed.], that those losses would be heavy. They were accepted without flinching. The mood of the officers and men of the Royal Flying Corps can be best depicted by a phrase used a generation later to describe the British people in a crisis even graver. They were grim and gay. The first quality was displayed in the air, the second in the Mess. However many

empty chairs there might be, the spirit of relaxation, which tradition decreed must prevail after toil, was never allowed to depart from the board. Critics there were of this behaviour, persons belonging for the most part to an older generation, cold, unimaginative, and without understanding. To them Sir Walter Raleigh[2] made an unanswerable reply, when he wrote: "The Latin poet said that it is decorous to die for one's country; in that decorum the Service is perfectly instructed."'

Although more than 600 Fokker monoplane types were produced, far fewer than this saw active duty with the German Air Service at the front. Even its designer, Anthony Fokker, admitted that it was not all that it should be, the aeroplane being tricky and unreliable. Its success was solely due to its interrupter gear, its reasonable (for the period) manoeuvrability, and to the skill and courage of the men who flew it, making a name for it and themselves, even if short-lived.

Combat ceiling was no more than 10,000 feet for the EI and 13,500 feet for the EIV. Even so it took the pilot in an EI forty minutes to reach this height, thirty minutes in an EIV. What, however, is not in dispute, is that the Fokker Eindecker and its handful of pilots changed the course of air combat – indeed, invented it – while for a period it gained air superiority over all-comers above the Western Front in the first air war ever known.

---

[2] Sir Walter Raleigh, author of the official history *The War in the Air*. One of his quotes in his six-volume opus (plus appendices), refers to the men of the RFC in this manner: 'They made courage and devotion the rule, not the exception.' (Vol 1, page 7.)

Chapter Eleven

THE TWILIGHT OF THE GODS

While much has been said and made about the Fokker Scourge, and the airmen of the British and French air forces being Fokker Fodder during the 1915-16 period, it was only a comparatively small number of German pilots who were inflicting these casualties upon the Allied airmen.

As already mentioned, the numbers of aircraft involved were fairly small in comparison to 1917-18, so any dramatic developments in the air war between July 1915 and the summer of 1916 obviously made an impact on the recipients, in their BEs, Farmans and Caudrons. Yet despite the small number of German aces scoring victories there were still quite a number of other pilots operating in Fokker and Pfalz monoplanes, who either did not score a victory, or scored the odd one, or perhaps two or three. Their presence made the air seem full of these deadly fighters, each spitting fire through the propeller arc. Many Allied pilots who succeeded in getting back across the lines to safety obviously took their stories back to squadron messes which only increased the tension for the listeners in days to come.

These early German aces quickly became well known names, not only amongst their fellow flyers but also to the general public at home in Germany. Once these handful of successful pilots had achieved, or been credited with eight victories, high honour came too, in the shape of the *Ordern Pour le Mérite*, that highly decorative and very noticeable pale blue enamel and gold cross that, once awarded, dangled at the neck of the wearer for all to see and admire. With it too came other medals, orders and decorations.

We have already seen how the first of these Blue Max decorations were given to Boelcke, Immelmann, Buddecke, Wintgens, von Mulzer, Frankl, Höhndorf, von Althaus and Parschau. These were the first nine, and in the early Jasta era, they were followed by Rudolf Berthold (12 October 1916), Gustav Leffers (5 November), Albert Dossenbach, the two-seater ace (11 November), and Hans Berr (4 December). Leffers, Berthold and Berr had each achieved early victories with the Fokker monoplanes.

Two days after Christmas 1916, Gustav Leffers was killed, less than a week before his 25th birthday. Yet another to join Jasta 1 following his successes with Kek B and AKN – five victories – he continued to score with the new formation and on 9 November he brought down his ninth. Even so, his Blue Max took almost a month to be bestowed, following his eighth victory on 7 October. Other than the Hohenzollern House Order, Knight's Cross, he had received two classes of the Oldenburg Friedrich August

Cross. On 27 December 1916 he was shot down and killed during a fight with FE2b machines from 11 Squadron, hit by fire from the 'pusher' crewed by Captain J B Quested and Second Lieutenant H J H Dicksee.

In April 1917, a month which was to prove the most disastrous month for the Royal Flying Corps in terms of casualties, two more former monoplane aces were lost. First was Hans Berr on the 6th.

Berr had been given command of Jasta 5 upon its formation, from men from Kek Avillers with whom he had scored two Fokker kills in March 1916. By 3 November 1916 Berr had raised his score to ten and been awarded the *Pour le Mérite* on 4 December, his eighth victory having been scored on 26 October, in fact two on this day, first an FE2b and then a balloon. So rapid had been these last few victories, seven since 7 October, that it took time to award him the Knight's Cross of the Hohenzollern House Order (that came on 10 November), which was a pre-requisite before the *Pour le Mérite* could be bestowed. He was the 13th recipient.

Following his awards he was temporarily detached to command the all-important Jastaschule at Valenciennes, but with the coming of spring 1917, and the offensives both sides were planning for April, Berr resumed his command of Jasta 5. During the interim, another former Fokker monoplane pilot with Kek Avillers now with Jasta 5, Hans Karl Müller, was seriously wounded on 26 December. Oddly, his score on this same day had risen to nine, but he did not receive the Blue Max! Nor did he see further active duty although he was commissioned and became a test pilot for the Siemens-Schuckert company. Seemingly, the Blue Max 'goal posts' had been moved.

Back with his Jasta 5 once more, Hans Berr, like Boelcke earlier, collided with a fellow pilot during a combat. Both attacking an FE2b of 57 Squadron on this Easter Good Friday morning, the two Albatros Scouts touched over Noyelles and both fighters crashed to earth. Berr (possibly in 2256/17) and Vizefeldwebel Paul Hoppe died instantly. Just nine days earlier, Berr had been awarded the War Merit Cross from the two German Principalities of Reuss to add to his laurels.

Another of Berr's former Kek monoplane pilots, Hans Gutermuth, had increased his Fokker score from two to four with the new formation. He had also been lost during this period, being shot down on 16 February 1917 in an Albatros DIII. He had fallen in Allied lines and his crashed machine was given the British identification serial G13.

On 8 April, just two days after Berr's death, Wilhelm Frankl leading his Jasta 4, was in combat with Bristol Fighters of No. 48 Squadron RFC and was shot down. His Albatros DIII biplane fighter (2158/16) was seen to break up in the air and Frankl, who had now achieved 20 victories, went down over Vitry-Sailly at 14.15 hours. Coincidentally, the pilot of the two-man crew who appear to have shot him down was Captain D M Tidmarsh MC, a former DH2 pilot. It may be recalled that it was Tidmarsh who was credited with bringing down Leutnant Schmedes of FA32 on 30 April 1916, without firing a shot. Later in the month, in fact three days later, Tidmarsh was shot down by Kurt Wolff of Jasta 11 and taken prisoner.

Of the other 1916 Blue Max winners, Buddecke survived until March

1918. After a late 1916 period with Jasta 4, during which he brought his score to ten, he returned again to the Turkish front, flying with Ottoman FA5. In March 1917 he brought his score to a round dozen. In early 1918 he returned to France once again, firstly to Jasta 30, gaining one further kill, but then moved to Jasta 18 as deputy leader to his old friend Rudolf Berthold. The type of air combat had changed considerably over the interim and within a couple of days, Buddecke fell to Sopwith Camel fighters of 3 Naval Squadron in the early afternoon of 10 March and was killed. He was probably shot down by Flight Lieutenant Art Whealy, a Canadian, who claimed an Albatros DV down 'out of control' east of Lens at the time Buddecke was lost. Berthold was wounded in the same fight.

For Rudolf Berthold, a wound or an injury was nothing new. With Kek Vaux he had been wounded in the leg, then injured in a crash on 25 April 1916, flying a Pfalz EIV (803/15) after scoring five victories. Upon recovery he was given command of Jasta 4 and being shot down in May 1917, he suffered a fractured skull. Then commanding Jasta 18 he was wounded on 12 August, a bullet shattering his right upper arm. Despite very limited use of this arm he returned to the front in the early spring of 1918 but was shot down again on 10 March.

Berthold, not for nothing named 'The Iron Knight' (although this was probably another title bestowed on him post-war), was given command of Jagdesgeschwader Nr.II. With his victory score at 29 by this time, he raised this to 44 during his final combat on 10 August 1918. However, he was seriously wounded yet again on this date, his crippled Fokker DVII fighter crashing into a house following a collision with his last victim – a DH4 bomber.

In 1919, the war lost, and despite his shattered body, Berthold joined the Freikorps during the post-war revolution and unrest in his native Germany. He was killed in Harburg, on the River Elbe, by rioters on 15 March 1920, strangled, it was reported, with the ribbon of his Blue Max. On his grave was inscribed: 'Honoured by his enemies – slain by his German brethren.'

The last of the 1916 *Pour le Mérite* winners, Ernst Freiherr von Althaus also commanded Jasta 4 later, with which he was wounded in March 1917, and then Jasta 10. He scored one more victory, his ninth, in July 1917, but failing eyesight made it necessary for him to relinquish this command. Taking over Jastaschule II for a while he later returned to army duties and was taken prisoner by American troops in October 1918 while commanding an infantry regiment on the Verdun front over which he had fought as a Fokker pilot more than two years earlier.

After the war he became a lawyer and barrister until his eyesight totally failed him in 1937. He continued studying law and during WW2 he was the Director of the County Court in Berlin. At the end of that war he was employed as an interpreter for the Allied Armistice Commission. Von Althaus died on 29 November 1946, aged only 56, thirty years after his glory days.

One other thing to record is the number of Eindecker pilots who served with the various Kek units and who did not achieve any victories. Success in air combat was more than just having a fighter plane and a machine gun.

Ability was everything, experience almost necessary. However, some who failed to score went on to do better things with the Jasta units, having cut their combat teeth with the Keks. One of these was Alfred Lenz from Munich, aged 26. He had gained one victory as a two-seater pilot with FA61 and later flew monoplanes with Kek Sud under Rudolf Berthold. He flew monoplanes for several months and in 1917 was with Jasta 14, but his next victories – five – were all achieved with Jasta 22 in 1918 while its commander! He served in front line units for 42 months and survived the war.

Others, like Josef Jacobs for example, who scored the odd one or two kills with Fokker monoplanes, went on to down 48 aircraft and balloons and be another *Pour le Mérite* winner in 1918. In fact, flying the Fokker DrI Triplane, he was the most successful exponent of the famed Driedecker, scoring more kills in them than Baron Manfred von Richthofen. There was also Bruno Loerzer, Kek Jametz, who ended the war commanding JGIII, winning the Blue Max and having 44 victories.

Stefan Kirmaier, two victories with Kek Jametz, took over command of Jasta 2 following Boelcke's death, adding a further nine victories before he too died in action, shot down by 24 Squadron's DH2s in late November 1916.

I should report too on those few two-seater airmen I have mentioned in this book. While not part of the main theme, they have all too often been ignored or overlooked in the past, but the opportunity to record their early successes was too good to miss in dealing with 1915-16.

Franz Josef Walz had, with his observers, achieved six victories by the end of July 1916. Going on to single-seaters he later commanded Jasta 2 for a while and gained his seventh and final victory with it. Going out to Palestine he led FA304 in that theatre and won the *Pour le Mérite* in August 1918. He had flown more than 500 war sorties, but ended it as a prisoner of war the following month. After the war he served in the Reichswehr and the State Police. Between the wars he joined the German Luftwaffe and attained the rank of General-leutnant in April 1941. Captured by the Russians he died as a prisoner of war in Breslau, Silesia, in December 1945, aged 60.

Albert Dossenbach and his observer Hans Schilling achieved nine and eight victories respectively with FA22 in 1916 (Dossenbach gained his ninth with another observer) and both men received the Knight's Cross of the Royal Hohenzollern House Order on 12 October. Flying with another pilot, Schilling was shot down by the French ace Charles Nungesser of Escadrille N65 on 4 December, and both men were killed.

Dossenbach received the Blue Max on 11 November, a week after Schilling's death. From the Black Forest region, Dossenbach was 25 by this time and had already been decorated by the army in 1914 as an NCO. Commissioned in January 1915 he had transferred to the air service. Following his FA22 days, he transferred to single-seaters and served with Jasta 2, but then took command of Jasta 36, and later Jasta 10. He added six more victories to his personal tally, but with a score of 15 he was shot down on 3 July 1917, either falling or jumping from his burning fighter.

Hans Rosencrantz's early victories still remain largely a mystery other than an RE7 downed on 9 July, but it is understood that he and his observer, Willi Fahlbusch gained their fifth victory on 31 August 1916 while with Kasta 1 of KGI. A week later they were both shot down and killed while in combat with Sopwiths of 70 Squadron over Malincourt.

Martin Zander, two victories with FA9's two-seaters, went on to gain three more kills with Jasta 1 after commanding Kek Nord. Transferred to command Jagdstaffelschule Nr.I at Valenciennes in November 1916 he did not see further front line action. He died in 1925.

* * *

One might question why Hans Karl Müller of Jasta 5 did not receive the *Pour le Mérite* following his eighth victory on 20 December, adding yet another on the 26th during the fight in which he was seriously wounded. The fact that he was an NCO pilot was probably the main reason, all the previous airmen having been commissioned officers. Even so, surely he deserved some recognition. Only a couple of weeks later Offizierstellvertreter Fritz Kosmahl of FA22 received the Member's Cross with Swords of the Hohenzollern House Order. The fact that Müller was commissioned on 14 January 1917 failed to sway judgement, it was almost as if it was not possible to back-date awards.

There is the distinct possibility that his qualifying eighth victory came just at a time when it was being discussed, if not decided, that too many airmen fighter pilots were receiving Germany's highest award for bravery, and that it was becoming a little too 'easy' to achieve eight victories. (Rather like the British who awarded Victoria Crosses to the first few airmen to bring down German airships, while later victorious pilots only received Distinguished Service Orders or Military Crosses for the same feat.) We know this was about to become fact as another of the first 'victims' of the change of policy was going to be non-other than Manfred von Richthofen.

Von Richthofen, still flying with Jasta 2, had, by the end of 1916 achieved fifteen victories! Number 14 had gone down on 20 December, nearly a week before Müller's last combat on the 26th, and Number 15 was scored the day afterwards, 27 December. And von Richthofen was an officer. There is no doubt that he was already harbouring his disappointment at not receiving his Blue Max following his own eighth kill, scored on 9 November (and his 11th victory on 23 November had been the British air hero, Major Lanoe Hawker VC DSO), so it has to be assumed that the 'goal posts' had been moved before that date. Obviously Hans Berr had been the last to struggle under the wire before the number was doubled to sixteen victories.

Baron von Richthofen scored his sixteenth victory on 4 January 1917 and received the *Pour le Mérite* on the 14th, which was nine days before he scored victory number seventeen. Almost immediately the qualifying number was changed again, for Werner Voss, who received the Blue Max on 8 April, had run his score to 24 two days earlier, so we can assume the qualifying number had risen to 20 victories. The next two pilots, Otto Bernert and Karl Emil Schäfer both scored around 20 too before they were honoured.

Of course, any number missed out. We met Hartmut Baldamus who flew monoplanes with FA20 and achieved four victories. He went on to greater things with Jasta 9 and by mid-April 1917 had scored 17 victories and had the Knight's Cross of the Royal Hohenzollern House Order. He too had brought his score to eight the previous December as the rules were changed. Within striking distance of 20 kills he collided with a French Nieuport Scout of Escadrille N37 near St Marie-à-Py on 14 April – credited as victory number eighteen – and was killed.

So ended this unique period dominated by the early German fighter aces. A period which found a handful of airmen willing, not to say eager, to exploit the merits of a fixed machine gun that fired bullets through the propeller blades of a fairly fast but otherwise unspectacular tractor-type aeroplane. An aeroplane that had few merits other than good visibilty, not being restricted by a pair of upper wings and interplane struts, and that it carried the first interrupter gun gear. Yet these pilots had shown the way, learnt their trade within a very few weeks or months, captured the imagination of their countrymen at home and overawed their opponents.

For almost a year the pilots who flew the Fokker, and Pfalz, monoplane fighters had demonstrated the use of fighter warfare, laid down basic tactics, and held sway over their British and French opponents. The arrival of better, more manoeuvrable opposition, in the shape of the British DH2 and French Nieuport Scouts finally overcame the Fokker monoplane menace. They in turn would be challenged in the air by the next generation of German biplane fighters, notably the Albatros DIII and DV Scouts.

What had begun as a moderate aeroplane in the Fokker Eindecker, had started the race for better machines with which each side challenged for air superiority. Already two factors had started to dominate the air war over France. One was the Royal Flying Corps' stance on taking the war across the trenches to the enemy and fighting over their side of the lines. The other, due to numbers and the desire to keep the secret of the Eindecker's interrupter gear from the Allies, meant the German fighter pilots invested in a largely defensive war.

The outcome of these policies became paramount in the final stages of the war. It became plain to see that the Allied policy enabled their air forces to dominate the battle grounds, support their artillery and assault vital lines of supply. Flying ground attack sorties with fighters as well as bombers, helped to stem the massive German assault in March 1918, and aided considerably to turn the tide of battles with the Allied attacks in August and September 1918. The German fighter pilots, good though they were, had fought themselves to a standstill and were unable to support or protect their comrades on the ground, who daily were harassed, bombed, strafed and pursued by the Camels, Dolphins, SE5s, Bristol Fighters, Big Acks, DH4s, Spads and Bréguet 14s in the final weeks of the Great War.

* * *

In Chapter Four I recorded an extract from the last letter written by Graham Price, the observer in 6 Squadron, killed in action by an unknown Fokker pilot, and unclaimed by one due, no doubt, because the German was unaware his victim had crashed. That last letter began as many thousands must have done, with reference to the normality of family life going on in England. It is poignant to read knowing this young man had only a few more days of life left to him.

The sadness and waste of war is always in the forefront of my mind in writing these books. I do not glory in war, but cannot ignore the sacrifices made by men of all nations in these often mindless conflicts which inflict themselves upon the human race. My books chronicle the events and hopefully record not only the horrors of air warfare but keep alive the memories, and not least the gallantry, of those who fought in them, and those who did not survive. As a finalé I record Graham Price's last letter home, at least the first part, not dealing with his war, but with ordinary domestic matters:

B Flight   *No. 6 Squadron*
5.3.16   *ROYAL FLYING CORPS*
In the Field   *B.E.F. FRANCE*

Dear Mother and Father.

I was very pleased to get your letters which arrived this morning. I began to think that I shouldn't have any letters from home this week. The post is taking much longer to come now and you have also probably heard that all leave is stopped until the end of July, so that anticipations of a leave in the near future are knocked on the head.

Congratulations to Mabel and Jack on the choice of such a pretty name for their daughter. I trust that she will grow up to be as pretty as her name. It is very good of Aunt Millie to give Audrey some Government stock.

I am glad to hear that Father is very much better. I expect he will have considerable trouble presently with the branch managers when they get called up as it doesn't look as though the committees are going to let many off.

Jeanie seems to think that Raymond will not be exempted when called up. I should hardly be inclined to take her view, but don't blame her for getting as many anticipatory thrills out of the matter as she can.

By the way, a special order has just been issued to the R.F.C. forbidding any officer to communicate with the Press. I only mention this as a reminder in order that you are double sure that none of my letters go into unknown hands.

I got the magazines alright, thanks. I will always write and let you know when I want anything.

If young Stafford wants to get into the R.F.C. the best thing he can do is to go to Sandhurst and it is of great advantage to them later on and counts considerably for promotion. I do not think the R.F.C. will take on many more civilian pilots as they prefer to train them themselves, and they can get as many pilots as they want.

I have just finished making up my log book for February . .

Yours affectionately,

Graham

Appendix A

FOKKER PILOTS ON OTHER FRONTS

While this book covers the main activities of the Fokker monoplanes on the Western Front, a number of these aircraft were sent to the Eastern Front in 1915 and a few pilots operated them successfully there. There was also a handful of Eindeckers with Home Defence Kest units (Kampfeinsitzer Staffeln), in December 1916, those known being an EIV with Kest 2 at Saarbrücken Nr. 180/16; an EIV with Kest 5 at Freiburg Nr. 183/16; and an EIV Nr. 161/16 with Kest 6 at Köln (Cologne).

One of the first recorded victories with a Fokker other than in France came on 18 October 1915 on the Russian front by Leutnant Karl Odebrett. He was flying with Flieger-Abteilung Nr.215 and shot down a Russian aircraft at Dryswiaty Lake, near Dunaburg. It was a pusher-type, either a Voisin or Farman and its Russian captain pilot was taken prisoner.

Karl Odebrett came from Schneidemuhl, born 31 July 1890, and had gained his flying certificate, No.659, on 9 February 1914. In August that year he volunteered for the air service and first served with FA47 in Russia and then attached to FA215. Wounded in May 1916 he later went to France and became a successful fighter pilot with Jasta 16 and then Jasta 42. His score may well have been around 21 but any chance of winning the Blue Max ended with the Armistice. He had received the Knight's Cross of the Royal Hohenzollern House Order in April 1918, with his score standing at 11. He died in Venezuela in 1930 from kidney failure.

Flieger-Abteilung Nr.6, operating in the Dardanelles in late 1915 had several Turkish pilots on strength, and as we read in Chapter 4, Hans-Joachim Buddecke had been posted to this unit at this time after scoring three victories with FA23 in France with Fokkers. Known as Ottoman FA6, his first action resulted in an unconfirmed victory over a Farman on 6 December 1915, near Nara.

On 6 January 1916, Buddecke made two claims, but this time one was confirmed but the other disallowed. The confirmed success was over a Farman being flown by Flight Commander H A Busk RNAS. Hans Acworth Busk came from London, was 21, and flying with 2 Wing RNAS. Buddecke's unconfirmed victory was another Farman he thought went down east of Jalova.

Two days later, the 7th (sometimes noted as the 9th), another German pilot with FA6, Oberleutnant Theodore Jakob Croneiss, claimed his first victory. Together with Buddecke, he engaged and shot down a Voisin III LAS (8502) of 2 Wing RNAS, in the Cape Hellas area. Lieutenant F D S

Bremner managed a forced landing and he and his observer, Midshipman H E Burnaby were able to set their aircraft on fire after first smashing it up with picks, shovels and a sledgehammer.

Theo Croneiss would become an ace flying in the Middle East and win the Hohenzollern House Order. Between the wars he was a famous sport-flyer and also test-flew the first Messerschmitt aircraft for his friend and aircraft designer Willi Messerschmitt, and later became a test pilot for the company.

On the following day, Buddecke and Croneiss again engaged the RNAS off Hellas and while Buddecke was recorded as having an unconfirmed victory, there are suggestions that Croneiss was given the victory. There are no RNAS losses, so perhaps the Farman was either seen to be going down on the Allied side, or it got away.

Buddecke lost out again on 11 January. In action against a 3 Wing RNAS Farman, piloted by Flight Sub-Lieutenant C H Brinsmead, he and Oberleutnant Hans Schüz shot it down at Sedd-ul-Bahr, off Hellespont. The victory was credited to Schüz for his first of ten victories. All his victories were achieved in the Middle East, which made him the most successful German pilot, in terms of kills, in the area during WW1. Cecil Horace Brinsmead was 22, and came from Sydney, Australia. He was buried at Lancashire Landing, Gallipoli.

This was becoming a productive time for FA6, for Buddecke, in company with Schüz, got his fifth victory on the 12th, a Farman off Hellas, near Galeta. The 3 Wing crew of Flight Sub-Lieutenant J S Bolas and Midshipman D M Branson were indeed brought down, Jim Bolas, 23, being killed, Branson wounded and taken prisoner.

Buddecke gained his sixth victory on 25 January, another Farman, downed in the Dardanelles area, another unconfirmed the next day, and his seventh, on the 27th – yet another Farman. However, it is believed that by this time Buddecke was flying a Halberstadt D-type fighter.

On the 29th Turkish pilots Lieutenants (Yuzbasi) Ali Riza Bey and Orkan Riza Bey claimed two British machines down at Sedd-ul-Bahr, but it is not clear if they were both flying Fokkers or a two-seater.

Over the Aegean on 4 February, Theo Croneiss claimed a British biplane at Baba Tepe, off Imbros for his second victory, but again it is unclear if he still flew a monoplane. It would be March before further action occurred which resulted in victories for the German pilots. The first recorded encounter with a Fokker came on the 17th; a 2 Wing Nieuport 10 (3921) on a recce mission over Gallipoli, was attacked by a Fokker and shot-up, the observer being wounded.

On the Macedonian front on 23 and 24 March, Hauptmann Stenzel flying a Fokker with FA66 claimed two two-seaters in the Lake Dorian area. Both are believed to be French aircraft, and one came down near Volovec in Bulgarian lines west of the lake and the pilot escaped. Another French Farman with Sergent Gerard and observer Albert Misran aboard, fell in Lake Dorian and both were killed, although some reports indicate that ground fire caused the loss.

Gustav Stenzel was born at Hoefen on 2 October 1888 and in May 1905 had joined the Pommerschen Infantry Regiment Nr.2. He transferred to aviation in 1912 and soon after the outbreak of war went to FA15 and then to BAO, going with this unit to the Eastern Front. Assigned to FA66 he gained his two kills. His Ehrenbecher was awarded on 15 April 1916. He returned to France to command Jasta 8 in the late summer of 1916 and gained two more victories in 1917 before being killed in action on 28 July 1917.

Leutnant Schiebel, also flying with FA66, shot down a Farman near the Bulgarian lines on 25 March for his first victory. On the 30th Buddecke's claim for a Farman was disallowed, as was another Farman on 4 April east of Felahie, Gallipoli. One Fokker Buddecke was using in 1916 was an EIII No. 345/15, which carried black squares on wings, fuselage and tail, those on the wings and fuselage being edged in white, whereas the whole rudder being white, the black square was not edged. This later became the national marking of Turkey although the black square was changed to red. Buddecke originally formed the black square by merely squaring off the white areas surrounding the black patée cross of Germany.

The reason for the black square was simple. Aircraft flying over and in support of Moslems were not able to retain the Christian 'cross', hence the black square had been devised.

Another pilot to gain his first victory was Vizefeldwebel Kurt Jentsch of FA66. He claimed a French Voisin or a Farman, on 8 April over the Kalinowa area, near the Bulgarian lines. This was followed by two more kills on the 16th, although only one was allowed, another French pusher in the Perdeci area.

Hans Schüz had now moved to FA2 and still flying fighters he downed a RFC Voisin on 13 February 1916 near Kut in the Tigris sector, unconfirmed. Two British aircraft followed on 26 April. The first was a RNAS Short 184 seaplane (8044) of 'D' Force flying a food-drop sortie to the beseiged town of Kut-el-Amara, which had been withstanding enemy attempts to capture it for more than 140 days. (It finally fell on 29 April 1916.) Flight Lieutenant C B Gasson RNAS was wounded and taken prisoner, while Second Lieutenant A C Thouless RFC, aged 19, was killed. A 30 Squadron BE2c on a similar mission also fell to the German, its pilot, Lieutenant D A L Davidson being wounded, although he managed to force land inside British lines.

Schüz was again successful on 7 May, shooting down a BE2c over the Euphrates River. This was another machine from 30 Squadron (4558). It was noted that the pilot was killed and the observer taken prisoner, although this has not been confirmed and in reality the pilot landed at Camp Wadi with fuel tank holed and several control wires cut. Schüz appears to have driven off another BE on this date, and both encounters have been translated into 'victories'.

Karl Jentsch claimed a Voisin on the evening of 6 May near Lake Artzan, by the Bulgarian lines and on the 8th claimed a Farman at 05.22 hours and later another. Both were again near Lake Artzan, but the second of these two was not made an official victory.

It is difficult to be absolutely certain if all the above combats were by pilots flying Fokkers, for some Halberstadt biplanes had arrived during 1916. We know that a 30 Squadron BE2c was shot up by a Pfalz monoplane on 13 August 1916 over Shumran aerodrome, its pilot being wounded. Another BE crew, Lieutenant T E Lander and E A D Barr engaged this monoplane and shot it down, which was the first German aircraft shot down on the Mesopotamian front. However, this may also have been a Fokker two-seater, as the recently arrived FA62 lost a crew this date.

Hans-Joachim Buddecke seems to have gained most of the limelight flying on the Turkish front during 1916 and received both German and Turkish decorations. His Knight's Cross of the Military St Henry Order came on 16 October 1915 while with FA23. The Ottoman Empire bestowed upon him its Imtiaz Medal with Clasp and Sabres in both Gold and Silver; its Liakat Medal with Clasp and Sabres in Gold and Silver, and its War Medal. The *Pour le Mérite*, as already mentioned earlier, came on 14 April 1916, the third fighter pilot so honoured. In addition, he also received the Knight's Cross of the Royal Hohenzollern House Order, the Bavarian Military Merit Order, 4th Class with Swords, and the Brunswick War Merit Cross, 2nd Class.

Upon his return to France he took command of Jasta 4 in August 1916 and he downed an FE2b on 16 September. With a further two victories that same month, he then returned to Turkey where he remained for most of 1917, but he only gained two more kills, on 30 March before returning to France once more. His last official victory was scored on 19 February 1918, his 13th, and then he was sent to Jasta 18 to help his old comrade Rudolf Berthold who was still suffering from earlier injuries. Buddecke was to lead the unit in the air, while Berthold retained command of the Jasta. On 10 March Buddecke was mortally wounded in combat with Camels of 3 Naval Squadron and fell to his death.

Another Ottoman FA6 pilot scored a couple of victories in a Fokker in early 1917, that being Leutnant Emil Meinecke. He shot down a 2 Wing Farman (N3021) on 12 February, with Flight Lieutenants C A Maitland-Herriot and W C Jameson being taken prisoner in the Imbros sector. This was followed by a 2 Wing Bristol Scout (8996) five days later near Nagara. Canadian pilot Flight Sub-Lieutenant G T Bysshe made a forced landing near Hamidiye and was captured.

Meinecke, from Mannheim, born 20 July 1892, had been a motor mechanic, a job which led him into aviation in 1910. Enlisting into the air service when war came, firstly as a mechanic, then a pilot he was to score six victories with FA6 in 1917-18. His first Fokker victory had been whilst flying 342/15. In later life he lived in Canada, where he died in 1975.

The Fokker Eindeckers were used as late as September 1916 on the Bulgarian front, Feldwebel Wagner, in company with two other Fokker pilots, taking off to chase a hostile machine on the 29th. Wagner claimed the Caudron 30 km north-west of Sofia. Its French pilot was Brigadier Rouable, his Serbian observer named as Naunowitsch. The machine was probably a Farman from Escadrille F384. This may have been Gilbert Wagner, from Mittersheim, born 27 July 1893. He later served on the Western Front with Jasta 29, gaining three more victories before being shot down and killed by the CO of 74 Squadron RAF, Major K L Caldwell MC, on 12 April 1918.

* * *

The Austro-Hungarians also flew a few Fokker monoplanes over Northern Italy. Only a few were purchased for use by the *kaiserluche und königliche Luftfarhtruppen* (k.u.k LFT), being given the designation A.III machines which were, it is understood, in a batch LFT serial-numbered 03.41 to 03.52. They were used as fighters, the only real fighter the LFT had in late 1915 and the first interception by a Fokker came on 12 November. Oberleutnant Hassan Riza Effendi Pieler took off to engage an Italian Caproni which was bombing the aerodrome of Flik 4 at Haidenscraft. As he closed in and began to fire his gun jammed and the Caproni escaped unharmed.

Hauptmann Mathias Bernath, führer of Flik 4, flying Fokker EI 64/15 (03.51 in the LFT numbering) claimed the first victory for the monoplane by shooting down a Maurice Farman near San Lorenzo di Mossa on 25 November 1915.

The Austro-Hungarians had the same limitation imposed upon them as the Western Front pilots, that no flights should be made or pursuits carried on over the enemy lines for fear of the interrupter gear being discovered. This limited the offensive sorties by LFT pilots.

Then on 18 February 1916 Italian Caproni Ca.1 bombers raided the Croatian city of Ljubljana, seven of the original ten completing the outward journey. Heinrich Kostrba, in 03.511 attacked one, supported by Bernath in 03.42, and in a running fight killed two of the crew and wounded the pilot, who eventually re-crossed the lines before making a forced landing at Palmonova.

Later that morning, having refuelled and rearmed, Kostrba intercepted a Caudron which he sent down in a steep dive towards Monfalcone. This too force landed behind the Italian lines and was credited as Kostrba's second victory.

Within a very short space of time Kostrba was attacking a Caproni whose gunner stitched some holes through the Fokker's fabric. Oberleutnant Ludwig Hautzmayer then attacked and damaged the Caproni further, and with another attack by a Fokker (03.41) flown by Fähnrich Brociner, the bomber went down to crash-land near Merna. This gave Kostrba three victories in one day because the Austro-Hungarian airforce allowed shared kills. Kostrba later commanded Flik 23 and raised his score to eight, but by this time he was flying Hansa-Brandenburg two-seaters. He was killed in an air accident in 1926.

Ludwig Hautzmayer also became an ace. As the Fokker monoplanes of Fliks 4, 8 and 19 were grouped together at Haidenschaft airfield – known machines being 03.41, 03.42, 03.51 and 03.52 – Hautzmayer was assigned to Flik 19 in February 1916. His first combat sortie was on the aforementioned 18 February, in which he shared a Caproni bomber.

Hautzmayer then flew a Brandenburg C-type, but on 9 August 1916 he was back in an Eindecker (03.42) and scored his third victory over an Italian Caudron. He later increased his score to seven victories, but on other fighter types. He too died in a flying accident at Croydon airport, England, on 6 December 1936.

Adolf Heyrowsky was another ace who flew a Fokker briefly, and scored a victory in one (03.42 again) on 15 August 1916, with Flik 19. He forced a Voisin to land in enemy territory near Cormons for his fifth victory. He went on to score 12 in all, but all the others were whilst flying two-seater Brandenburg machines. He ended the war as Hauptmann and in WW2 was Oberst in the German Luftwaffe. He died in 1945 aged 63.

Appendix B

FOKKER EINDECKER ACES

Hauptmann Oswald Boelcke

1915

1	4 Jul	Morane L Parasol	MS15		Valenciennes
	(observer Wühlisch)				
2	19 Aug	Bristol Biplane		eve	Front lines
3	9 Sep	Morane 2s		eve	French front lines
4	25 Sep	Farman	MF16	am	Pont-à-Mousson
5	16 Oct	Voisin B1 (V839)	VB110	am	St Souplet
6	30 Oct	Voisin B1		am	S of Tahure

1916

7	5 Jan	BE2c (1734)	2 Sqn	0930(A)	Pont-à-Vendin
8	12 Jan	RE7 (2287)	12 Sqn	1040	NE Turcoing
9	14 Jan	BE2c (4087)	8 Sqn	1015(A)	Nr Bapaume
10	12 Mar	Farman	MF63?	1130	S of Fort Marre
11	13 Mar	Voisin		1300	E Malancourt
12	19 Mar	Farman	MF19	1300	S of Cuisy
13	21 Mar	Voisin (V1417)	VB109	1115	Fosses Wood
14	28 Apr	Caudron		am	S of Vaux
15	1 May	French Biplane		eve	Pfafferrückos
16	18 May	Caudron G4	C56	eve	S Ripont
17	21 May	Nieuport	N65	am	S Mort Homme
18	21 May	Nieuport	N65	eve	Bois de Hesse
19	27 Jun	Nieuport		eve	Douaumont

Victories 20-40 scored as Staffelführer of Jasta 2 between 2 September and 26 October 1916, flying D-type biplane fighters. Killed in Action 28 October 1916.

Oberleutnant Max Immelmann

1915

1	1 Aug	BE2c (2003)	2 Sqn	0615	Brebières, Douai
2	26 Aug	French biplane			Nr Souchez
3	21 Sep	BE2c (2004)	10 Sqn	1000(A)	Nr Willerval
4	10 Oct	BE2c (2033)	16 Sqn	1500	Nr Verlinghem
5	26 Oct	VFB5 (5462)	11 Sqn	1005	Ecoust St Mein
6	7 Nov	BE2c (1715)	10 Sqn	1545	Quiery
7	15 Dec	Morane Parasol (5087)	3 Sqn	am	Raismes

1916

8	12 Jan	VFB5 (5460)	11 Sqn	0900(A)	Beaumetz

9	2 Mar	Morane BB (5137)	3 Sqn	1035	Somain, E of Douai
10	13 Mar	Bristol C Scout (4678)	4 Sqn	1330	Serre, Hill 181
11	13 Mar	BE2c (4197)	8 Sqn	1740	Pelves, Arras
12	29 Mar	FE2b (6352)	23 Sqn	1110	Quéant
13	30 Mar	BE2c (4116)	15 Sqn	1115	Ablainzeville
14	23 Apr	VFB5 (5079)	11 Sqn	1106	Monchy-le-Preux
15	16 May	Bristol C Scout	11 Sqn	1655	S of Drocourt

Killed in Action 18 June 1916 in combat with 25 Squadron. He had scored victories on this date but his death prevented him receiving confirmation.

Leutnant Kurt Wintgens

1915
1	15 Jul	Morane			
2					
3	9 Aug	Voisin	VB112		Gondrexange

1916
4	20 May	Nieuport XII	N68		S Château Salins
5	21 May	Caudron G4	C43		NE Château Salins
6	17 Jun	Farman	MF70		S Château Salins
7	23 Jun	Nieuport XVI (1334)	N124		N Verdun
8	30 Jun	Farman	MF7?		S Château Salins
9	19 Jul	Sopwith 1½ Strutter	70 Sqn		Arras
10	21 Jul	BE2c (2100)	12 Sqn	0937	Cambrai
11	21 Jul	Morane N (A128)	60 Sqn	eve	Nr Combles
12	30 Jul	Martinsyde G100 (7471)	27 Sqn	pm	E of Péronne
13	2 Aug	Morane BB (5177)	60 Sqn	1630	SE of Péronne
16	15 Sep	BE12 (6583)	21 Sqn	1130	Manancourt

It is difficult to ascertain if Wintgens ever flew an Eindecker with Jasta 1 during September 1916, during which time he increased his victory tally to 19 before being killed in action on 25 September. However, he was flying one on 15 Sept, downing victory No.16. (Possibly victories 18 and 19 too.)

Leutnant Max Ritter von Mulzer

1916
1	30 Mar	VFB5 (5071)	11 Sqn	1107	N of Wancourt
2	23 Apr	FE2b (5210)	25 Sqn	1130	Nr Estaires
3	31 May	FE2b (6345)	23 Sqn	1120	Inchy-en-Artois
4	18 Jun	FE2b (6940)	25 Sqn	1732	Noyelles, Lens
5	22 Jun	FE2b (5209)	25 Sqn	0955	E of Hulloch
6	26 Jun	FE2b (5212)	25 Sqn	0655	Mazingarbe
7	2 Jul	BE2c (2654)	9 Sqn	1400	Miraumont
8	8 Jul	BE2c (5765)	4 Sqn		Miraumont
9	22 Jul	EA			E of Hulloch
10	3 Aug	FE2b (4272)	25 Sqn	0730	Sallaumines, Lens

Killed in Flying Accident, 26 September 1916.

Leutnant Otto Parschau

1915

1	11 Oct	Farman	MF2		Argonne
2	19 Dec	BE2c (2074)	12 Sqn	1100	Oostkamp, Bruges

1916

3	12 Mar	Nieuport	N49		Verdun
4	21 Mar	Voisin			N of Verdun
5	29 Jun	DH2 (5963)	24 Sqn		N of Péronne
6	2 Jul	Caudron CIV (2235)	C106		NW of Noyon
7	3 Jul	Balloon			La Neuville
8	9 Jul	Balloon	55 Cie		N of Grévillers

Died of Wounds following combat, 21 July 1916.

Leutnant Wilhelm Frankl

1915

1	10 May	Voisin			Flanders
	(as an observer, claimed aircraft shot down using a carbine.)				

1916

2	10 Jan	Voisin LB (991)	RFD		Woumen
3	19 Jan	Voisin			Woumen
4	1 Feb	Voisin			Chaulnes
5	4 May	BE2c (4109)	7 Sqn	pm	Ploegsteert Wood
6	21 May	FE2b (5206)	20 Sqn		Nr Houthem
7	2 Aug	Morane BB (5181)	60 Sqn	pm	Pouilly
8	9 Aug	Voisin?		1225	SW of Bapaume
9	9 Aug	EA (Nieuport?)			SW of Bapaume

After this date it is probable that Frankl began to fly D-type biplanes. Brought his score to 20 victories by 7 April 1917 but died in combat with 48 Squadron RFC the next day.

Leutnant Walter Höhndorf

1916

1	17 Jan	Voisin (V1096)	VB105		Medevich, Alsace
2	19 Jan	Voisin	VB101?		Nr Thiaucourt
3	10 Apr	Nieuport Scout	N68		NE Château Salins
4	2 Jun	Caudron (C2474?)	C42		W of Mörchingen
5	17 Jun	Nieuport XVI	N124		S Château Salins
6	22 Jun	Caudron	C66		Lembach
7	25 Jun	Caudron G4 (1202)	C9	pm	Raucourt
8	15 Jul	Nieuport XVI (1392)	N62		SW of Péronne
9	19 Jul	Farman	F207		Péronne
10	21 Jul	Nieuport	N3 or N37		S Bapaume
11	30 Jul	Martinsyde G100 (7304)	27 Sqn	1630	Sapignies

Höhndorf's 12th victory was scored on 17 September flying with Jasta 1, a French Caudron G4 of C43. Killed on test flight 5 September 1917 at Ire-le-Sec, near Marville.

Hauptmann Rudolf Berthold

1916

1	2 Feb	Voisin	VB108		Chaulnes
2	5 Feb	BE2c (4091)	13 Sqn	am	Grévillers-Irles
3	13 Mar	BE2c (4151)	8 Sqn	pm	Bourlon
4	1 Apr	Farman			Lihons
5	16 Apr	BE2c (2097)	9 Sqn	1115	S of Maurepas
6	24 Aug	Nieuport (1552)	N37	1900	Péronne

Berthold went on to score a total of 44 combat victories by the war's end. Of his many wounds and injuries, those on 10 August 1918 brought his fighting to an end. This very brave German was killed in Harburg, on the Elbe, by rioters while serving with the Freicorps, on 15 March 1920.

Leutnant Gustav Leffers

1915

1	5 Dec	BE2c (2049)	13 Sqn	1500	Achiet-le-Grand
2	29 Dec	BE2c (2039)	8 Sqn	1200	Marquion

1916

3	20 Feb	BE2c ((2054)	13 Sqn	0945(A)	Nurlu, SW Cambrai
4	14 Mar	BE2c (4153)	15 Sqn	1320	S of Bapaume
5	9 Jul	FE2b (6952)	11 Sqn	0740	Bucquoy
6	31 Aug	Martinsyde G100 (7479)	27 Sqn	0840	Moislains

Leffers scored three more victories in September, October and November, thought not to be while in a Fokker, and one at least in a captured Nieuport Scout (3 September). Killed in action in a fight with an FE2b of 11 Squadron around noon on 27 December 1916, in the Nieuport.

Oberleutnant Ernst Freiherr von Althaus

1915

1	5 Dec	BE2c (4092)	13 Sqn	1500	W of Roye
2	28 Dec	BE2c (2670)	8 Sqn		Sancourt

1916

3	2 Feb	Nieuport 2-seater	N3		Biaches
4	19 Mar	Caudron G4			W Lihons
5	30 Apr	Farman			St Mihiel
6	2 May	French 2-seater			Caillette Wood
7	2 Jul	Nieuport XI			Somme front
8	21 Jul	Farman	F16		Roye

Von Althaus' ninth and final victory came as leader of Jasta 10 on 24 July 1917, after which failing eyesight forced his retirement from operational flying.

Hans-Joachim Buddecke

1915
1	19 Sep	BE2c (2008)	8 Sqn		W of St Quentin
2	23 Oct	BE2c (2017)	13 Sqn	pm	W of St Quentin
3	11 Nov	BE2c (1725)	8 Sqn		German lines

1916
| 4 | 6 Jan | Farman | 2 Wg RNAS | | E of Kap Nara |
| 5 | 12 Jan | Farman | 3 Wg RNAS | | off Hellas |

Buddecke claimed a further two aircraft in the Middle East plus a number of unconfirmed successes, but it is understood these claims were not whilst flying a monoplane. Returning to the Western Front in the spring of 1917 he scored three more kills with Jasta 4 before returning to Turkey. He did not add to his score until he returned once more to France. With a final score of 13 he was killed in combat on 10 March 1918.

(A) approximately.

Appendix C

TWO-SEATER CLAIMS JULY 1915 – SEPTEMBER 1916

In order not to convey the impression that Fokker Eindecker pilots dominated totally the air fighting and victory claims by the *Luftstreitkräfte* during the period under review, listed below are the known/recorded victory claims by two-seater *Flieger-Abteilungen* over the Western Front. Although this book is all about the Fokker period, this list also gives us the opportunity of listing these claims for historical information.

Date	Crew	Unit	Claim	Location
1915				
4 Jul	Ltn O Boelcke Oblt Heinz H von Wühlisch	FA62 Alb C	Morane L MS15	Beaulicourt area
21 Jul	Oblt Wolfgang J G Weese Lt Christian von Scheele	FA32	Voisin 4 Sqn	Bapaume
1 Aug	Oblt Eduard Wimmer Hptm Stadelmayr	FA3 Alb CI 62/15	Farman	Malzaville raid
9 Aug	OfStv Franz Nüssel Ltn Philipp Cherdron	FA6	Voisin VB110	Harboucy
9 Aug	Ltn Pheredron Ltn von Sprunner	?	Voisin GB4/VB110	
20 Aug	?	Alb CI	Voisin	Challerange
31 Aug	Uffz Kandulski Ltn Bilitz	FA48	Morane MS49	Nr Belfort
6 Sep	OfStv Heinrich Metz Ltn Walter Lichtenberger	FA6	Voisin VB105	Saarbrücken raid
7 Sep	Gefr Emil Thuy Oblt Cranz	FA53	Farman MF8	
25 Sep	Hptm Martin Zander ?	FA9	BE2c	Nr Moeuvres
7 Oct	Ltn Schlemmer Oblt Baer	FA3	Farman	
10 Oct	Oblt Fritz Hempel Ltn Robert Greim	FA3	Farman	Deuxnouds Bois

Date	Crew	Unit	Claim	Location
11 Oct	Hptm Martin Zander Oblt Lerche	FA9	BE2c 8 Sqn	NW St Quentin
12 Oct	Oblt Kirsch Ltn Kaehler	FA25	Voisin VB112	Chalons area
14 Oct	Ltn Wunderlich Ltn Zimmer	FA2		
11 Nov	Ltn Bethke Ltn Eckstein	FA24 Alb CI 451/15	FE2a 6 Sqn	Ploegsteert 1100
16 Nov	Ltn Hermann Göring Ltn Otto Bernert	FA25 Alb CI 486/15	Farman	Tahure 1430 hrs
18 Nov	Ltn Hugo Gregold Oblt Rudolf Schonger	FA8	?	Corcieux – French lines
30 Nov	Oblt Illing Oblt Kraft	FA5 LVG C	BE2c 16 Sqn	W La Bassée 1230
14 Dec	Ltn Otto Pfältzer Ltn Kurth	FA48(68?)	Caudron C61	Mülheim
14 Dec	Hptm Martin Zander Ltn Lerche	FA9	VFB5 11 Sqn	Bapaume
1916 17 Jan	Uffz Krause Ltn von Lersner	KG1	BE2c 15 Sqn	Paschendaele
23 Jan	? Ltn C von Scheele	KG2 Alb CI	Voisin VB102	NE Metz
24 Feb	Ltn Karl Persch Ltn Walter Veigl	KG1	Fr a/c	
26 Feb	unknown crew		Fr a/c	
29 Feb	Ltn Kühl Ltn Kurt Haber	FA6	Voisin GDE	NW Soissons
1 Mar	Ltn Kühl Ltn Kurt Haber	FA6	Farman	W Karlsruhe
8 Mar	Uffz Schade Uffz Wirtz	FA(A)211	Farman C18	Fort St Michel
8 Mar	Ltn Lothar von Hausen Oblt Heymann	KG2	Caudron C11	Verdun front
9 Mar	Uffz Gröschler Ltn Patheiger	FA(A)213	Morane N 1 Sqn	Wytschaete
14 Mar	Ltn Hermann Göring Ltn Graf von Schaesberg -Boje (M)	FA(A)203 AEG G 49/15	Caudron C6	

Date	Crew	Unit	Claim	Location
14 Mar	Vfw Paulisch Ltn Kommoss	FA(A)211	Fr a/c C6	S Montzeville
25 Mar	Ltn Renatas Theiller ?	FA44	Farman MF35?	Caillette Wood
30 Mar	Oblt Eduard Wimmer Oblt Kraft Oblt Lieberts (but credited to Mülzer)	FA4 FA62	VFB5 11 Sqn ditto	N Wancourt 1107 hrs ditto
31 Mar	OfStv (E von?) Mellenthin Ltn Simon	FA60	Nieuport 11 N57	Nr Etan
31 Mar	Uffz Becker Ltn Moeller	FA44	Fr a/c	
1 Apr	Uffz Gröschler Ltn Patheiger	FA(A)213	BE2c 5 Sqn	Messines
9 Apr	Oblt Franz Walz Ltn Gerlich	KG2	Caudron C27	Douaumont
11 Apr	Oblt Georg Zeumer ?	KG1	Nieuport N68	N Verdun
23 Apr	Ltn Seibert Ltn Karl Rieger	FA5 LVG CII	Br a/c FTL	Br lines
20 May	Ltn Seibert Ltn Karl Rieger	FA5 LVG CII	Martinsyde 27 Sqn	La Bassée noon
21 May	Oblt Franz Walz ?	KGI	Nieuport RNAS	Sea/Dunkirk
4 Jun	Vfw Friedrich Wendland Ltn Bruhn	FA34	Fr a/c	
20 Jun	Uffz Eugen Weiss Ltn Albert Dietlen	FA60	Nieuport	Bois de Ville
20 Jun	Vfw Adolf Wellhausen Oblt Otto Schmidt	FA25	Gitterumpf	
1 Jul	Vfw Wendt Ltn Geerkens	FA(A)209	Nieport XVI N57	
2 Jul	Ltn Walter Dingel Ltn Bartsch	FA32	FE2b 11 Sqn	Vaulx 1350 hrs
3 Jul	Ltn Hohberg Oblt Viebig	FA32	BE2c 4 Sqn	Grandcourt
3 Jul	Oblt Franz Walz Oblt Gerlich	KGI	BE2c 13 Sqn	S Péronne

Date	Crew	Unit	Claim	Location
9 Jul	Oblt Franz Walz Oblt Gerlich	KGI		W Neuville
9 Jul	Ltn Wilhelm Fahlbusch Ltn Hans Rosencrantz	KGI	RE7 21 Sqn	Marcoing
11 Jul	Ltn Renatus Theiller Oblt Otto Schmidt	FA25	Balloon	Dombasle
15 Jul	Oblt Franz Walz ?	KGI	Caudron C106?	W of Somme
29 Jul	Oblt Franz Walz ?	KGI	Fr a/c?	Somme area
1 Aug	Ltn Hans Wacker ?	KG4	EA	
3 Aug	Vfw Fritz Bärmann Ltn Friedrich Vordenfelde	FAA235	Fr a/c	SW Arras am
5 Aug	Oblt Mollberger ?	FA22 Rump CI	BE2c 4 Sqn	NW Bapaume 0730 hrs
12 Aug	?	Roland	DH2 32 Sqn	Courcelette
13 Aug	Ltn Albert Dossenbach Obltn Hans Schilling	FA22	BE12 19 Sqn	E Bapaume
24 Aug	?	Kasta 18 Roland	Nieuport	Somme
26 Aug	? Ltn Schatz	FA57	BE12? 19 Sqn	Biefvillers 2005 hrs
28 Aug	Ltn Karl Spitzhoff Oblt Friedrich Schilling	FA57	Sop $1^1/_2$ 70 Sqn	
31 Aug	Ltn Willi Fahlbusch Ltn Hans Rosencrantz	KGI Roland C	Martinsyde 27 Sqn	Moislains 0820 hrs
31 Aug	Ltn Alexander Kutscher Ltn Erbelding	FA32 Rumpler CI	FE2b 23 Sqn	S Haplincourt late am
2 Sep	Uffz Wendroth Oblt Jollase	FA32 Rumpler CI	FE2b 11 Sqn	S of Mesnil eve
2 Sep	? ?	FA22 Roland C	FE2b 11 Sqn	Villers au Flos?
2 or 3 Sep	Ltn Willi Fahlbusch Ltn Hans Rosencrantz	KGI Roland C	? ?	
3 Sep	? Oblt Walter Veigl	KGI	Morane	Sapignies

Date	Crew	Unit	Claim	Location
5 Sep	Vfw Jüterbock Oblt Groehle	FA(A)224	Voisin	
15 Sep	? Ltn Diers	FA22	Martinsyde 27 Sqn	Bourlon am
15 Sep	Ltn Alexander Kutscher Ltn Erbelding	FA32 Rumpler CI	FE2b 11 Sqn	Haplincourt eve
15 Sep	Vfw Hey Ltn von Cornberg	FA32 Rumpler CI	BE12 21 Sqn	Rocquigny late pm
22 Sep	Ltn Julius Fichter Oblt Hasso von Wedel	KG5	FE2b 25 Sqn	Longueval am
24 Sep	Ltn Albert Dossenbach Oblt Hans Schilling	FA22	BE12 19 Sqn	Morchies 1810 hrs
26 Sep	Ltn Albert Dossenbach Oblt Hans Schilling	FA22	Sop $1^1/_2$ 70 Sqn	Ervillers 1315 hrs

Appendix D

The following maps show the locations of Max Immelmann's victory claims between August 1915 and June 1916 (noted by a number in a square), and those of Max Mulzer between March and August 1916 (a number in a circle).

It is strange that the so-called, or so-named – presumably post war – Immelmann, should be given the sobriquet of The Eagle of Lille, as he operated from Douai, some way to the south of Lille, and only one victory was achieved in the vicinity of that town. As can be seen, most of his victories were east and west of Bapaume, and between Douai, Arras and Lens.

Even his last battle was over Lens, nearer to Arras in the south than to Lille further

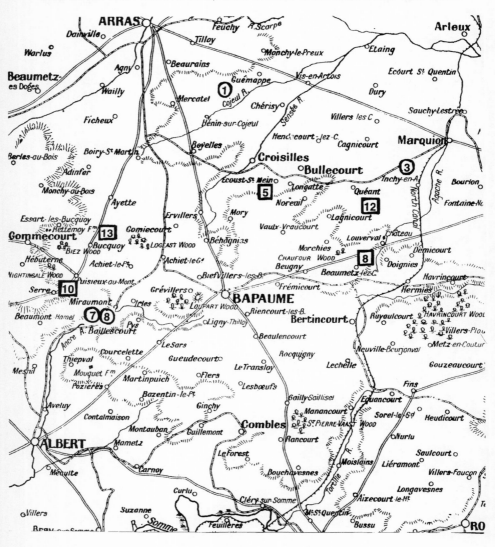

170

to the north. And strangely, Franz Immelmann's book about his brother Max says of his death: 'Downward he plunged in his headlong fall; as the lights of Lille sparkled upwards to him . . .' Perhaps he had meant to entitle the book, *The Eagle of Lens*!?

The area of his last air battle is noted with an 'X', where too his final victory or victories, were located, but not officially credited.

As for Mulzer's victories, five were in the general area of Lens, just one well west of Lille and the others east of Bapaume or south-east of Arras. The victory sites of both pilots should be read in conjunction with their claims recorded in Appendix B.

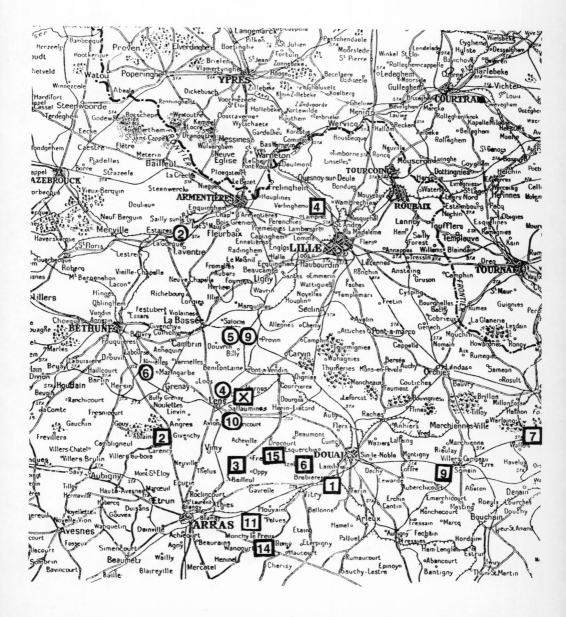

BIBLIOGRAPHY

Above the Lines, by N Franks, F W Bailey & R Guest, Grub Street, 1993.
Ace of the Iron Cross, by Ernst Udet, (trans by R K Riehn), Doubleday & Co, 1970.
Aeroplanes of the Royal Flying Corps, by Jack Bruce, Putnam, 1992.
An Aviator's Field Book, by Oswald Boelcke, (trans R R Hirsch) Battery Press, 1991.
Casualties of the German Air Service, by N Franks, F W Bailey & R Duiven, Grub Street, 1999.
Flying Fury, by James McCudden VC, John Hamilton Ltd, 1930.
German Aircraft of the First World War, by Peter Grey & Owen Thetford, Putnam, 1962.
Germany's First Air Force 1914-1918, by Peter Kilduff, Arms & Armour Press, 1991.
Knight of Germany, by Prof. Johannes Werner, John Hamilton Ltd, 1933.
Over the Front, by N Franks & F W Bailey, Grub Street, 1992.
Per Ardua, by Hilary St.George Saunders, Oxford University Press, 1944.
The Eagle of Lille, by Franz Immelmann, John Hamilton Ltd, 1935.
The Jasta Pilots, by N Franks, F W Bailey & R Duiven, Grub Street, 1996.
The Sky Their Battlefield, by Trevor Henshaw, Grub Street, 1995.
Years of Combat by Lord Douglas of Kirtleside, Collins Ltd, 1963.

Various articles in *Cross & Cockade* and *Over The Front* Journals: Societies of WW1 Aviation Historians.
The *Aviation Awards* books of Neal W O'Connor, Vols I to VI, Foundation for Aviation WW1, 1988-1999.

Index of Names

ERAU-PRESCOTT LIBRARY